Law and Liberty in Early New England

Law and Liberty

 ## in Early New England

Criminal Justice and Due Process, 1620–1692

EDGAR J. MCMANUS

AMHERST The University of Massachusetts Press

Copyright © 1993 by
The University of Massachusetts Press

All rights reserved

Printed in the United States of America

LC 92-18719

ISBN 0-87023-824-8

Designed by David Ford

Set in Plantin by Keystone Typesetting, Inc.

Printed and bound by Thomson-Shore, Inc.

Library of Congress Cataloging-in-Publication Data

McManus, Edgar J.
   Law and liberty in early New England : criminal justice and
due process, 1620–1692 / Edgar J. McManus.
      p.   cm.
   Includes bibliographical references (p.   ) and index.
   ISBN 0–87023–824–8 (alk. paper)
   1. Criminal justice, Administration of—New England—
History—17th century.   2. Criminal law—New England—
History—17th century.   I. Title.
KF9223.M38   1993
345.74'05—dc20   92–18719
[347.4055]   CIP

British Library Cataloguing in Publication data are available.

TO JANE ORTON YOUNG

We shall be as a city upon a hill, the eyes of all people are upon us.

—John Winthrop (1630)

Marvelous it may be to see and consider how some kind of wickedness did grow and break forth here in a land where the same was so much witnessed against and so narrowly looked into and severely punished.

—William Bradford (1642)

Contents

Preface

The New England colonies began as a dream in the minds of Puritan idealists who envisioned holy communities free of sin and corruption. Pilgrims and Puritans alike came to the American wilderness for nothing less than to found a New Jerusalem covenanted with God and giving testimony to His glory. His laws would be their laws, not just as moral abstractions, but literally, as binding rules for good Christian living. They committed New England law to the formidable task of conforming society to the highest standards and ideals. While the dream of a New Jerusalem faded almost from the beginning, the legal institutions of the founders proved much more durable. They held sway for so long primarily because no generation of Americans put greater faith in the law as a formula for social living. Everything in life had a legal aspect sometimes even more compelling than the claims of conscience. Yet the system was not authoritarian in the modern sense of an all-encompassing state. Strict limits were set on the power of government, and individual rights were carefully protected. Some of the key guarantees of American constitutionalism first took root and flourished in the legal culture of Puritan New England.

This book traces the development of Puritan criminal law and justice from the period of settlement until the colonial reorganization of the 1690s brought New England more into line with the legal institutions of England. The Puritans were at first practically unhampered in imposing their values and beliefs on the region. While bound in theory to adopt no laws repugnant to English law, they in fact did precisely as they pleased for more than half a century. The story has been told before, but the focus of previous accounts has been almost exclusively on Massachusetts. While the seminal importance of the Bay Colony certainly demands special emphasis, legal developments in the other colonies deserve attention as more than mere offshoots of Massachusetts law. Massachusetts influenced all of New England to some extent, but not at the same time or in identical ways. All the Puritan colonies shared common beliefs, but none was an exact clone of the Massachusetts model. Rhode Island, which rejected the Puritan hegemony, remained outside the orbit of Massachusetts law almost completely and looked to England instead for legal models. This study takes a comparative approach that examines indigenous developments and puts similarities and differences into perspective.

While every book must ultimately speak for itself, it may be useful to make clear now what this study is and what it is not. It is not another foray through the archives in search of new manuscript data. Its focus instead is the vast amount of primary material already available in underutilized printed collections. The hundreds of statutes and thousands of court cases in these collections provided the main building blocks for this study. The importance of these sources cannot be exaggerated. They reveal the legal thinking of New Englanders on religion, morality, and government, as well as on the more mundane problems of everyday life. All were grist for a legal system that both defined and enforced community mores. While archival material has been used to fill in gaps in the printed records, the emphasis throughout is on the analysis and synthesis of the mountainous data already available.

The emphasis placed on primary sources has not precluded consideration of important secondary material. The writing of American legal history has undergone explosive growth in recent years, and much of it relates to early New England. The key monographs and journal articles are cited extensively, not just for their intrinsic value, but to provide readers with alternative interpretations of particular topics. While a conscious effort has been made not to confuse history with historiography, my goal throughout has been to provide balanced coverage. To ignore or gloss over differing conclusions is tantamount to writing history blindfolded. This study attempts to present a point of view without falling into the trap of solipsism.

A note on style and organization may also be helpful. Those sources that are frequently cited throughout the notes are abbreviated. A list of these abbreviations precedes the notes. Other sources cited in the notes are abbreviated when repeated in the same chapter. Relevant dates not in the text or citation can be found in parentheses following the page reference. Where two dates appear in parentheses following a code citation, the first indicates the year of the code, and the second, following the pagination, the year in which the law was first enacted. The citation *Massachusetts Colonial Laws* (1660), 43 (1648), for example, is to a law passed in 1648 which appears in the 1660 code. All materials quoted in the text retain their original grammar and syntax, but spelling and punctuation have been modernized for the reader's convenience. Abbreviations, except those in common usage, have been spelled out, and unnecessary italics eliminated. Dates have been left in the Old Style (Julian calendar), but with the year beginning on January 1 instead of March 25. Split annotation for dates before March 25 has been dispensed with to avoid confusion. A citation to the fourteenth day of the first month of 1647 appears simply as March 14, 1648 (not 1647/48), putting it unmistakably in the new year. These adjustments improve clarity but change nothing of substance.

Many people generously gave their time and valuable assistance to help in the book's preparation. I am grateful to the late George L. Haskins for sharing his vast knowledge of early New England law with me. My thanks also to William Nelson and Kai T. Erikson for assistance and advice. Barbara Black helped clarify some problems of appellate jurisdiction in Massachusetts, and John P. Demos was generous with information about witchcraft accusations. A note of thanks is also due to Sanford J. Fox for clarification on the legal definition of insanity in the seventeenth century and to John M. Murrin for information about jury trial in early New England.

I also owe a large and now unpayable debt to the late Richard B. Morris, one of the pioneers in the field of American legal studies. We met during my student years at Columbia University, and he impressed me from the beginning as the most brilliant person I had ever known. That was long ago, but nothing has happened over the years to change that first impression. Talking with him was like opening the windows or turning up the lights. Cobwebs blew away and everything became clear and comprehensible. His advice and assistance contributed significantly to this study, and for that I am grateful. But I am grateful most of all for the privilege of having known him.

Parts of the book were written in Norway in 1989 during a Fulbright lectureship at the University of Oslo. It is a pleasure now to acknowledge the many courtesies extended there in helping the project along. I am grateful to Barbara Lysholt Petersen, executive director of the Fulbright Program in Norway, for her kindness and assistance in making my stay so pleasant. I am also grateful to Dorothy Burton Skårdol and Per Winther for arranging a lecture schedule allowing me ample free time to work on the

Preface

book. My thanks also to the librarians and staff of the Universitetsbiblio-
teket and Deichmanske Bibliotek in Oslo for their unfailing courtesy and
cooperation. I will not soon forget these kind people who helped in so many
ways.

Edgar J. McManus

Queens College
City University of New York
March 1992

Law and Liberty in Early New England

A commonwealth without laws is like a ship without
rigging and steerage.—Increase Nowell (1648)

I   Laws for Living Saints

The Pilgrim and Puritan founders brought to New England ideas about law
shared by most Calvinists of the seventeenth century. The basic idea was
that people everywhere were free moral agents with power to choose between right and wrong and responsibility for their actions implicit in that
freedom. Puritans made individual conscience and judgment the pivot of
public policy. While no authority could legitimately coerce them, individuals had to accept the consequences of moral choices. Politically, these
assumptions fostered liberty and progress by treating people not as a mass
but as an aggregate of individuals covenanted with one another in society
and accountable to God in the hereafter. But such thinking also fostered notions of vindictive justice and of the necessary connection between wrongdoing and retribution. If wrongdoing went unpunished, people would soon
lapse into the moral anarchy from which God's grace had raised them.

Puritans believed that God's moral law flowed in a continuum through
natural law and Scripture to the human laws and statutes known as positive
law. So obvious was God's law that all right-thinking persons could per-
ceive it without prompting or coercion by the state. But not everyone was
right-thinking and able to make the right choices unassisted. Positive law
was needed because original sin had so corrupted human nature that most
people had lost the capacity to distinguish between right and wrong.
Churchmen during the Middle Ages had regarded canon law as the highest
expression of positive law, but the Protestant Reformation shifted the
emphasis to secular law. Protestants substituted the state for the church as
the main conduit for divine law and therefore strove to bring secular law
more into line with Scripture. While Reformation ideas about church
organization met official resistance in England, the new legal thinking won
general acceptance.[1] Adding moral muscle to secular law strengthened the

3

state and reinforced the dominant role of the official Anglican church in the life of the nation.

These trends in Reformation law reached their fullest development in Puritan New England. The Puritans had a free hand in matters of law and government. They were in the majority, had no official opposition to overcome, and so were able to legislate their principles into concrete public policy. Their vision of a New Jerusalem could only be realized by building bulwarks against the frailties of human nature. But they had no intention, not even in the beginning, of creating primitive Bible states. The new order they sought to build would be English as well as Christian. Puritans had no quarrel with the legal and constitutional traditions of England. They saw them as a national heritage to be improved upon but not discarded. While Puritans considered themselves bound by the moral commands of Scripture, they did not feel bound to rules and practices peculiar to the circumstances of the ancient Hebrews.[2] Their task would be to combine what was morally essential in Scripture with traditional rights equally essential to them as seventeenth-century Englishmen.

The everyday administration of justice at first claimed priority over lawmaking in the early settlements. The Assistants, as the Pilgrim and Puritan magistrates were known, had to determine not only how offenders should be punished but whether the offense should be punished at all.[3] They had few guidelines other than Scripture and their own sense of moral equity to assist them in maintaining order. Their only role model during the early years was the English justice of the peace, whose commission from the crown granted broad powers to deal with local offenders.[4] By the time the Puritan migration to New England began, justices of the peace had become key officers in the local administration of justice. The decline of manorial law shifted to them responsibility for trying a wide range of offenses formerly tried in courts leet and baron. So a precedent of sorts existed for the sweeping powers assumed by the Puritan magistrates.[5]

But New England was not England, and the magistrates were not English justices. Written commissions limited the authority of the latter, while the former had almost unlimited discretion in the administration of justice. In Massachusetts the Assistants for a time dispensed justice as a governing elite. Since statutes passed by the General Court covered only a fraction of the offenses committed, they had a virtually free hand in dealing with offenders. While the magistrates did not abuse their powers, doubts nevertheless surfaced about the desirability of giving any public officials a blank check. Many feared that so much power in so few hands could pose a

4

threat to personal liberty. Widespread dissatisfaction with the arrangement helped promote the dispersion of population beyond the borders of Massachusetts. Most of the Rhode Island settlers and to a lesser extent those who settled Connecticut objected to the freewheeling powers of the Bay Colony magistrates.[6]

The magistrates for the most part used their powers with moderation and good sense. They dispensed justice fairly, making allowance for the circumstances of the offense and the past record of the offender. Persons convicted of fornication, for example, got off more lightly if they intended to marry, and the harshest punishments were reserved for casual or promiscuous sex.[7] Moreover, the magistrates were never completely free to do as they pleased with regard to their judicial functions. If the offense was covered by statute, they had to follow the statute whether they agreed with it or not. And no matter how serious the offense, they hesitated invoking the death penalty unless a statute directed them to impose it. In 1630 the New Plymouth magistrates debated long and hard before sending John Billington to the gallows for murder. The crime had not yet been covered by statute, and they were reluctant to order the death penalty on scriptural authority alone.[8] Similar qualms the following year saved a Massachusetts adulterer from the gallows. The magistrates let him off with a whipping because the statutes had not yet made adultery a capital crime.[9]

But whether the magistrates used their power responsibly was not the real issue. What disturbed people was the power itself and its potential for abuse. However fairly and reasonably the magistrates handled ordinary cases, there was reason to fear that they might not deal fairly with political offenders. If they had confined their law-finding functions to clear-cut criminal cases, the system might not have been challenged so sharply. But they failed on this score, particularly in Massachusetts, where political and religious dissidents were treated harshly. Law-finding to punish thieves and common criminals was one thing, but law-finding to punish persons who questioned the Puritan establishment was quite another. The treatment accorded Thomas Morton, Anne Hutchinson, and Roger Williams must have alarmed even those who deplored their behavior and beliefs.[10] If the rights of dissidents meant nothing, then the rights of all might be in jeopardy.

Sentiment for a change in the justice system surfaced in Massachusetts during the first decade of settlement. John Winthrop, the leading magistrate, noted that by 1635 support for a body of written laws "in resemblance to a Magna Charta" had taken hold among the people. Winthrop himself opposed the idea, fearing that written laws would put judges in a straitjacket and prevent them from punishing offenses not covered by the statutes. He thought that judges needed a free hand to mete out justice on a case-by-case basis that made allowance for extenuating circumstances.[11] A system of prescribed statutory penalties allowing no flexibility in sentencing would almost certainly cause hardship and injustice. If, for example, judges could not take into account the offender's financial means in assessing fines, poor offenders would suffer disproportionately more than the wealthy. Such things had to be taken into account. no set of statutory penal   e for "any special wisdo   dge," Winthrop asked   lties according to the let

Wir   ws might pose a politic   xpressly forbade laws re   ifficult to square with m   nony in politics and rel   nd at odds with the cha   nterests of Massachuse   le and putting nothing   e government. Laws ba   use trouble for the colo

Winth   written laws consider   than preserving the   saw an uncomfortable resemblance between the Massachusetts justice system and the functioning of the English Court of Star Chamber. The magistrates meted out justice according to the same vague standards of moral equity that made Star Chamber unpredictable and notorious. In 1631 the Assistants Court sentenced Phillip Ratliffe to a whipping and loss of both ears for making seditious speeches against the government and church in Salem. These were Star Chamber punishments for Star Chamber offenses, and harsh even by the standards of Star Chamber.[14] In 1642 Daniel Fairfield was sentenced to have his nostrils slit for debauching young girls. Though no statute covered the offense, the Assistants, in typical Star Chamber fashion, not only made it punishable but imposed a punishment not authorized by statute.[15] Five years later Dr. Robert Child was fined and imprisoned for appealing a court decision to England.[16] He was punished for conspiracy, a Star Chamber offense, for not accepting the finality of colony adjudications.[17]

[Handwritten note: Worries that if they codified what they were already doing, the "autonomy" of the colony might be in trouble]

6

The flood of immigration to New England in the 1630s made legal reform inevitable. Discretionary justice worked well enough in the early settlements, where people shared similar views and the magistrates were respected as a natural elite. But the new wave of immigrants contained many discordant elements, and the dispersal of population complicated the administration of justice in areas without a resident magistrate. The General Court reacted by increasing the number and scope of the criminal laws. As the moral consensus weakened, more explicit laws were needed to enforce the official morality. But this in turn caused confusion as to the actual state of the law. The growing body of legislation made it only a question of time until all the measures were brought together and rationalized in readily accessible codes.

The deputies in the Massachusetts General Court put codification high on their political agenda. As the representatives of the freemen, they reflected public opinion, and public opinion had come to regard discretionary justice as inimical to personal liberty.[18] Supporters of codification made it a point not to reproach the magistrates for abusing their authority. This would have been divisive and counterproductive, for magistracy had a key place in the Puritan scheme of things. They contended instead that the concentration of so much power was bad public policy. People could never be sure where they stood in relation to the law until the law had been separated from the discretion of those who enforced it. Since even God had made His laws explicit and ascertainable in Scripture, New Englanders had a right to expect as much from the state. The codification of man-made laws would also ensure closer conformity with God's laws by providing a basis for textual comparison.[19]

Movement toward codification began in 1635 when the General Court, at the insistence of the deputies, appointed a drafting committee to work on a written compilation. All the members were magistrates unsympathetic with the project, and they predictably accomplished nothing. The greatest obstacle to codification, even after the decision to codify had been made, was that the officials most qualified to complete the project had no enthusiasm for the task. Another attempt was made the following year when the General Court appointed a new committee, this one with clergy as well as magistrates as members. They were directed to prepare a set of laws "agreeable to the word of God" for submission to the next session of the General Court.[20]

This foot-dragging by the magistrates enabled New Plymouth to take the lead from Massachusetts in codification. A rudimentary code was adopted in 1636 that reduced the law-finding functions of the magistrates, regulated trial procedures, and guaranteed the right to jury trial. The magistrates retained considerable discretion in sentencing but lost their blank check to determine what should be punished. New Plymouth took the lead primarily because political conditions there were more favorable to codification than in Massachusetts. The colony had no charter, only a political consensus based on the Mayflower Compact.[21] The freemen controlled the government from the outset, and the magistrates could claim no powers as a matter of charter right. Because they stood to lose nothing, the magistrates did not actively oppose codification.[22] The situation in Massachusetts was completely different. The authority of the magistrates came not from the freemen but from the colony charter, and they were loath to give up powers that they considered theirs as a matter of constitutional right.[23] Some took the position that the powers of magistracy could not be altered without changing the charter itself.[24]

The adoption of a law code by New Plymouth therefore had no immediate impact in Massachusetts. The magistrates on the second drafting committee continued their foot-dragging, and nothing would have been accomplished had not John Cotton, one of the clerical members, prepared his own draft of laws for submission to the General Court. Cotton relied heavily on Scripture, and quoted the Old Testament extensively with regard to criminal prohibitions.[25] His basic assumption seems to have been that the proper function of secular law was to restate and emphasize the eternal commands of God.[26] The major defect in his proposed code was not excessive biblicism, however, but its failure to reduce the authority of the magistrates. Indeed, adoption of the code would have strengthened their position by granting them life tenure and shielding them completely from political accountability.[27]

Cotton's proposals were not what proponents of codification had in mind. For one thing, the provision for life tenure for magistrates ran counter to the movement toward greater accountability in government. For another, Cotton allotted too much space to details of government already covered by the charter and not enough for listing the laws in force. Most of the colony's law was left as vague and uncertain as before. The code was so riddled with defects that it almost certainly would have been rejected if put to a vote. Since this would have been a setback for codification, the General Court tabled it instead until a revised and more acceptable version could be drafted.[28]

The events of 1637 left the General Court no time to pursue legal reform. First the Pequot war and then the antinomian attack on orthodoxy preempted the attention of the lawmakers. They did not take up codification again until the spring of 1638, and this time they tried a different approach. Instead of appointing still another drafting committee, probably with no better results than before, they appealed directly to the people to get the project started. The plan called for the freemen to hold discussions at the town level and present their proposals to a new committee of magistrates, ministers, and freemen who would then consolidate and combine them with the laws already in force.[29] The final compilation would then be submitted to the General Court for approval.[30]

The grass-roots approach prevented foot-dragging by the committee but not disagreements among its members. The details of what happened can only be guessed at, but when the dust had settled, not one but two separate drafts of laws were submitted to the General Court. One was the code prepared by Cotton in 1636 and already tabled by the Court, and the other was a draft prepared by Nathaniel Ward, a clerical member of the committee.[31] Like Cotton, Ward was a prominent minister, but before turning to the church he had been a common-law attorney in England. His legal training gave his proposals a high professional gloss not found in Cotton's draft. Instead of putting either draft to a vote, the lawmakers appointed still another committee, the fourth so far, to revise and combine them. The new committee submitted a consolidated version based mainly on Ward's proposals. But Cotton was not ignored completely, at least not with regard to the criminal provisions of the code. The latter owed their form and most of their content to his proposals. Before putting the compilation to a vote, the Court sent it to the towns for further recommendations. Whether any changes resulted is not known, but the local discussions consumed another year.[32] So it was not until 1641, six years after the project had begun, that the General Court finally voted on and adopted a law code for Massachusetts.[33] The new code, aptly captioned the *Body of Liberties,* would have landmark importance in the legal development of New England.

But the *Body of Liberties* in many key respects more resembled a bill of rights than a law code. Article I set the tone by declaring that no one might be deprived of life, liberty, or property except under laws enacted by the General Court.[34] The government thus bound itself to an English constitutional principle going back to Magna Carta. The articles then went on to list other traditional rights as well as some not yet recognized in England. The space allotted to everyday law, the main purpose of an ordinary code, was disproportionately small. Most of the substantive law in force remained as vague and uncertain as before.[35] Aware that the *Body of Liberties* fell short of the compilation desired and needed, the General Court adopted it only provisionally until a more complete set of laws could be drafted.[36]

Seven additional years were needed to complete the project. The delay, as before, can be attributed to foot-dragging by the magistrates. Some, like Winthrop, thought that the *Body of Liberties* sufficiently protected the liberty of the people and that a comprehensive code was not needed. He feared that any attempt to summarize all the laws of the colony would create loopholes enabling wrongdoers to escape punishment. So the project languished until 1646, when Dr. Robert Child and other critics of the Puritan hegemony accused the government of violating the laws of England.[37] This was the sort of charge likely to attract attention in England and possibly bring intervention by the home government. The vagueness of Massachusetts law now gave plausibility to the charge of lawless government. Child's protest made further delay on codification politically risky. Even opponents recognized the need to refute the appearance of arbitrary government.[38]

Everything thereafter went smoothly. New drafting committees were appointed, and within two years a comprehensive code was ready for the General Court. Most of the guarantees of the *Body of Liberties* were included, along with a summary of the colony laws already in force.[39] Topics were arranged alphabetically, making it easy to find particular provisions, and any old laws not included were deemed repealed and no longer binding.[40] While gaps here and there were inevitable, nothing really important was omitted. Completing the code had taken nearly seven years, but the final product fully justified the long wait.[41] Passed by the General Court in 1648 under the caption *The Laws and Liberties of Massachusetts*, it set a new legal standard for the rest of New England.[42]

The preamble of the *Laws and Liberties* affirmed adherence to the law of God as the foundation for all man-made laws. Scripture pervaded its criminal provisions, many of which carried Old Testament citations. This was consistent with the mandate of the drafting committees to frame laws "agreeable to the word of God," and gave the stamp of legitimacy to the final product.[43] Allowance was made for possible loopholes by providing that offenses not covered in the code should be dealt with according to Scripture.[44] Not to have made God's law part of colony law would have defeated the purpose that brought Puritans to New England.

But the code was much more than just a Puritan restatement of Scripture. Care was taken to safeguard and improve upon rights guaranteed by English law. Within the framework of Scripture, the framers incorporated procedural guarantees of their national heritage that were unknown in Old

Testament times. The technical terminology and legal fine-tuning were as important as the more obvious reliance on Scripture. Nowhere is this more apparent than in the provisions governing the rights of defendants. Had the framers looked only to Scripture, defendants would not have had the right to bail, jury trial, and other guarantees of the English common law.

The *Laws and Liberties* followed the English model of dividing all offenses into the two broad categories of felonies and misdemeanors. Felonies entered the criminal law first as a feudal conception brought to England by the Normans. They originally involved breaches of the fealty and loyalty owed by vassals to their suzerain, and their punishment was forfeiture of estates and chattels. But the concept gradually extended to offenses that in Anglo-Saxon times called for the loss of life as well as property. Capital punishment, which became the characteristic feature of felonies, was historically one of its last accretions.[45] Felony absorption of more and more serious crimes over the years had the political effect of extending the jurisdiction of the royal courts. By the seventeenth century felonies covered a wide range of crimes punishable by death and forfeiture of property.[46] But not every felony led straight to the gallows. Parliament complicated the felony concept by creating statutory felonies calling for penalties less than death. Even some of the capital felonies could be mitigated by a procedural device known as benefit of clergy, while others could not.[47] The *Laws and Liberties* rationalized felony law by discarding the historical baggage and treating all felonies as simply serious crimes punishable by severe penalties.[48]

Misdemeanors entered English criminal law sometime after felonies. They were an offspring of trespass, and their prosecution originally resembled civil litigations more than trials for felony. Although the local courts had dealt with a great deal of minor crime, the common-law courts did not become seriously involved with nonfelony offenses until the late thirteenth century. But thereafter assault and the asportation of chattels rapidly came under the jurisdiction of the king's courts, and by the fourteenth century most other forms of civil trespass would support a criminal prosecution as well. Still, before Tudor times, everything outside felony was basically trespass, very little of which came before the central courts by way of indictment. It was only after Star Chamber with its discretionary powers invented a riot theory of trespass that the misdemeanor concept began to take form as a separate criminal category.[49] By the sixteenth century the term "misdemeanor" was used to distinguish the criminal forms of trespass from the purely civil variety.[50] The *Laws and Liberties* adopted the concept of misdemeanors as a criminal category but discarded the technical

Laws for Living Saints

distinctions. Misdemeanors were simply minor offenses calling for less severe penalties than felonies.

The English common law entered New England through legal handbooks and commentaries readily available in the early seventeenth century. The most important by far was Michael Dalton's *The Country Justice*, an alphabetized summary of contemporary law and procedure in England.[51] Dalton, a justice of the peace in Cambridge, wrote the book for the guidance of justices who had no formal legal training. His simple, direct style made the handbook popular in England and the colonies. An earlier unalphabetized handbook by William Lambarde, the *Eirenarcha*, was also available, having gone through thirteen editions by 1619.[52] While the *Laws and Liberties* was being prepared for publication in 1647, the General Court ordered two copies each of Dalton's *Country Justice*, Sir Edward Coke's *Commentary upon Littleton*, Coke's *Reports*, the *Book of Entries* (probably also by Coke, but possibly William Rastell's earlier *Collection of Entries*), and *New Terms*, probably by Rastell, a popular law dictionary that went through numerous editions between 1527 and 1624.[53] The Court noted that these works were needed to provide "better light for making and proceeding about laws."[54]

The common law was not the only law source available to Puritan lawmakers. England in the seventeenth century had more than a dozen systems of law, each with traditions and procedures distinct from the common law.[55] They would all eventually be absorbed or superseded by the common law, but in the early 1600s they still functioned as separate systems.[56] The church courts still enforced canon law; town and borough courts administered local laws known as custumals; and courts merchant applied mercantile law in commercial cases.[57] So there was not one but many systems from which colonial lawmakers could borrow what was suitable for their circumstances and needs.

One non-common-law system from which the Puritans borrowed heavily was the body of church law enforced by the ecclesiastical courts of England. Despite the break with Rome, the church courts were far from outworn relics of the old papal system.[58] They still had the power to punish immorality and sin, and boasted a vigorous legal tradition.[59] The Church of England did not claim to be a new church. In theory, it was the original Catholic church, purged of popery and superstition, but retaining the powers and traditions of the true apostolic church. There was nothing connected with church matters over which the church courts might not take cognizance, providing that in so doing they did not violate a statute.

12

Because they claimed jurisdiction over private morality, these courts were, in effect, the moral policemen of the time. They enforced on the people of England a way of life chosen for them by the official Establishment.[60]

Although still powerful, the church courts of the early seventeenth century were less powerful than they once had been. Their decline began during Queen Elizabeth's reign as the Reformation undermined the disciplinary authority of the official church. Defendants could appear by proxy, and abuse of the process fostered disrespect for ecclesiastical penalties. Excommunication, once the most feared penalty of all, meant nothing to people who had no respect for the official religion.[61] The ineffectiveness of church discipline was originally deplored by English Puritans and other Elizabethan reformers, but Puritan dissatisfaction turned to rage when the Stuart kings used the ecclesiastical courts against Nonconformists. The most significant development in early Stuart times was the way Puritans came to be treated as a subversive and potentially dangerous element in the English church.[62] The Book of Common Prayer became the test of conformity, and clergymen who refused to accept it were removed from office. Ecclesiastical repression intensified in 1611 when Archbishop Laud became primate of England. The Laudian persecution that followed drove thousands of English Puritans to New England.[63]

Their hatred for the ecclesiastical courts did not prevent the Puritans from adapting ecclesiastical methods to their own use in New England. Though victims of the system themselves, they found Anglican methods of church discipline useful in safeguarding religious orthodoxy. Compulsory church attendance and civil disabilities for Nonconformists made perfect sense to the Puritan establishment.[64] Although the Puritan congregations never had the formal judicial powers of their Anglican counterparts, their disciplinary powers were formidable enough. Members who resisted church authority faced censure and excommunication, and the state stood ready to impose additional penalties as well.[65] To be excommunicated was a serious matter in colonies where the right to vote and hold public office depended upon church membership.[66] Excommunicated persons had six months in Massachusetts to gain reinstatement or face fine, imprisonment, and possibly expulsion from the colony.[67]

Anglican church law also provided models for regulating sexual morality. Fornication, incest, and adultery were offenses dealt with in England by ecclesiastical rather than secular courts. The latter could issue support orders in bastardy cases, but only the former could punish the parents for fornication. The English Puritans often complained that the ecclesiastical penalties were too weak and that such offenses should be more severely punished. So it is not surprising that they made the regulation of private morals primarily a state function in New England. The reach of the secular courts was longer and the range of penalties available more extensive.[68]

Although they had reason to hate it as an institution, the Puritans borrowed heavily from the body of criminal law developed by the English Court of Star Chamber. Star Chamber was a so-called prerogative court set up by the crown to deal with offenders too powerful for the regular courts.[69] It had no jurisdiction to take life or property, but it could punish perjury, riot, fraud, libel, extortion, and other serious misdemeanors. Actually, its reach was even longer, for it claimed jurisdiction to punish any wrongdoing not covered by the laws in force.[70] Had the Puritans not looked to Star Chamber for precedents, a vast amount of misconduct not covered by the common law would have gone unpunished. The influence of Star Chamber extended to judicial procedure as well. The fact that Star Chamber did not employ juries provided a precedent for assigning many misdemeanors to judges for trial without juries. The abolition of Star Chamber by Parliament in 1641 shifted its jurisdiction to the regular English courts and transferred to the general body of English law the offenses formerly tried in Star Chamber. This was essentially the same sort of fusion that had been achieved in New England from the outset. And the progress of the codification movement after 1640 eliminated the last objectionable Star Chamber features from the system.[71]

No English law source had greater conceptual importance than the local laws known as custumals. The most important thing about them was that they were in writing and readily ascertainable. Most Englishmen were exposed to these laws in one way or another, and the experience almost certainly contributed to their support for written laws in New England.[72] Not surprisingly, the first New England codes followed the format of the custumals. They began by listing the rights of the people and the constitutional basis for the assumption of lawmaking functions. The New Plymouth laws of 1636 cited the Mayflower Compact, the patent of 1629, and finally the inherent right of Englishmen to live under laws of their own making.[73] The *Body of Liberties* adopted by Massachusetts in 1641 cited divine law, the will of the people, and the need to safeguard public order.[74] And the *Laws and Liberties* adopted seven years later had a preamble asserting the right of the General Court to enact such a compilation.[75]

While the codifications of 1641 and 1648 clearly made Massachusetts the leader in New England's legal development, commentators have disagreed on which code was the more important. Most give primacy to the *Laws and Liberties*, which was published and printed, rather than to the *Body of Liberties*, which was published but not printed. George Lee Haskins does not think the latter was a law code at all but really a bill of rights protecting the liberty of the people. He notes that it neither summarized the statutes in force nor reduced the judge-made laws to written form. The *Laws and Liberties*, he believes, was the first real code. Not only was it the crowning legal achievement of Massachusetts, but "the first modern code of the Western world, antedating by twenty years the project of Colbert in France and by even more those of Austria and Prussia in the eighteenth century."[76]

Max Farrand agrees with Haskins on the importance and primacy of the *Laws and Liberties*. He describes it as "the first attempt at a comprehensive reduction into one form of a body of legislation of an English-speaking country."[77] It became the basis of all subsequent Massachusetts law and influenced legislation throughout New England. Stefan Riesenfeld goes even further: he describes the *Laws and Liberties* as "a legislative precedent *par excellence*," one which served as a model for other colonial codes and "determined noticeably the path of early American law." What made the code particularly important, Riesenfeld believes, is that "it recognized and enshrined, in an early age, a number of the civil liberties which have come to be considered the necessary and priceless pillars of a free society."[78]

These views have not gone unchallenged. Thomas Barnes regards the *Body of Liberties* as much more important than the *Laws and Liberties*. He dismisses the latter as a "highly-touted source of early Massachusetts law" but one that was definitely inferior to the former. Indeed, he questions whether it was a code at all, noting that it did not include all the laws of the colony and took the form of an abridgment or handbook of existing law rather than a comprehensive code. Barnes concludes that the *Laws and Liberties* was little more than a colonial adaptation of Dalton's *Country Justice*, which followed the same alphabetical format. The *Body of Liberties*, on the other hand, was both a real code and "a structured, rational, moderate, and compelling articulation of human rights." Its only shortcoming, the one leading to its replacement by the *Laws and Liberties*, was that it failed to quiet the popular clamor for limiting the power of the magistrates.[79] But this was a political matter unrelated to its intrinsic merit as a law code.

Barnes is correct in describing the *Body of Liberties* as a true law code. That it was less comprehensive than the *Laws and Liberties* did not make it less of a code in its own right. But his assertion that the *Laws and Liberties* was not also a code really cannot be taken seriously. The argument that it was not a code simply because it did not encompass all the colony laws would be equally applicable to the *Body of Liberties,* which contained even less substantive law. Besides, because the *Laws and Liberties* provided for the repeal of all laws not included, it can be argued that it represented the totality of colony law.[80] Nor does its alphabetical arrangement make it a mere legal manual or handbook. The format, as the preamble notes, was adopted to facilitate the finding of specific provisions. On balance, the *Laws and Liberties* was not only a true code but a more important one than the *Body of Liberties.* Their relative importance can be gauged from the fact that the General Court anticipated a successor code when it adopted the *Body of Liberties* only provisionally. Although its enactment was a landmark event, its successor immediately became the basic law source for Massachusetts and most of New England.[81]

The seminal influence of Massachusetts law was most apparent in Maine and New Hampshire. Both entered its orbit as territories claimed and governed by Massachusetts. The Maine settlements were annexed in the 1640s, and the New Hampshire settlements were taken over a decade later despite the protests of their English proprietors.[82] Both annexations were probably illegal, but the settlers themselves preferred the law and government of Massachusetts to rule by absentee proprietors in England. The annexation of Maine was legitimized by purchase in 1677, but New Hampshire was lost two years later when the home government made it a royal province.[83] Political separation, however, had almost no effect on New Hampshire's legal system.[84] The inhabitants had no desire to abandon laws under which they had lived for a quarter of a century nor to upset judicial orders and decrees.[85] The first laws adopted by the provincial government were almost verbatim restatements of the laws previously in force. The new assembly even provided that any gaps in the provincial laws should be filled by reference to Massachusetts law.[86]

Massachusetts exerted an almost equally powerful influence over legal developments in New Plymouth. Although New Plymouth adopted the first rudimentary law code in 1636, leadership in legal matters shifted in the 1640s to Massachusetts. Both the *Body of Liberties* and the *Laws and Liberties* were far superior to the Plymouth compilation. The Bay Colony attracted a higher caliber of settlers, and by midcentury New Plymouth had become a sort of backwater overshadowed by its more dynamic and powerful neighbor.[87] A new law code adopted by Plymouth in 1658 reflected the Massachusetts influence. While its substantive provisions remained fairly independent, its form and organization closely followed the Massachusetts *Laws and Liberties*. The 1658 code marked New Plymouth's last real attempt at independent lawmaking. The next code, adopted in 1671, was almost completely based on Massachusetts law. By the time they merged in 1691 to form a single jurisdiction, their legal institutions were virtually identical.[88]

Massachusetts law entered Connecticut and New Haven Colony with the first settlers. Many had lived in the Bay Colony and felt no need to abandon familiar forms of law and government.[89] Ultra-Puritan New Haven followed the Massachusetts rule that only members of the official churches should have the right to vote and hold public office.[90] Both colonies originally gave their magistrates sweeping discretion as to law-finding and the punishment of offenders.[91] When Massachusetts began to curb the power of the magistrates in the 1640s, Connecticut closely followed. A written set of laws adopted by the colony in 1642 put some limits on judicial discretion. Though more a listing of capital offenses than a real code, the compilation marked the beginning of movement toward a system of written and ascertainable laws. In 1650, two years after Massachusetts adopted the *Laws and Liberties*, Connecticut enacted its first comprehensive law code. Not surprisingly, whole passages were lifted almost verbatim from the Massachusetts model.[92]

New Haven Colony was the last New England jurisdiction to adopt the code idea. The founders and apparently most of the early settlers preferred the pure rule of Scripture to man-made laws of any sort.[93] For more than a decade justice was dispensed by magistrates who assumed the role of Old Testament patriarchs and judges.[94] Their principal law source during these years was the Bible, supplemented by the draft of laws prepared by John Cotton for Massachusetts. A copy had been brought from Boston, and for nearly two decades it served as a convenient handbook of Bible law. Although it had no legal standing, the magistrates applied it as a sort of unofficial law code.[95]

New Haveners seem to have had few apprehensions about entrusting so much power to their magistrates. They practiced the strictest form of Puritanism untroubled by the thought that authority might be abused. In the end, it was practical necessity rather than popular pressure that brought codification to the colony. As the General Court legislated on various matters over the years, the body of statute law eventually required adjustment and consolidation.[96] In 1655 a drafting committee was finally appointed to gather all the laws in force into a single compilation. The committee was directed to use Cotton's unofficial code and the Massachusetts *Laws and Liberties* as models. Since nothing original or innovative was expected, the task was completed with dispatch. A draft submitted to and adopted by the General Court in 1656 combined the criminal provisions of Cotton's code with the civil provisions of the *Laws and Liberties*.[97] Despite the heavy emphasis on Scripture, adoption of the code brought New Haven well within the orbit of Massachusetts law.

Only Rhode Island had a separate and independent legal development. Many of the settlers were refugees from the Bay Colony with bitter memories of Puritan law and justice. Their commitment to religious freedom and to local self-government set the colony apart from the rest of New England.[98] Rhode Island looked not to Massachusetts but to England for legal models. The adoption of English law not only provided a better basis for the separation of church and state but also reassured the home government that the colony was politically reliable.[99] The support of the home government was important because both Massachusetts and New Plymouth had territorial claims that might have obliterated Rhode Island as an independent jurisdiction. The threat of annexation continued until 1644, when Parliament granted a charter authorizing the settlers to set up a colony government.[100] The charter directed them to adhere to English law, which they probably would have done in any case, but left them otherwise free to run their own affairs.[101]

The civil war in England delayed implementation of the charter. It would have been politically risky to put it into effect until Parliament had actually won the war. In 1647, with Parliament finally victorious, representatives from the towns met in general assembly at Portsmouth to create a colony government.[102] They adopted a constitution setting up a federal system of government that reserved considerable authority to the towns. The central government got general lawmaking power, but the towns retained the right to vote as political entities on all proposed legislation. Provision was also made for the submission of proposed laws to the people and for the repeal of unpopular ones by referendum. These arrangements made Rhode Island the most democratic and decentralized jurisdiction in New England.[103]

The assembly also adopted a colony law code. This was the first code in New England adopted from the very beginning of colonywide government. It was based almost entirely on English common law and statutory precedents. Certain crimes were listed under New Testament captions, but their content was English, not scriptural. The Bible citations that punctuated the

Puritan codes were noticeably absent, and the precedents cited were to the laws of England instead.[104] Parts of Dalton's *Country Justice* were incorporated almost verbatim.[105] This reliance on English legal models became a characteristic feature of Rhode Island law over the years. A statute passed in 1673 required a copy of current English laws to be available at all legislative sessions and judicial proceedings of the colony government.[106]

Reliance on English law never made Rhode Islanders slavishly imitative. The idea of constructive crime, for example, was rejected out of hand. The concept had been used in English treason cases to circumvent the provision in Magna Carta that punishment should be inflicted only for violating some particular law of the land. The courts of England permitted treason convictions for acts within the spirit or intent of the law even though not within its letter. The code adopted by Rhode Island in 1647 expressly rejected such thinking. It provided that no one should be convicted and punished for anything not covered by the actual letter of the law.[107] This was the strongest safeguard enacted by any New England colony against specious prosecutions. While the Puritan codes cited the guarantee of Magna Carta, they did not repudiate what the English courts had done to it in treason cases.[108] The guarantee was further reinforced in Rhode Island by a provision that law officers should do no more than their official duties required.[109] This safeguarded people against officiousness and nit-picking. To a far greater extent than in the Puritan colonies, Rhode Islanders had protection against overreaching by government.

One of the more humanitarian features of the Rhode Island code virtually abolished imprisonment for debt. Debtors who agreed to pay installments or work off their debts could not be sent to jail, "there to lie languishing to no man's advantage."[110] This was at a time when England and most of the colonies treated insolvent debtors as though they were criminals. Connecticut allowed creditors to clap defaulting debtors into jail, and Massachusetts originally did the same.[111] The *Laws and Liberties* of 1648 imposed some limitations on imprisonment for debt but allowed defaulting debtors to be sold into bondage for the benefit of their creditors.[112] Not until 1672 did Massachusetts take the first tentative step toward discharging all impoverished debtors. Unless the creditor agreed to pay jail fees, an insolvent debtor worth less than five pounds would be unconditionally freed.[113] New Plymouth more closely followed Connecticut in the treatment of defaulting debtors. They were subject to arrest and imprisonment on the complaint of creditors.[114]

Despite its humane and progressive features, and perhaps in a way because of them, Rhode Island law never became a threat to the legal leadership of Massachusetts. Bay Colony law more closely reflected the assumptions of the age, and its coverage was more comprehensive. Rhode Island was also too out of step with the rest of New England in religion and politics to serve as a suitable model for anything. A refuge for malcontents and dissidents, it stood for everything that Puritans deplored. The progressive features of Rhode Island law served as more of a model for later non-Puritan generations.[115]

Although English law influenced lawmaking in all of New England, nowhere did it apply automatically just because it was the law of England. No one could be punished for an offense in Massachusetts that was not covered by a statute or the law of God.[116] Connecticut had a similar provision making offenders liable only under colony laws and Scripture.[117] Not even Rhode Island attempted to apply all of English law. The letter-of-the-law guarantee of the 1647 code applied only to laws passed by the assembly.[118] The laws of England applied only to the extent that the assembly incorporated them into colony law. Not until 1701 was provision made for applying English law in cases not covered by colony law.[119]

Legislative autonomy ended for Massachusetts in 1684 with the revocation of its charter. The old government ceased to function, and the colony became part of the Dominion of New England. The Dominion government appointed a law committee to bring the colony laws into closer conformity with the laws of England.[120] Until new ones were adopted, the old laws previously in effect remained in force. Instead of replacing the old laws completely with a comprehensive new code, the committee made piecemeal changes that caused uncertainty and confusion.[121] Some of the laws were new or revised old laws while others remained in effect unchanged from the charter period. Only in 1692 after its merger with New Plymouth did Massachusetts get a completely new law code.[122] But since the approval of all laws thereafter was up to the home government, the era of independent legal development effectively ended. The future of New England would no longer be decided by New Englanders alone.

The judicial laws of God as they were delivered to Moses
. . . shall be accounted of moral equity and generally bind
all offenders and be a rule to all the courts in
this jurisdiction.—New Haven Colony Laws (1644)

2   Crime and Scripture

The New England Puritans were not alone in looking to Scripture for legal models. All the English colonies relied upon it to some extent in drafting their criminal laws. Its influence had taken hold in Reformation English law, and the settlers brought the new legal thinking with them as part of their intellectual baggage. By the early seventeenth century English judges routinely cited Scripture to put the stamp of divine approval on their decisions. Sir Edward Coke, the greatest contemporary expert on the common law, asserted that the law of England was no ordinary system of positive law, but a body of law "grounded on the law of God."[1] This sort of thinking was common not only among lawyers but among most educated Englishmen in the early seventeenth century. Even if New England had been settled by non-Puritans, Scripture would have been an important factor in its legal development.

Still, while all Englishmen revered Scripture, the Puritans revered it most of all. Its influence on their conception of what law should be was stronger than among other Protestant reformers. They believed that the moral commands handed down to Moses on Mount Sinai still bound God's people across the ages. The Puritans saw themselves as God's special people, the successors of the ancient Hebrews in a new divine covenant. It was not mere hyperbole when they spoke of New England as their Wilderness Zion and looked to God's laws to keep it holy. The Hebrew language was as important as Greek and Latin among educated Puritans. It was the original language of the Old Testament and an essential instrument for understanding God's law.[2]

Puritan lawmakers automatically looked to Scripture for authority in legislating the death penalty. The list of capital laws adopted by New Plymouth in 1636 covered Old Testament as well as common-law crimes.[3]

Massachusetts cited scriptural precedents directly; eleven of the twelve capital offenses listed in the *Body of Liberties* of 1641 carried citations attesting their scriptural legitimacy.[4] The *Laws and Liberties* adopted seven years later followed the same format.[5] Connecticut, which closely followed Massachusetts, did likewise.[6] New Haven Colony went even further with regard to Scripture. For nearly two decades the Bible and Cotton's unofficial code served as the basic law of the colony. When an official code was finally adopted in 1656, the lawmakers included a provision that in all capital cases Scripture should be followed to the letter.[7]

Some of the scriptural offenses calling for the death penalty were not capital crimes in England. On the other hand, some punishable by death in England were left off the Puritan capital lists because the death penalty was not authorized by Scripture. The questionable legality of taking life outside the authority of English law did not disturb Puritan lawmakers. They felt morally bound to follow Scripture in such cases, fearing that not to do so would leave them open to the charge of rejecting God's law. Whether judges and juries would send offenders to the gallows for such offenses as adultery, blasphemy, and idolatry was not their concern. Their primary obligation as lawmakers was to make all colony laws an authentic restatement of divine law.

The discrepancy between English law and Scripture appeared clearly enough in the Puritan treatment of adultery. Secular law did not punish the offense at all in England, because adultery came under the jurisdiction of the ecclesiastical courts. The penalties imposed by the latter often fell short of what English Puritans deemed appropriate. Puritan criticism of the Anglican church courts sprang in part from their failure to enforce moral and spiritual discipline.[8] The Root and Branch Petition submitted to Parliament in 1640 blamed the ecclesiastical courts for "the great increase and frequency of whoredoms and adulteries occasioned by the prelates' corrupt administration of justice in such cases." The specific complaint was that they imposed only fines, thus turning justice "into monies for the filling of their own purses."[9] The lenient treatment of adultery ended in 1650, when Parliament made the offense a capital felony without benefit of clergy.[10]

The New England Puritans made adultery a hanging offense almost from the beginning. The issue of whether adulterers should be punished with death first surfaced in 1631, when John Dawe was brought before the Massachusetts Assistants Court for having sexual relations with a married Indian woman. Because no colony law authorized the death penalty for such an offense, the Assistants let him off with a whipping. But they also

22

issued an order, which presumably had the effect of law, that anyone committing the offense in the future would be punished with death.[11] The order was approved by the General Court in 1638, thus resolving all doubts about the status of adultery as a capital crime.[12] Three years later, the *Body of Liberties* unequivocally put adultery on the capital list.[13]

The Puritans deviated significantly from the English canon-law definition of the offense. They adopted the narrow Old Testament rule that the offense could be committed only with a married woman.[14] The marital status of the male partner did not count, only that of the woman. A married man could not be punished for relations with a single woman, nor could a single woman be punished for relations with a married man. Under canon law, the only law applicable to adultery in England before 1650, the offense occurred if either of the parties was married.[15] This remained the rule until Parliament made it a capital offense and adopted in the process the scriptural rule that the crime could be committed only with a married woman.[16] This brought English adultery law essentially into conformity with laws already passed by the New England Puritans.

But the New England definition of adultery still differed in one significant respect from the English definition. The latter covered only married women, while the former covered women under contract to marry as well. Puritan lawmakers followed the scriptural command that such offenses should be punished with death.[17] Since the point of the adultery prohibition was to protect the husband's bloodline against spurious progeny, it made no difference whether the offense occurred before or after marriage. A bride unfaithful before marriage was as much a danger as an unfaithful wife. The only points on which Puritan adultery law departed from Scripture had to do with penalties and evidence. No colony authorized the Old Testament penalty of death by stoning, nor was the scriptural rule adopted that a married woman discovered in bed with a man other than her husband was presumptively guilty of adultery.[18] Puritan law required direct proof that sexual intercourse had actually occurred.

The quest for scriptural legitimacy sometimes led to tortured interpretations of biblical events. In order to justify the death penalty for conspiracy, rebellion, and political subversion, the Massachusetts lawmakers cited the fate of Korah in Numbers 16 as a precedent.[19] Korah and his followers had challenged the right of Moses and Aaron to act as intermediaries between God and the Hebrews. When they dared approach the Trysting Tent to worship Yahweh directly, they were destroyed by divine fire as an object lesson that no one might enter the sacred precincts uninvited. Since Korah had not challenged the leadership of Moses and Aaron, only their exclusive access to the deity, his offense hardly amounted to conspiracy or rebellion in the political sense. More likely, he was punished for sacrilege for intruding upon the divine presence. Equating this with resistance to the Puritan hegemony required a considerable stretching of Scripture.

Many of the capital offenses adopted from Scripture were capital crimes under English law as well. Two obvious examples were sodomy and bestiality, offenses which had called for the death penalty in England since the time of the Tudors. The execution of Lord Castlehaven for sodomy in 1631 demonstrated that not even a peerage could save such an offender.[20] The New England Puritans followed the letter of Scripture with regard to bestiality, but modified the sodomy prohibition considerably. They began by waiving the death penalty for sodomites under the age of fourteen, which was also the cutoff age for sodomy executions in England.[21] New Haven Colony expanded the scriptural definition of sodomy. Mosaic law prohibited only offenses between males, leaving heterosexual sodomy uncovered.[22] New Haven punished heterosexual offenses as well. It proscribed "carnal knowledge of another sexual vessel than God in nature appointed to become one flesh," a ban so sweeping that almost any deviation from normal intercourse might be deemed a capital offense.[23]

New Plymouth alone among the Puritan colonies did not cite Scripture to legitimize the death penalty. While the preamble of its 1658 law revision declared compliance with "the ancient platform of God's law," the substantive provisions carried no biblical citations.[24] Since the lawmakers were as well versed in Scripture as their Massachusetts counterparts, the omission is curious. Perhaps lack of a colony charter made them hesitant to underscore any deviations from English law. But that should have been a minor consideration, if indeed it was a consideration at all. Connecticut and New Haven began without charters, and neither hesitated to cite Scripture. More likely, the omission can be attributed to the simple, less didactic style of Pilgrim piety. New Plymouth was less concerned with legal biblicism than with making religion an everyday part of life.[25] Not until the law revision of 1671 was Scripture cited to justify the death penalty for idolatry and blasphemy.[26] But by then the colony had moved into the orbit of Massachusetts law, where scriptural citations were part of the legal format.

One glaring omission from the Puritan capital lists was the scriptural prohibition against incest. The complicated marriage regulations of the ancient Hebrews would have conflicted with the tendency toward endogamy in the early settlements.[27] Adoption of some of the scriptural prohibitions but not the others would have been tantamount to repealing Scripture. So Massachusetts and New Plymouth enacted no incest prohibitions at all, leaving it to the magistrates to deal with the matter pragmatically. Only ultra-Puritan New Haven adopted the Old Testament regulations verbatim.[28] But these lapsed in the 1660s when the colony merged with Connecticut to form a single jurisdiction. Connecticut itself had no incest law until 1673, when the death penalty was prescribed for father-daughter and mother-son relationships. The courts were authorized to deal with other forms of incest according to the seriousness of the offense.[29]

The absence of incest statutes did not prevent the Massachusetts courts from dealing with such offenses. In 1690 the Assistants Court belatedly broke up the marriage of Samuel and Rebekah Newton of Marlborough. Rebekah was the widow of Samuel's uncle, a relationship which the Court declared made their marriage incestuous and void "by the word of God, and also by the law of England." Although Rebekah and Samuel already had two children, they were henceforth forbidden to have "any cohabitation or fellowship together as man and wife." The Court threatened them with severe penalties if they violated the order of separation. The following year the marriage of Josiah and Hannah Owen was broken up on the ground that Hannah was the widow of Josiah's brother, which made their marriage incestuous "by the word of God & statutes of England."[30] When English law coincided with Scripture, as in these cases, the courts did not hesitate to cite it.

But Puritan lawmakers were seldom slavishly imitative in their reliance on Scripture. Some Old Testament prohibitions were modified and updated to conform with contemporary legal thinking. In prescribing the death penalty for rebellious sons, they set the cutoff age at sixteen, making rebelliousness by younger offenders less than a capital crime.[31] Scripture had no cutoff age at all for the offense.[32] Similarly, Puritan laws against blasphemy applied only to persons who "wittingly and willingly" denied God and the truth of religion. This incorporated the contemporary notion of criminal intent into the law of the ancient Hebrews. Massachusetts and New Haven also gave blasphemy a secular twist by extending it to dissidents who derided religion as a political device "to keep ignorant men in awe."[33] Not even the English Court of Star Chamber could have given such a purely religious prohibition a more creative secular interpretation.

One of the sharpest departures from English law appeared in the Puritan homicide statutes. Puritan law followed Scripture and made no distinction between manslaughter and premeditated murder. English law did make a distinction, and persons convicted of manslaughter were not sent to the gallows. The common-law crime of manslaughter emerged in seventeenth-century English law in response to statutory limitations on the availability of benefit of clergy in murder cases (see chapter 6). Defendants could no longer save their lives by interposing the plea in cases involving a deliberate or premeditated killing. Since the latter seemed more culpable than the former, the notion of "chance medley" (accidental killing not without the killer's fault but without evil intent) was expanded to cover sudden, unpremeditated, but still intentional killings. The distinction between murder and the less serious crime of manslaughter came to be whether the killing had been committed in "hot" or "cold" blood. To qualify as manslaughter, the killing had to result from a sudden quarrel or altercation that eliminated the possibility of premeditation. While murder and manslaughter were both capital crimes, only manslaughter was clergyable and therefore not punished with death.[34]

Scripture recognized no middle ground between premeditated killing and accidental killing without intent or malice by the perpetrator. Only the latter called for penalties less than death. That the common law allowed for additional categories of homicide was well understood by Puritan lawmakers. But they consciously chose to ignore English law and follow Scripture instead. The Massachusetts lawmakers went even further. The *Body of Liberties* enacted in 1641 expressly provided: "If any person slayeth another suddenly in his anger or cruelty of passion, he shall be put to death." They reiterated in their murder statute that all intentional homicides were capital offenses. If the defendant took life "not in a man's necessary and just defense, nor by mere casualty against his will, he shall be put to death."[35] The lawmakers endorsed the scriptural position that all intentional homicides deserved the same punishment. Killing in cold blood was more reprehensible, but killing in hot blood also deserved the death penalty.

Connecticut also rejected the distinction between murder and manslaughter. The capital laws adopted in 1642 did not recognize manslaughter as a separate crime, but dealt with it under the murder statute, which read: "If any person shall commit any willful murder, which is manslaughter committed upon malice, hatred or cruelty, not in a man's necessary and just defense, nor by mere casualty against his will, he shall be put to death."[36] The omission of the word "premeditated" from the definition of murder obliterated completely the common-law distinction between homicides committed with malice aforethought and those committed upon sudden provocation. Although cast in common-law terminology, the statute was more in line with Scripture than with English law. The approach was similar to the definition of murder proposed by John Cotton in his 1636 draft of laws for Massachusetts. He defined it as "willful manslaughter, not in a man's necessary defense, nor casually committed, but out of hatred or cruelty, to be punished with death." While there is no evidence that Cotton's code was consulted by the lawmakers, its use in neighboring New Haven strongly suggests the possibility.[37]

The Massachusetts *Laws and Liberties* passed in 1648 recognized manslaughter as a distinct form of homicide, though not in the common-law sense of killing upon sudden provocation. What the Bay Colony version covered was really justifiable homicide committed in self-defense. It read: "If any person in the just and necessary defense of his life, or the life of any other, shall kill any person attempting to rob or murder in the field or highway, or to break into any dwelling house, if he conceive he cannot with safety of his own person otherwise take the felon or assailant, or bring him to trial, he shall be holden blameless."[38] The Connecticut code adopted two years later incorporated the Massachusetts definition of manslaughter almost verbatim.[39] While both statutes essentially restated the common-law definition of justifiable homicide, unlike the common law they did not make the defense of property a legal justification for taking life. Moreover, they required the endangered party to use nonlethal means if possible to bring the culprit to justice. English law granted what amounted to a license to kill under such circumstances.[40]

Massachusetts and Connecticut rejected the notion that anything but imminent peril to life justified the taking of life. The homicide laws of both colonies remained the same after 1650, though Connecticut did delete the word "manslaughter" from its murder statute in 1672. But the deletion had no substantive effect on how the law applied. Unpremeditated homicides committed upon sudden provocation remained capital crimes. The lawmakers may have deleted the word simply to avoid confusion. The term *manslaughter* was increasingly used in seventeenth-century England to describe intentional but noncapital homicide, a type of homicide not recognized in Connecticut. The only justifiable form of intentional homicide remained, as under the 1650 code, killing in self-defense.[41] Deletion of the term also helped keep the capital laws unambiguously scriptural.[42]

New Plymouth adopted essentially the same homicide rules as Massachusetts. The code adopted in 1636 made no distinction between premeditated and unpremeditated killings. The capital laws simply prohibited "willful murder," which apparently covered both planned and unplanned intentional killings. The code revision of 1658 reiterated this broad prohibition, leaving it to the courts to find mitigating circumstances justifying lesser penalties. No further change occurred until 1671, when the General Court adopted the Massachusetts homicide law almost verbatim. The new murder statute read: "If any person shall commit willful murder by killing any man, woman or child upon premeditated malice, hatred or cruelty, not in a way of necessary and just defense, nor by casualty against his will, he shall be put to death." The manslaughter statute was also clear and to the point: "If any person slayeth another suddenly in anger and cruelty of passion, he shall be put to death."[43] These provisions brought New Plymouth into line with Massachusetts, Connecticut, and Scripture, but considerably out of line with contemporary homicide law in England.

Surprisingly, New Haven, the strictest jurisdiction in matters of religion, was the only Puritan colony to deviate significantly from Scripture in dealing with homicide. The code adopted in 1656 was straightforward in prescribing the death penalty for all forms of homicide not committed accidentally or in necessary and just self-defense. But the manslaughter statute differed from those adopted in the other Puritan colonies. It read: "If any person in the just and necessary defense of his own life or the life of another, shall kill any person attempting to rob or murder in the field, highway or other place, or to break into any dwelling house, if he cannot otherwise prevent the mischief, or with safety of his own person take the felon or assailant and bring him to trial, he shall be holden blameless."[44] What made this statute different were the words "if he cannot otherwise prevent the mischief," for the mischief to be prevented included the threat to property as well as to life. A burglar fleeing from a dwelling house with stolen goods, for example, could be killed to "prevent the mischief" even though he posed no threat to the owner of the property. This was consistent with contemporary English law but contrary to Scripture and to homicide law in the other Puritan colonies.[45]

Puritan lawmakers sometimes wrote contemporary legal concepts into Scripture to prevent unjust results. For example, they made the scriptural offense of bearing false witness in a capital case punishable by death only if the witness had lied deliberately in order to convict the accused. Criminal intent was an English legal concept and not an element of the scriptural offense.[46] The Puritans also limited the scriptural offense of cursing or striking a parent to children over the age of sixteen. Younger offenders were not punishable by death.[47] On the other hand, Puritan lawmakers lowered the

28

level of accountability for the offense. Scripture made gluttony and drunkenness substantive elements of the offense, but Puritan law eliminated these preconditions completely.[48] Similarly, while the scriptural crime of manstealing applied only to males, Puritans included females by extending its coverage to "mankind."[49]

The influence of Scripture on legal developments stopped at the borders of Rhode Island. Lawmaking there was not complicated by a need for scriptural legitimacy, and the capital lists were therefore shorter and more in line with contemporary legal thinking. Roger Williams, whose ideas about religion and government helped set the course of institutional development, explicitly rejected the value or binding nature of Old Testament precedents. He asserted that the temporal penalties of Mosaic law had been superseded in the Christian era by spiritual remedies and that secular coercion was not needed for the salvation of mankind. The laws of the ancient Hebrews had only limited contemporary relevance. He wrote: "To make the shadows of the Old Testament and the substance or body of the New, all one, is but to confound and mingle heaven and earth together, for the state of the law was ceremonial and figurative, having a worldly tabernacle and vanishing beggarly rudiments."[50] As Williams saw it, the present was not bound by the dead hand of the past.

Unlike the Puritan colonies, Rhode Island did not prescribe the death penalty for any crime not punishable by death under the laws of England.[51] There were none of the scriptural constraints that complicated Puritan homicide law. Manslaughter was specifically covered in the 1647 code and defined as "the killing of a man feloniously, to wit: with a man's will, though without any malice forethought." Although the penalty prescribed was death, the death sentence could be canceled, as in England, by a plea of benefit of clergy. The availability of the plea can be inferred from the murder statute which made premeditated killing a "felony of death without remedy." Since benefit of clergy was the only remedy at common law for the death penalty, the lawmakers by implication made it a part of colony law. In any case, the code provided that homicide should be punished according to the "divers laws of England," which recognized manslaughter as a clergyable crime.[52]

Any attempt to quantify the influence of Scripture on Puritan law must inevitably be tentative and subjective. The problem is that Puritan lawmakers were selective about what they adopted and always distinguished between the realities of seventeenth-century life and circumstances peculiar to the ancient Hebrews. One attempt at quantification rates the Puritan laws against adultery and blasphemy as 100 percent biblical in origin.[53] But while their origin indeed may have been 100 percent biblical, they were modified in significant ways by the Puritan lawmakers. Scripture made being in bed together presumptive proof of adultery, whereas Puritan law required direct proof that sexual intercourse had actually occurred. A couple discovered in bed together could be punished for presumed immorality, but not for the crime of adultery. Moreover, although Scripture ordered that adulterers should be stoned to death, no colony authorized such punishment. The 100 percent biblical rating accorded to blasphemy also overstates the scriptural content of the colonial crime. By making intent a substantive element of culpability, the colonies brought the scriptural offense into line with seventeenth-century legal thinking.

While adding some offenses to the capital lists, Scripture excluded others that in England would have been punishable by death. Absence of scriptural authority made the Puritans reluctant to order the death penalty for common-law capital offenses such as burglary and robbery. Only after a third offense were such offenders punished by death.[54] Massachusetts initially treated burglary and robbery as forms of theft, and not until 1642 were more severe penalties imposed.[55] But it took another five years for the General Court to order the death penalty for third-offenders. In 1650 Connecticut also adopted this test for sending burglars and robbers to the gallows.[56] New Haven delayed until 1656, when death was prescribed for third-offenders.[57] Since Puritans blinked at taking life to punish offenses against property, the death penalty was justified on the ground that third-offenders deserved to die for refusing to mend their ways. New Plymouth did not put burglary and robbery on the capital list until 1671, when third-offenders were marked for the gallows.[58] Rhode Island was the only New England colony where, as in England, burglars and robbers faced the death penalty for a first offense.[59]

Reluctance to take life for crimes against property did not prevent the Puritans from punishing burglars and robbers severely. For a first offense, Massachusetts prescribed branding on the forehead, plus loss of an ear for offenses committed on the Sabbath.[60] Similar penalties were imposed in the other Puritan jurisdictions. Connecticut ordered branding and ear amputations, while New Haven ordered branding but settled for an additional whipping for Sabbath offenses.[61] New Plymouth branded burglars and robbers on the hand instead of the forehead, reserving the forehead for offenses committed on the Sabbath.[62] Such punishments were harsh but at least left culprits alive to mend their ways. Burglars and robbers got no second chances in Rhode Island.[63]

Scripture provided no useful models for punishing rape or the sexual abuse of underage females. Mosaic law allowed the rapist to square things by marrying his victim and paying damages to her family.[64] This was far too lenient by the legal and moral standards of the seventeenth century. Scripture prescribed no penalties at all for consensual relations between adult males and underage females. English law treated such offenses as a form of rape, but Scripture ignored them completely. The upshot was that for more than a decade the Puritan colonies passed no laws punishing the sexual abuse of young females.

A scandalous case of child abuse finally forced the hand of the Massachusetts lawmakers. The colony was outraged in 1641 by disclosures that Daniel Fairfield and two male servants had debauched the three young daughters of John Humfry, one of the magistrates. The affair had gone on for some time, and the girls had apparently been willing participants. But their extreme youth (one had been under the age of ten when the affair began) made the issue of consent irrelevant. Although nothing in the colony laws or Scripture covered the case, an outraged public demanded the death penalty. But the authorities were reluctant to take such a step without some basis in law; public anger, no matter how justifiable, was a dangerous precedent for taking life. So the culprits got off with severe whippings plus additional punishments for Fairfield. The latter had apparently been the ringleader, so he was sentenced to have his nostrils slit and wear a rope about his neck to remind people of the heinousness of his offense.[65]

The General Court reacted by passing a complicated rape law prescribing the death penalty for rapes against married or engaged women and for consensual relations with females under the age of ten. The death penalty was also authorized for rapes against other females, though the courts could impose lesser penalties if the circumstances warranted.[66] The scriptural rationale for punishing consensual relations with underage females was that such offenses were unnatural and akin to sodomy, for which Scripture prescribed the death penalty.[67] But this tortured interpretation of Scripture left doubts about the legitimacy of the measure. The *Laws and Liberties* adopted seven years later deleted the provisions of the rape law covering married or engaged women as well as the provisions punishing consensual relations with underage females. The only offenses left covered were rapes

31

against unmarried females over the age of ten.[68] While rapes against married or engaged women could still be punished under the adultery statute, females under the age of ten were left completely unprotected against either rape or consensual abuse.

This gap in the statutes went undetected until 1669, when Patrick Jennison was accused of raping an eight-year-old girl. Since the rape law covered only rapes against females older than ten, Jennison was technically guilty only of fornication, a noncapital offense. Uncertain how to proceed, the Assistants Court referred the case to the General Court for a full debate of the legal issues. Although some doubted the legitimacy of a death sentence without explicit legal authority, a majority of the Court decided that the rape law in force applied, by implication, to rape victims under ten as well as to older victims.[69] So Jennison went to the gallows, but only because he had actually raped the girl. Had she consented, as in the Fairfield case, there would have been no basis for a capital conviction, not even by implication. The loophole in the laws was closed the following year when the General Court made both forced and consensual relations with females under the age of ten a capital offense.[70]

Rape law in the other Puritan colonies also had a checkered history. In 1636 New Plymouth put rape on the capital list but did not expressly order the death penalty. The law code adopted in 1671 followed the Massachusetts model and made the death penalty prescriptive both for rapes and for consensual relations with females under the age of ten.[71] Rape law in Connecticut originally followed Scripture by allowing the rapist to square things by marrying his victim. The crime was finally promoted to the capital list in 1642 under a law prescribing the death penalty for rapes against married or engaged women.[72] But no provision was made for punishing consensual relations with underage females or rapes against single women. The latter finally got protection in 1673, but underage females remained as unprotected against consensual abuse as before.[73]

New Haven had a rape law protecting unmarried women against rape, but not married ones. Rapes against the former were punished by death, but the latter were left unprotected. The lawmakers probably assumed that married and engaged women were already protected by the law against adultery and that protecting them again under the rape statute would have been redundant. New Haven also prescribed death for consensual relations with females under the age of ten. Stretching Scripture for justification, the lawmakers characterized such relations as a form of sodomy because they were nonprocreative.[74] That this line of reasoning might be used to criminalize relations with postmenopausal women apparently did not bother them. Of all the New England colonies, only Rhode Island took a straightforward approach uncomplicated by Scripture. Rape was made a capital offense from the outset, and the death penalty was prescribed for consensual relations with females under the age of ten.[75]

Another offense covered by English law but not by Scripture was the potentially lethal crime of arson. The offense had not been particularly dangerous in Old Testament times, among pastoral people living without permanent habitations. But it was extremely dangerous in the seventeenth-century world of highly flammable wooden buildings. Even accidental fires could cause catastrophic losses of life and property. The Puritans put arson on their capital lists primarily to protect life rather than property. In 1636 New Plymouth took the lead and prescribed the death penalty for setting fires aboard ships or in human habitations.[76] The Massachusetts General Court did not make arson a capital crime until 1652, and then only for fires posing a threat to human life.[77] New Haven made arson a hanging offense in 1656, and seventeen years later Connecticut also made it a capital crime. Both colonies distinguished between fires posing a threat to life and those threatening only property; the latter were punished by whipping and civil damages, while the former called for the death penalty.[78] Only Rhode Island, which followed English law in such cases, made arson a capital crime whether directed against life or property.[79]

Since witchcraft called for the death penalty under both English law and Scripture, there was never the slightest doubt about making it a capital crime in New England. The witchcraft statutes adopted generally followed the English law of 1603 making all forms of witchcraft a capital offense. The English prohibition covered "white magic," as the harmless variety was called, and "black magic," the malevolent practices directly linked with Satan.[80] Although any dabbling in the occult could get a person into serious trouble, the New England lawmakers were mainly concerned with Satanism. They made dealing with the devil the key legal element in witchcraft; indeed, they made such dealings a capital offense regardless of the results.[81] Although the New Haven statute did not specifically require satanic contacts, the courts applied it as though such contacts were a substantive element of the crime.[82] Only Rhode Island made no distinctions with regard to occult practices. All such practices were capital offenses whether the devil was involved or not.[83]

Scripture, in taking crimes off the capital list, often prescribed alternative penalties. The Puritans found some of these, like restitution, particularly useful in dealing with crimes against property.[84] Requiring the thief to restore what had been stolen made more sense than inflicting the brutal penalties prescribed by English law. The latter would have been excessive in the early settlements, where there was no real criminal class and crimes against property seldom went beyond petty pilferage or the misappropriation of farm animals.[85] Restitution was enforced by the courts of Massachusetts and Connecticut even before it was required by statute.[86] New Plymouth showed the way by passing a restitution law applying to apprentices and servants. They were bound to repay double what they had stolen, a principle subsequently extended to all forms of theft.[87]

All the New England colonies adopted some form of the restitution principle. The details varied, but the rule was everywhere the same: the culprit had to make good what had been stolen plus an additional amount as punitive damages to the victim. New Haven provided that thieves unable to make double restitution should be bound out to service for the benefit of the victim until full payment had been made.[88] Massachusetts and Connecticut raised the stakes by requiring thieves to make triple restitution.[89] Rhode Island supplemented restitution with corporal punishments of the sort inflicted in England. Besides having to restore what they had stolen, thieves guilty of stealing more than twelve pence were whipped for the first offense and branded for the second. Fines of up to four times the value of the goods were also assessed, and those unable to pay were committed to the house of correction.[90]

The same rules applied to fraud and embezzlement. New Plymouth ordered simple restitution plus fines for falsifying legal documents, while Massachusetts required double restitution in such cases. Massachusetts also barred such offenders from serving on juries or testifying in the courts of the colony.[91] Connecticut and New Haven also sought to make the victim whole and punish the culprit by authorizing the courts to devise penalties geared to the circumstances of the case.[92] Rhode Island combined restitution with other penalties. Besides having to make good the victim's losses, offenders had to pay heavy fines or face imprisonment if unable to pay.[93]

Restitution made so much sense that it was applied even in assault cases. The culprit had to compensate the victim for the injuries inflicted as well as face additional criminal penalties. New Plymouth and Massachusetts provided for compensation by giving the victim a statutory civil action against his assailant. The amount of the damages to be paid would be up to the jury.[94] Even in the absence of an authorizing statute, the courts of Connecticut awarded damages as a matter of judicial discretion.[95] Both New Haven and Rhode Island had detailed legislation on the subject. New Haven granted the victim medical costs plus compensation for time lost as a result of the injury.[96] Rhode Island not only provided for medical expenses but allowed the victim to recover for pain and suffering.[97]

The restitution principle even became a part of homicide law. Money damages were routinely awarded by the Massachusetts courts to compensate the victim's family for accidental killings attributable to negligence. In 1683 the Assistants Court ordered John Dounton to pay damages plus a fine in a negligent shooting death.[98] Dounton got off lightly, because a fatal negligent shooting was technically a capital offense.[99] But juries were unwilling to bring in capital convictions in such cases. Jury nullification of the law was common both in England and the colonies in the seventeenth century.[100] Connecticut juries were no different. The jury trying John Allen on a murder indictment for the negligent shooting of a woman let him off with money damages and an order forbidding him to carry firearms for a year.[101]

Puritan lawmakers relied less upon Scripture with the passage of time. For one thing, scriptural principles had already been incorporated into the key criminal laws; for another, Scripture became less relevant to everyday needs after 1650. As population grew and the colonies prospered, problems arose for which Scripture had no answers. The trend away from Scripture appears clearly enough in the growing list of capital crimes unknown in Old Testament times. The capital offenses listed in New Plymouth's 1636 code more than doubled by 1671.[102] Connecticut's capital list increased from twelve offenses in 1642, to seventeen in 1650, and finally to eighteen in 1673.[103] The capital laws of Massachusetts grew over the years until by 1686 twenty-seven offenses called for the death penalty.[104] Only in New Haven, where the capital list shrank after the merger with Connecticut, was the process reversed.[105] Everywhere else Puritan capital lists became progressively longer. Of all the New England colonies, only Rhode Island had a fairly stable capital list throughout the seventeenth century.[106]

Scripture influenced not only Puritan substantive law in capital cases, but procedural law as well. The lawmakers adopted the scriptural rule that no one could be put to death unless convicted on the testimony of at least two eyewitnesses to the crime.[107] No amount of circumstantial evidence could dispense with the need for eyewitness testimony in a capital case. Every Puritan colony adopted some version of the two-witness rule. The only significant modification made by the lawmakers was that failure to appear in court to answer the charge counted as one witness against the accused when the case finally came to trial.[108] Rhode Island was the only colony not to adopt the rule for all capital offenses. Following English law, it required eyewitness testimony only in treason cases. This made it the only jurisdiction in New England where a person could go to the gallows on purely circumstantial evidence.[109]

The Puritan colonies used Scripture as a backup system of law to remedy defects in the statutes. Massachusetts authorized the courts to refer to Scripture whenever necessary to fill in gaps in the colony laws.[110] Connecticut and New Haven gave their courts similar leeway. All legislation was subject to judicial construction by the light of Scripture.[111] New Plymouth adopted the rule that anything not covered by statute should be dealt with by reference to Scripture.[112] In 1630 John Billington was sent to the Plymouth gallows for murder solely on the authority of Scripture. Murder had not yet been made a capital crime, so Scripture had to be invoked to deal with the case.[113] Connecticut executed Thomas Rood for incest in 1672 under similar circumstances. Rood was sent to the gallows for committing the offense with his daughter, though incest had not been made a capital crime. The court cited Scripture to justify the death penalty.[114] The following year a statute was passed adding the offense to the capital list.[115]

Puritan statutes typically gave the magistrates considerable discretion in meting out punishments. Though bound by the law as to what could be punished, they had much of the sentencing flexibility of Old Testament judges. Most of the criminal laws governing noncapital crimes provided for a wide range of penalties from which they might choose.[116] New Plymouth even granted sentencing discretion with regard to about one-fourth of the offenses on its 1671 capital list.[117] Indeed, all the Puritan colonies allowed for at least some judicial leeway in matters of life and death.[118] There was no way the statutes could be fine-tuned sufficiently to cover every situation. But Rhode Island judges had less sentencing flexibility than their Puritan counterparts. For one thing, they had no authority to invoke Scripture to fill in gaps in the statutes; for another, they worked under a statutory constraint to enforce only the letter of the law. The capital laws of the colony also tended to be more prescriptive with regard to the death penalty, leaving them no alternative to the death sentence.[119]

The influence of Scripture was not a step backward in the legal development of New England. Actually, Scripture became a force for progress and legal reform. The Bible provided lawmakers with a rationale for breaking with existing institutions. It took precedence over the historical freight of the common law that in England made law reform so difficult. Puritan reformers in England had to overcome obstacles that did not exist in the colonies, where English law had not struck deep roots. New England lawmakers seized the opportunity to modify English law by the light of Scripture, eliminate its archaisms, and turn it into a more dynamic and progressive body of American law.[120]

If you stand for your natural corrupt liberties . . . you will
not endure the least weight of authority but will murmur
and oppose and be always striving to shake
off that yoke.—John Winthrop (1645)

3   The Reach of the Law

Puritan law had goals higher than just keeping the streets safe and protecting life and property. The whole point of lawmaking was to promote public
morality by translating God's moral precepts into criminal statutes and
regulations. Calvin had warned that reliance on positive law would be
necessary because moral perfection could never be found in a community of
men. People were so inherently wicked that "it is the function of the law, by
warning men of their duty, to arouse them to a zeal for holiness and
innocence."[1] Promoting a zeal for holiness became the prime goal of public
policy in every Puritan colony. Good citizenship meant more than merely
paying taxes and serving in the militia; it also meant leading a good Christian life and accepting the official morality. That the standards set might be
unrealistically high and unlikely to be met was no reason not to set them.
The function of law was to provide moral instruction, and if people sometimes went astray, to return them, forcibly if necessary, to the path of
righteousness.

Social pressure made it relatively easy to enforce morality in the early
settlements. The churches functioned as powerful social regulators, and
neighbors could be relied on to admonish one another about lapses from
Christian living. People who initially needed one another in the daily
struggle for survival could not afford to be indifferent to community standards. Social cohesion was so important that aberrant behavior was viewed
as a form of disloyalty to friends and neighbors. The pressure to conform
was reinforced by the Puritan idea that the community was ultimately
responsible for the behavior of its members. While the Puritans gave it
moral dimensions, the idea had even older roots in the accountability of the
Anglo-Saxon hundred for individual wrongdoing.[2] But if the Puritans did
not invent communal responsibility, they raised it to a level where private

morality could not be separated from official morality. Every man was expected to be his brother's keeper and nip bad tendencies in the bud before they undermined good Christian living.

The family acted as the surrogate of the state in many matters of moral discipline. Family living was expected to foster good habits among the young and prepare them for responsible citizenship. Puritan social theory regarded living alone without family supervision as undesirable for the individual and dangerous for society. A Massachusetts law of 1641 ordered all unattached persons to move in with suitable families and warned that those who failed to make private arrangements would be assigned to families by the local authorities.[3] The law was difficult to enforce because most families had no room for outsiders. Colonial households were so overcrowded that finding space for family members was difficult enough without bringing in strangers. Still, universal family living was a social goal wherever possible. That anyone should live without accounting to someone undermined the ideal of an interdependent communal morality.[4]

All the Puritan colonies had statutes mandating some form of family living. New Plymouth gave unattached persons the choice of making suitable arrangements or facing unspecified penalties.[5] New Haven and Connecticut had similar laws, the latter ordering a fine of ten shillings for each week lived outside family authority.[6] All these measures specifically targeted unattached males, probably because the lawmakers assumed that females would remain at home until marriage. New Haven abandoned the gender distinction in 1656, perhaps because by then some women as well as men lived outside family authority. The new law ordered all single persons to make living arrangements with suitable families.[7] But the tightening of regulations probably did not improve enforcement where already crowded households could not accommodate everyone subject to the law.

If bad for single persons, living alone was even worse for married ones. In 1647 the Massachusetts General Court blamed spouses who lived apart for much of the "lewdness and filthiness here among us." A law was passed ordering the deportation of separated spouses who could not prove that they would soon be reunited.[8] Married settlers arriving alone from England had to bring their spouses over within a reasonable time. Connecticut set a two-year limit on bringing them over, and those who failed to do so were subject to a forty-shilling fine for each month the separation continued.[9] New Haven set fines as high as twenty pounds for spouses who failed to reunite.[10]

Both courtship and marriage were regulated in New England. Their

39

social ramifications made them more than simply private matters. In 1636 New Plymouth took the lead with a law forbidding anyone under parental authority to marry without first obtaining consent. If the parents were unavailable, the couple had to apply to a magistrate "whose care it shall be to see the marriage be fit before it be allowed by him." A law was passed two years later forbidding clandestine courtships. Men attempting to win the affections of young women without parental consent faced penalties ranging from fines to corporal punishments. The courts in such cases had authority to mete out penalties according to the circumstances of the offense.[11]

Massachusetts dealt with the matter by first prohibiting secret marriages. A law passed in 1639 required publication of the marriage banns at least fourteen days before the event took place. This afforded parents, guardians, and other interested parties an opportunity to raise objections. Secret courtships were forbidden in 1647 under a law prescribing stiff penalties for suitors who attempted "to draw away the affections of young maidens" without first getting parental consent. First-offenders had to pay a fine of five pounds; second-offenders, ten pounds; and third-offenders faced imprisonment at the discretion of the court. Not even the absence of parents gave suitors a clear field to proceed. They had to apply in such cases to a magistrate for permission to court the young woman.[12]

Connecticut had similar courtship rules. A law passed in 1640 prohibited secret marriages and engagements. The banns had to be published in some public place as well as announced at a public meeting in the town where the couple resided. No marriage might take place until at least eight days after the announcement. While this prevented secret marriages, it did not prevent secret courtships. So another law was passed in 1643 to close the loophole. It prohibited anyone living under the authority of parents, guardians, or masters to enter into a marriage contract without first obtaining consent.[13] The law had the curious and probably unintended effect of banning unauthorized courtships only if the couple intended to marry. Since couples who had no intention of marrying were not covered, the law actually encouraged illicit relationships.

New Haven had the most detailed courtship regulations in New England and stiff penalties to back them up. The code adopted in 1656 made it an offense "to inveigle or draw the affections of any maid . . . by speech, writing, message, company-keeping, unnecessary familiarity, disorderly night meetings . . . or any other way" without the consent of her parents or guardians. Offenders faced heavy penalties: fines of forty shillings plus civil damages for a first offense; four pounds if the offense was repeated; and additional fines, imprisonment, and corporal punishment for subsequent offenses. The declared purpose of the law was to prevent "the irregular and disorderly carriage of young persons of both sexes," the sort of conduct that today would be considered harmless dating.[14] Such relations were too important in the Puritan scheme of things to be left unregulated.

The Puritans assumed that courtship and marriage had to be regulated to maintain family authority and stability. Good marriages produced stable families, and stable families were likely to produce God-fearing children. Parents were regarded as surrogates for the state in the rearing of children, and any resistance to their authority was severely punished. Every Puritan colony followed Scripture in making the striking or cursing of parents a capital crime.[15] Although no one was ever executed for such an offense, John Porter, Jr., probably would have gone to the Massachusetts gallows in 1665 had his mother not refused to join in the complaint his father filed against him.[16] For ordinary defiance of parental authority, any magistrate in Massachusetts might order up to ten lashes or remand the case to a county court for more severe penalties.[17] Connecticut dealt with children who defied their parents by sending them to the house of correction "for hard and severe punishment."[18]

Family heads were accountable to the state for how they used their authority. They had a duty to provide children and apprentices living in the family with the education and training needed to earn a living. Every family head was expected to set a good example and inculcate the moral values considered essential for good citizenship. Periodic checks were conducted by the local authorities to make sure these duties were not neglected. The children would be questioned about such things as the capital laws to determine whether they had been instructed about the consequences of crime and what was expected of them as members of the community.[19] Parents who failed to provide proper instruction could be deprived of the custody of their children. Such children would be placed in suitable families willing to take responsibility for raising them.[20] The interests of society in how the children turned out superseded the rights of parents.

Children and young people with free time on their hands were particularly difficult to control on the Sabbath. Adults complained about the noisy play of children in the streets and the spectacle of young men and women walking "uncivilly" in the fields. Some young people, and older ones as well, spent their free time drinking excessively in taverns. In 1653 Massachusetts banned all such conduct during the daylight hours of the

Sabbath. Fines were ordered for the parents of offenders under fourteen years of age, with heavier fines and possible whipping for older offenders. Since the law covered only the daylight hours, the hours after sunset were left completely unregulated. The law had been passed during the summer when the sun set fairly late, and the lawmakers apparently assumed that by then it would be too late for young people to be out of doors in any case. They forgot that when sunset came progressively earlier in the fall, young people would have plenty of time to make the most of the evening hours without breaking the law. The loophole was finally closed in 1658 when the General Court extended the law to the hours after sunset as well.[21]

The reach of Puritan law extended to dress and fashions. Personal vanity was frowned upon as unworthy of God-fearing people and an obstacle to good Christian living. It was particularly reprehensible for people to deck themselves out in expensive clothing and adornments beyond their means and standing in society. This was not only wasteful but a tacit rejection of the role God had assigned them. The Puritans believed in hierarchy and thought that rank and position in society reflected God's will. This in turn made acceptance of one's lot an act of pious submission. Attempts by members of the lower class to emulate their betters by dressing elegantly were viewed as a form of rebellion against God's plans. Such problems likely never arose in the early years when the everyday struggle for survival left little time for elegance or social envy. But once the settlements took hold and people began to prosper, attitudes changed dramatically. Drabness in dress became unacceptable, and a fascination took hold with silks, laces, and jewelry. All the classes were affected, much to the chagrin of moralists who saw the preoccupation with fashions as evidence of the weakening of spiritual values.[22]

Massachusetts took the lead in sumptuary legislation. A law passed in 1634 mandated frugality and modesty in apparel. Gold and silver buckles, laces, and silks were prohibited as "superfluous and unnecessary." The manufacture or purchase of slashed clothes, which were then the height of fashion in England, was restricted. Only garments with just "one slash in each sleeve, and another in the back" were permitted. One slash was as far as the lawmakers were willing to bend; any further concession to fashion would have been frivolous and un-Puritan. Gold and silver girdles were also prohibited, along with embroidered caps, hat bands, fancy belts, and beaver hats. Anyone already owning such apparel might wear it out, provided the garment was not showy or offensive. The law listed no penalties, but left it to the magistrates to deal with offenders according to the circumstances of the case.[23]

Fashion-conscious people almost immediately discovered a loophole in the law. Because bone lace and some other kinds of lace were not expressly prohibited, these legal forms of lace enjoyed a brief vogue until the General Court outlawed all kinds of lace in 1636. The new law forbade lace adornments under penalty of five shillings per yard for every yard of lace made or sold. One minor concession was made to the growing fascination with fashion. Garments with "small edging laces" were allowed if they did not offend moral sensibilities.[24] Anything more conspicuous fell under the general ban against excessive adornments.

Enforcement of the sumptuary regulations proved almost impossible because they ran counter to popular tastes. Noting the many complaints about the continued "wearing of lace and other superfluities," the Massachusetts lawmakers conceded failure in 1639. They deplored the growing popularity of "immoderate great sleeves, great breeches, knots of ribbon, broad shoulder bands, and . . . double ruffles and cuffs." The trend toward immodesty was even more alarming. Women had apparently begun to wear short sleeves, "whereby the nakedness of the arm may be discovered." The sale of such garments was prohibited, and those already owned might not be worn in public "unless they cover their arms to the wrist with linen or otherwise." Realizing that enforcement would be difficult, the lawmakers urged the church congregations to discipline members who persisted in wearing prohibited apparel.[25]

Such measures found little support among the classes able to afford fancy clothing. People of means preferred elegance to drabness, and their pressure finally forced a change in the law. Shifting ground in 1651, the Massachusetts lawmakers narrowed the prohibition against excess in general to excess "amongst people of mean condition," a modification legalizing expensive apparel for those who could afford it. Moral outrage was now directed against men of mean condition who wore gold or silver lace and against women of the same rank who appeared in silk hoods and scarves. While such attire was "allowable to persons of greater estates and more liberal education," it was "intolerable" that persons of mean condition should make such displays. So a law was passed limiting the wearing of gold or silver lace or buttons of that sort to families worth two hundred pounds or more. But even those who qualified might not wear lace costing more than two shillings a yard, and silk hoods and scarves were banned completely. Penalties were set at ten shillings for each infraction.[26]

The new policy made fashionable attire an upper-class prerogative. The problem now became determining who could wear it rather than whether it should be worn at all. This was not easy, because almost anyone could claim to be worth two hundred pounds and shift the burden of proving otherwise to the authorities. So local officials were directed to note the sort of clothing worn and tax those wearing costly apparel at the rate paid by persons with estates assessed at two hundred pounds or more. The upshot was that lower-class persons who wore upper-class apparel had to pay upper-class taxes for the privilege.[27]

Some people were not subject to any means test to justify what they wore. The law left the families of magistrates and other public officials "to their own discretion in wearing of apparel." A similar exemption was granted to persons "whose education and employment have been above the ordinary degree, or whose estate have been considerable though now decayed."[28] These exemptions made the means test essentially a form of class discrimination applicable only to servants, workers, and persons without education or social standing. Keeping such persons in line may have been the real purpose of the regulations.

But members of the lower classes refused to accept drabness as a class condition. There were so many violations of the law that in 1662 the General Court increased the penalties for persons who wore apparel "exceeding the quality and condition of their persons or estate." The lawmakers were particularly concerned that the fascination of young people with showy fashions would leave them "corrupted and effeminated." The new law ordered admonitions for a first offense, fines of twenty shillings for a second, and forty shillings for each subsequent offense. Tailors were forbidden to make costly apparel for youths or servants without the consent of their parents or masters. Those who failed to obtain the requisite consent were reprimanded for a first offense and fined twice the value of the apparel for a second. Grand jurors were urged to assist the constables by keeping a lookout for offenders.[29]

Long hair and immodest fashions eventually replaced expensive attire on the regulatory agenda. In 1675 the General Court wondered out loud whether the problems besetting Massachusetts might not be the result of God's anger at the "manifest pride openly appearing amongst us in that long hair, like women's hair, is worn by some men, either their own or others' hair made into periwigs." Women, on the other hand, were rebuked for apparently doing the opposite—"cutting, curling and immodest laying out of their hair, which practice doth prevail and increase especially amongst the younger sort." The lawmakers also denounced the growing trend in female fashions toward "naked breasts and arms" and the wearing of "superfluous ribbons" on their heads and apparel. They blamed the problem on lax law enforcement and urged local officials to hold the line more forcefully.[30] But this was the last rhetorical blast in a war already lost, and no further attempt was made to control fashion through legislation.

The sumptuary laws enacted by Connecticut were no more effective. In 1641 the local constables were ordered to note any "excess in apparel" and require "all such as they judge to exceed their condition and ranks . . . to appear at the particular court."[31] This gave the constables the unenviable task of making fashion judgments that ranked people invidiously in society. Predictably, the order was poorly enforced. The General Court passed new regulations in 1676 based on the Massachusetts models. But instead of setting property qualifications for wearing upper-class apparel, the law simply made persons who wore "gold or silver lace, or gold or silver buttons, silk ribbons, or other superfluous trimmings" subject to a higher tax rate. Only those obviously attired beyond their means and social position were liable for a ten-shilling fine.[32]

Puritan lawmakers took for granted that the state had a duty to protect the Sabbath and compel regular church attendance. Compulsion was needed because many people found Sabbath services tedious and boring. The morning sermon lasted about two hours, during which the congregation was exposed to religious exhortation and moral nit-picking. Then, several hours later, the congregation had to return for the evening sermon, shorter than the first but likely just as boring.[33] Some members of the congregation found the services so dull that they could not resist falling asleep. The ministers themselves noted the tendency toward narcolepsy on the Sabbath. After one sleep-inducing sermon in 1646, the Reverend Samuel Whiting complained that he seemed "to be preaching to stacks of straw with men sitting here and there among them." Whiting once remarked that he sometimes wished for the Anglican service so that the frequent rising and standing would keep the congregation awake.[34] Many Puritan churches probably would have been half empty without laws compelling attendance.

When it had become apparent by 1635 that religious zeal alone would not fill the churches, Massachusetts made attendance compulsory under penalty of a five-shilling fine for each absence.[35] But people still continued to absent themselves in such numbers that sterner measures were needed. A new law was passed in 1646 to deal with persistent absentees. The five-shilling fine remained in force for occasional absences, but persistent absences were now treated as a renunciation of church connections. The penalty for the latter was forty shillings for each month the separation continued. The same law punished misconduct during church services as well as contempt toward the ministers at any time.[36] Some of the most distinguished ministers had reason to complain bitterly about the latter. A member of John Cotton's congregation had the temerity to follow him home after a Sabbath service to inform him that his sermons were dark and flat.[37] Anyone who interrupted a minister's sermon or falsely accused him of doctrinal error had to post bond not to repeat the offense. A second-offender had to pay a five-pound fine or stand in public "upon a block four feet high, on a lecture day, with a paper affixed on his breast with AN OPEN AND OBSTINATE CONDEMNER OF GOD'S HOLY ORDINANCES written in capital letters."[38]

But what bothered the ministers even more than occasional interruptions and discourtesies was the implacable indifference of many in the congregation. The Reverend Thomas Shepard noted that by the 1640s large families often arrived late, that young people came with only marriage in mind, and that the old habit of taking sermon notes was dying out. Even the most famous preachers complained that their efforts were not appreciated. Thomas Hooker deplored the behavior of some congregations. People talked or read during the sermon, and children played and ran about the churches.[39] All in all, despite the backing of the state, the lot of the ministers was not an easy one.

The Massachusetts attendance law did not compel people to remain for the entire Sabbath service. The loophole was soon discovered by bored churchgoers who slipped away before the sermon was over. By 1654 untimely departures had become so common that the General Court ordered the towns to keep track of persons who left services before the proper time. They were to be warned and then brought before a magistrate if the warning went unheeded. The lawmakers tacitly admitted that long-winded sermons had something to do with the problem. They politely recommended shorter sermons. With shorter services, they predicted, "none shall be ordinarily occasioned to break off from the congregation before the full conclusion of public exercise."[40]

But this was not the sort of advice ministers were likely to follow. The idea that their sermons might be long and boring was for many simply unthinkable. So churchgoers continued to shorten services themselves by leaving early when the sermon dragged on for too long. In 1675 Massachusetts finally passed a law ordering church doors to be closed and guarded to make sure that no one left before the proper time.[41] But the measure backfired by reducing overall church attendance. Even devout churchgoers resented being virtual prisoners until the services were over. The upshot of the closed-door policy was that more and more people absented themselves completely on one pretext or another.

The growth of absenteeism led the General Court to strengthen the machinery of enforcement. A law passed in 1677 provided for the appointment of tithingmen in every town to report Sabbath violations. Each had responsibility for supervising ten families, and they were authorized to make arrests and bring violators before the nearest magistrate for a hearing. Anticipating wholesale arrests, the lawmakers ordered cages to be set up in Boston and the other towns to hold offenders until their cases could be heard.[42] But mass arrests did not occur, for the tithingmen had no stomach for the assignment. Most were reluctant to make trouble for neighbors among whom they had to live the rest of the week. They made so few arrests that they were finally authorized to act outside their neighborhoods where they were less likely to jeopardize personal relationships.[43] But this did not improve enforcement much because tithingmen were unlikely to know of infractions outside their own neighborhoods. The system had little impact on absenteeism or Sabbath violations generally.

Massachusetts also tried restricting travel on the Sabbath in order to keep people in their home communities where they could not avoid the Sabbath regulations. In 1653 all unnecessary travel was banned completely, even to the extent of forbidding people to go aboard ships on the Sabbath.[44] But the law contained a loophole that prevented effective enforcement. Since only Sabbath travel was forbidden, people were able to get out of town on Saturday night without incurring penalties. The pre-Sabbath exodus from Boston reached such proportions in 1679 that the General Court restricted the flow of traffic on Saturday night. Watchmen were stationed to halt traffic and turn back anyone without a good explanation for leaving. All the towns were authorized to adopt similar measures against Saturday night departures.[45] The law probably worked no better than the other Sabbath regulations. The watchmen appointed were not eager to make enemies, so almost any explanation generally sufficed to justify a departure.

Sabbath regulations in New Plymouth were somewhat more detailed than those enacted by Massachusetts. The lawmakers banned unnecessary work and travel, required regular church attendance, prohibited sleeping and game-playing during services, required churchgoers to bring along firearms, and forbade the Indians to hunt, fish, or work whether they were Christian or not. The exodus from the towns to avoid Sabbath services was

47

so great that in 1658 the General Court banned unnecessary departures under penalty of a fine or a turn in the stocks. The problem of keeping churchgoers sober was also addressed. To prevent excessive drinking, the taverns were ordered not to serve wine or liquor until religious services were over. Whether churchgoers simply made other drinking arrangements cannot be ascertained, but it is reasonable to assume that those who wanted a drink brought their own. To underscore the seriousness of the Sabbath, the lawmakers made it a capital crime to violate the regulations "proudly, presumptuously and with a high hand."[46] But no one ever went to the gallows for such an offense.

Connecticut and New Haven enacted similar controls. In 1650 Connecticut made church attendance compulsory on the Sabbath and all other days set aside for public worship.[47] New Haven prohibited unnecessary work as well as sports or recreation likely to disturb the piety of the Sabbath. Offenders faced penalties ranging from fines and imprisonment to corporal punishment, depending upon the seriousness of the violation. As in New Plymouth, the death penalty was authorized for offenses committed "proudly, presumptuously, and with a high hand."[48] The death penalty provision lapsed after the merger with Connecticut in the 1660s. The code adopted in 1673 for the combined jurisdictions punished all Sabbath violations, high-handed or otherwise, with a five-shilling fine or a turn in the stocks if the fine was not paid.[49] These measures apparently worked no better than the controls adopted elsewhere. Sabbath offenses proliferated so rapidly that in 1676 the lawmakers raised the fine to ten shillings and ordered a whipping for failure to pay.[50]

The Puritans had no monopoly on Sabbath legislation. Despite its commitment to church-state separation, Rhode Island enacted what might be called nonsectarian Sabbath regulations. Noting the misuse of free time granted on the Sabbath, the lawmakers took steps to prevent "tippling and unlawful games and wantonness." Parents and masters were admonished to keep children and other dependents out of trouble, though not necessarily by compelling them to attend church services. To play down the religious implications, the lawmakers did not mention the Sabbath by name, but rather "the first day of the week." In 1679, and again without mentioning the Sabbath or religious worship, a partial work ban was promulgated against "evil-minded persons" who worked their servants a full seven-day week. Masters who worked their servants unnecessarily on the first day of the week or hired them out to work for others faced a five-shilling fine. The measure also banned sports, shooting, and drinking in taverns under penalty of a fine or a turn in the stocks.[51] These were Sabbath controls in everything but name. Their obvious purpose was to make the Lord's Day special by banning ordinary activities. Still, they did not compel church attendance, nor were people forbidden to travel or to work for their own benefit.

The most difficult social problem to manage in colonial times was the widespread abuse of alcohol. Excessive drinking not only harmed the drinker but imposed heavy costs on society in the form of impoverished families and destitute children. The problem was complicated by the fact that total prohibition was out of the question. Social drinking had broad popular support as well as the approval of Scripture.[52] Besides, alcohol was safer to drink than ordinary water, which in colonial times often contained lethal bacteria. Water mixed with a little alcohol was much safer than untreated water. The danger to health posed by the latter made wine and beer essential household items.[53] So despite its potential for abuse, alcohol came close to being a universal beverage. It was imbibed on all occasions, public as well as private, and even at legislative sessions of the Massachusetts General Court.[54] While there is no way to gauge its possible impact on lawmaking, some of the loopholes in the statutes may have had as much to do with drinking as with careless draftsmanship.

With total prohibition impossible, the only realistic goal had to be moderation in drinking. For a time Massachusetts banned toasting on the theory that it encouraged excessive consumption. Drinking to one another's health or success thus became unlawful, while drinking for the sake of drinking remained perfectly legal. The ban could not be enforced, partly because it was obviously foolish, but also because toasting was regarded as a basic social amenity.[55] Regulating the production and distribution of alcohol made much more sense, and every colony tried this approach.[56] While the measures adopted did not prevent alcohol abuse, they did manage to keep the problem under control and limit its social consequences.

The heart of the problem was that excessive drinking could not be quantified. An amount of alcohol sufficient to make one drinker drunk might have no effect on another. So the regulations had to target the effect on the drinker rather than the quantity consumed. Massachusetts made it unlawful for the drinker to become "disabled in the use of his understanding," a definition loose enough to cover everything from slight to total intoxication.[57] New Plymouth had a similar law with detailed guidelines for enforcement. A person who lisped, staggered, vomited, or could not work as a result of drinking was considered legally drunk.[58] The working test made even moderate drinking unlawful if it interfered with earning a living.

Inns and taverns were closely regulated to curb drinking abuses. Limits were set on business hours, on the amount of time patrons could spend drinking, and on how much liquor might be consumed. Taverns failing to enforce the rules faced fines and possible loss of their license to do business. Massachusetts taverns could not serve alcohol after nine o'clock at night or allow patrons to drink for more than an hour at one time.[59] Taverns in Connecticut could not serve patrons more than half a pint of wine per visit.[60] While nothing prevented a drinker from leaving and then returning for another half pint, he might not be served if he appeared to be intoxicated. New Haven limited drinking to one hour at a time and imposed a nine o'clock curfew on business hours.[61] New Plymouth for a time permitted only lodgers to drink in taverns, forcing the local inhabitants to make other drinking arrangements.[62] Every colony banned games, dancing, and most other things likely to draw people to taverns for companionship and relaxation.[63] The more people enjoyed themselves in taverns, the more likely they were to spend too much time drinking in such places.

New Plymouth tried to shame excessive drinkers into moderation by publishing the names of known drunkards. Alcohol sales to anyone on the list were forbidden without official approval.[64] New Haven had a similar law restricting purchases by anyone convicted of drunkenness.[65] Connecticut tried to nip excessive drinking in the bud before it became a compulsive habit. The constables had a duty to keep track of tavern patrons and admonish any who spent too much time there drinking.[66] Tavern keepers in Massachusetts had a duty to summon the constable if any of their customers became intoxicated.[67] New Plymouth and New Haven also had laws making the proprietor responsible for reporting problem drinkers.[68] It seems unlikely that such regulations were strictly enforced. A tavern keeper who informed on his patrons would have soon been out of business.

The courts were usually more concerned with reforming alcohol abusers than with punishing them. They took into account that many of the offenders brought before them were victims of an uncontrollable habit.[69] Some were required to post bond that the offense would not be repeated, while others were kept in jail long enough to break their habit.[70] Shock tactics were sometimes used to reclaim drunkards to sober living. They might be disfranchised or made to wear the letter *D* (for drunkard) until they pulled themselves together.[71] The harshest treatment was reserved for offenders who were not compulsive drunkards but whose drinking could be attributed to self-indulgence. They were treated as ordinary lawbreakers, and the penalties meted out ranged from fines to whippings.[72]

The strictest alcohol controls were those relating to Indians. The regulatory ideal was total prohibition, for experience had shown that even friendly Indians could turn lethal when intoxicated.[73] When total prohibition proved impractical, every colony did the next best thing by closely regulating liquor sales to the Indians.[74] Massachusetts assessed fines of forty shillings for each illegal transaction, with part of the proceeds going to informers who reported offenses.[75] Connecticut and Rhode Island punished unauthorized sales at the rate of five pounds for every pint sold, and both colonies allotted part of the fine to informers who reported such transactions.[76] Massachusetts put pressure on drunken Indians to disclose the source of their supply. They could be jailed indefinitely until they revealed who had sold them the liquor.[77] Because evidence in such cases was difficult to obtain, Massachusetts, New Plymouth, and Connecticut allowed sellers to be convicted solely on the testimony of Indian witnesses. While Indian testimony was generally considered unreliable, it was usually the only evidence available.[78]

While posing less of a threat to society, tobacco was in even greater official disfavor than alcohol. Unlike drinking, smoking had neither long-standing popular nor scriptural approval. None of the health benefits could be claimed for it that could be claimed for beer and wine as substitutes for unsafe drinking water. Smoking took hold and spread in England over bitter official opposition, and the controversy carried over to the colonies.[79] Smokers were denounced by nonsmokers as a nuisance and a hazard. They increased the risk of fires and posed a threat to life and property. A single careless smoker could cause incalculable harm to the whole community.[80] Smoking was also annoying and dangerous to the health of nonsmokers. While drinkers harmed only themselves, smokers contaminated the air breathed by everyone. The arguments made against smoking in the seventeenth century have a remarkably modern ring.

Most of the restrictions on smoking sought to reduce the risk and annoyance to nonsmokers. Massachusetts banned smoking around crops and buildings, and authorized fines and civil damages for smoking-related fires.[81] New Plymouth outlawed smoking within a mile of any habitation under penalties ranging from fines to whippings according to the seriousness of the offense.[82] New Haven banned smoking in the streets as a hazard to property and a nuisance to nonsmokers.[83] These regulations made legal smoking difficult and inconvenient. Even smoking at home was technically unlawful under New Plymouth's one-mile-from-habitations prohibition. Connecticut went even further and tried to stamp out the habit completely. In 1650 the General Court prohibited smoking by anyone under the age of twenty. The lawmakers apparently assumed that a total ban would work among younger people who had not yet become addicted. Older smokers unable to give up the habit might continue to smoke if a physician certified that they were addicted to tobacco and unable to function without it.[84] The plan was to eliminate smoking by attrition as the older generation of smokers gave way to a new nonsmoking generation.

But the law attempted too much, and in the end failed for lack of implementation. Connecticut would have needed an army of nonsmoking constables and law enforcers to make the prohibition effective. The code adopted in 1673 finally abandoned prohibition and fell back upon regulation.[85] The approach taken by the other colonies provided a useful model. Massachusetts permitted smoking in taverns only if the nonsmokers present did not object. If anyone did object, the smoking had to stop under penalty of a fine.[86] New Plymouth had the most detailed regulations of all. Besides its one-mile-from-habitations prohibition, the colony banned smoking in the fields during working hours and within two miles of the meetinghouse on the Sabbath. Persons serving on juries were forbidden to smoke during the trial. Smoking was thought to interfere with clear thinking and therefore to be incompatible with jury duty.[87]

Gambling was banned everywhere as a waste of time and money. Massachusetts made it an expensive pastime by fining gamblers three times the amount of the stakes and earmarking part of the fine for informers who reported the offense.[88] Games involving cards or dice were banned completely whether played for stakes or not. The mere possession of cards or dice was a punishable offense.[89] Since proving a gambling case was not easy, convictions were allowed on the testimony of one witness to the offense, even the testimony of an informer claiming part of the fine.[90] Although tainted by self-interest, such testimony was often the only evidence available.

The measures enacted against gambling varied only in detail from colony to colony. New Plymouth banned all betting under penalty of a fine and made the owner of the premises doubly liable for permitting the offense. If the premises happened to be a tavern, the fine quadrupled.[91] Any game played with cards or dice was illegal whether betting was involved or not. In 1663 three married couples were fined by a Plymouth court for playing a friendly game of cards at home.[92] Cards were too obviously associated with gambling to be tolerated under any circumstances. While all forms of betting were outlawed, Connecticut reserved the heaviest penalties for organized gambling. Lighter fines were imposed for casual betting than for gambling involving more than three players.[93] New Haven and Rhode Island made the sensible distinction between gambling in taverns and other public places and games among friends for nominal stakes. The latter were lawful unless they involved organized gambling.[94]

Every aspect of social behavior had to pass moral scrutiny in the Puritan colonies. Sports, dancing, and even singing were all regulated to protect public morality.[95] While virtually nothing went unregulated, the regulation of sexual morality had the highest priority of all. The Puritans regarded sex not as a private pleasure, but as something to be enjoyed only in marriage pursuant to God's plan for the procreation of the human race. Nor were secular considerations lacking for the strict enforcement of sexual morality. The sex drive, which in marriage bound people together in a network of relationships, outside it became a force for social disorganization. Unless kept in check by the state, extramarital sex would destroy family life and burden society with hordes of illegitimate children. With effective contraception virtually nonexistent, illicit sex meant spurious progeny whose growing numbers would stretch public resources to the breaking point. Even if morality had not been an issue, society still had to protect itself against the consequences of unbridled sexuality.[96]

The penalties for sexual misconduct ranged from fines and whippings to hanging for the most serious offenses. Since God's moral law provided the theoretical basis for the regulatory measures, scriptural punishments were often prescribed. In dealing with fornication, for example, Puritan lawmakers adopted the Old Testament rule that the offenders could partially square things by agreeing to marry.[97] The same rationale enabled engaged couples to get off more lightly than persons who engaged in casual sex. New Plymouth fined the latter at twice the rate assessed against engaged couples.[98] But no one got off completely in cases of premarital sex.[99] Even married couples had to appear in court and pay fines when their premarital affairs came to light.[100] Wiping the slate clean would have encouraged such relationships.

Fornication cases usually came to light through the pregnancy of the female partner. This would be enough to convict the woman, but not always enough to convict the man responsible for her condition. Her testimony alone might not be sufficient because of the possibility that she might lie in order to shield the real culprit or mitigate her punishment. Not to know who was responsible would be an admission of promiscuity and probably add to her sentence. On the other hand, knowing but refusing to tell showed lack of remorse. In 1676 a Massachusetts court sent Deborah Corliss to the whipping post "for refusing to challenge any man but taking all upon herself."[101]

Fearing shame and punishment, some unwed women tried to conceal their pregnancy as long as possible. Even married women concealed their condition and gave birth secretly if the child had been conceived before marriage.[102] There is convincing evidence that some unwed mothers killed their infants at birth and concealed their bodies in the hope of avoiding disgrace.[103] If the body should be discovered, they could plausibly claim that the child had been born dead and that they had concealed the birth to avoid punishment for fornication. Such tragedies may have been more common than the conviction rates indicate.[104] English law made concealment of the death presumptive evidence of murder unless a witness to the birth testified that the child had been born dead.[105] But the English rule was not enforced in Massachusetts until the last decade of the seventeenth century, so there was no presumption of wrongdoing. This made infanticide almost impossible to prove and probably contributed to its incidence.[106] The most a suspect could usually be convicted of was fornication, a noncapital offense. No woman who did not admit her guilt was executed for infanticide before the 1690s.[107]

Sexual misconduct falling short of fornication came under the heading of "lascivious behavior." This was a broad category of offenses covering everything from lewd remarks and gestures to open solicitation. A Massachusetts court sent John Leigh to the whipping post in 1673 for talking lewdly with a woman while she sat on his lap.[108] John Baldwin was fined by a New Haven court for behaving "suspiciously" with a woman, though no actual offense was even alleged.[109] The courts sometimes issued restraining orders to break up questionable relationships. The court sentencing John Leigh for the lap-sitting incident also ordered him to stay away from the woman in the future.[110] The New Plymouth court that fined John Barlow for "lascivious carriages" with a woman ordered him not to see her again.[111] Orders of separation were issued on mere suspicion. In 1660 a Maine court ordered Joseph Davis and Ann Crockett to spend less time together in order to quiet the rumor mills. Defiance of such orders could result in fines and other penalties for contempt of court.[112]

Seduction and sexual solicitation were punished severely. The courts were particularly hard on offenders who sought sexual favors under a false promise of marriage. In 1642 the Massachusetts Assistants Court fined William Collins one hundred pounds for such an offense and banished him from the colony. The same court sent John Davies to the whipping post and ordered him to wear the letter *V* (for *unclean*) for making advances to several women.[113] In 1642 a New Haven court sent William Harding to the whipping post and banished him from the colony for his "base carriages and filthy dalliances with divers young girls." The same court sentenced William Elliott to a fine and whipping for seducing a young girl under the pretext of marriage.[114] Although sexual solicitation was predominantly a male offense, women also sometimes turned up in court as defendants. In 1640 the Massachusetts Assistants Court sent Mary Rugs to the whipping post "for enticing and alluring George Palmer."[115]

Adultery was one of the sexual offenses for which Scripture and Puritan law prescribed the death penalty. It was far worse than fornication because it undermined marriage and family relations and raised doubts about the legitimacy of heirs (see chapter 2). But even more abhorrent were sodomy and bestiality, offenses for which every colony ordered the death penalty.[116] While the bestiality statutes applied to both men and women, the sodomy laws, with only one exception, applied only to males. New Haven was the only colony to make heterosexual as well as homosexual sodomy a capital offense.[117] While the death penalty for adultery was almost never enforced, capital punishment was virtually automatic for sodomy and bestiality (see chapter 10).

Prostitution was not legislated against until relatively late, most likely because it was not much of a problem in the early settlements. But by the 1670s it had become common enough in Boston to outrage moral sensibilities. In 1672 the General Court noted with disgust that attempts had been made "to erect a stews, a whorehouse, or brothel house" in the town. A law was passed prescribing severe penalties for prostitution. Anyone convicted of the offense was to be whipped through the streets at the tail of a cart and then confined to the house of correction for an indefinite term, where ten lashes were to be administered weekly for as long as the sentencing court ordered her to be detained.[118] No penalties were prescribed for males who patronized prostitutes. The latter were considered more culpable because they committed fornication for gain, while their clients committed it out of human weakness.[119] While New Plymouth had no special antiprostitution statutes, women convicted of sex for profit were punished more severely than ordinary fornicators. Their offenses were treated as much more serious than those attributable to sexual passion. Persons convicted of fornication had a good chance of getting off with a fine for a first offense, but an offense committed for money would usually be punished by at least a whipping.[120]

The Puritans were not alone in setting high moral standards. The enforcement of good morals was one of the primary goals of colonial governments everywhere. The upper classes considered it part of their governing responsibility to prescribe appropriate forms of morality for society. Such legislation also served as a useful instrument of social control. The seventeenth century made no distinction between public crime and private immorality. Since God's moral law was the basis of the criminal law, the secular and spiritual interests of society were closely intertwined. They could not be separated without calling into question the legitimacy of the state. Given the long tradition of such regulation in England, the only thing really original about Puritan attempts to legislate morality was the exceptionally high standard set.[121]

Rhode Island enforced the moral commands of Scripture nearly as strictly as the Puritan colonies. The separation of church and state never became a pretext for social permissiveness or lax morality. Drunkards, gamblers, and sex offenders got the same short shrift as in the Puritan colonies. On the other hand, government made fewer demands on the people, and there was less pressure for moral perfection. There were no laws dictating fashions and hairstyles, nor judicial orders of separation breaking up social relationships. Since people were held only to the letter of the law, there was less opportunity for nit-picking by the official custodians of morality.[122] What made Rhode Island different from the rest of New England was the right of its people to be left alone.

The execution of the law is the life of the law.
—Massachusetts Laws (1648)

4   Enforcing the Laws

Legislating morality was only the first step toward keeping New England Puritan and holy. Compliance could not be taken for granted, because every colony attracted sinners as well as saints. Even the *Mayflower* carried misfits and troublemakers who forced a delay in landing until a compact could be framed for maintaining law and order.[1] All the Puritan colonies assumed that they would succeed where others had failed to hold society to high moral standards. Their measure of success would not be the standards set but the extent to which compliance could be obtained. In Geneva Calvin had sought to make the criminal law less severe but more enforceable, and the Puritans put similar emphasis on enforcement. "You have . . . given us power to make these laws," the framers of the Massachusetts *Laws and Liberties* declared to the people, "we must now call upon you to see them executed."[2] Without the best efforts of those charged with enforcement, even the best of laws would amount to nothing.

Law enforcement began at the local level with town constables, who were among the first public officials appointed in every colony. They were chosen in New Plymouth by the townspeople, and they assumed office after taking an oath to enforce all the laws passed by the General Court.[3] In Massachusetts they were originally chosen by the General Court, but as the population dispersed and new towns sprang up their selection became a town function.[4] Constables were appointed for Hartford, Windsor, and Wethersfield even before Connecticut had a governor.[5] Originally chosen by the General Court, their selection was later transferred to the towns along with other functions of local government.[6] The New Haven settlements chose their constables from the beginning, subject only to the approval of the General Court.[7] The selection of constables was a function of local government in politically decentralized Rhode Island from the outset.[8] The towns elected their own constables a decade before colonywide government was established.

The authority of constables was more broadly defined than that of most public officials. New Plymouth gave them a mandate to "advance the peace and happiness of this corporation and oppose anything that shall seem to annoy the same." Although later enactments detailed their duties more specifically, constables still retained considerable flexibility as to the limits of their authority.[9] The only constraint imposed on them by Massachusetts was to enforce all laws and ordinances without favor or bias.[10] Their other duties included carrying out the orders of the General Court and keeping the peace in their respective towns.[11] Connecticut required them to enforce all colony laws as well as their own town ordinances.[12] Such guidelines left them with a fairly free hand as to how they would discharge their duties.

Although they were primarily concerned with local law enforcement, constables had a duty to cooperate with one another in the capture and return of fugitives from justice. When apprehended, a fugitive would be passed along from one constable to another until finally back in the town where the offense had occurred. Cooperation among the constables was vital, because the New England colonies did not employ sheriffs to coordinate law enforcement at the county and colony levels. As the principal law officers of the crown, English sheriffs were held in such disesteem for their high-handed treatment of Puritans that there was no inclination to make them a part of the system when county government was established.[13] The result was a highly decentralized police system in which local accountability discouraged abuses. Not until the governmental reorganization of the 1690s was the office of sheriff created to tighten law enforcement beyond the town level.[14]

Only Rhode Island had a law officer resembling the English sheriff. Known as the sergeant general, he had colonywide duties which included serving writs, enforcing the orders of the colony government, and bringing offenders before the courts. The office was considered so important that a candidate for appointment had to be "an able man of estate, for so ought a sheriff to be whose place he supplies."[15] In everything but title, the sergeant general functioned as a sheriff. He served as the law enforcer of the central government and freed it of complete reliance on the local constables. Given the political tendency toward decentralization, he played a key role in bringing central authority to bear on the largely self-governing towns.

Although constables had considerable discretion as to whether an arrest should be made, they had to follow strict guidelines after they had made one. The arrested person had to be brought before a magistrate or some other judicial officer for a hearing on the legality of his detention.[16] Most arrests required a warrant from a magistrate spelling out the charges against the accused and authorizing the constable to take him into custody. Constables could make arrests without warrants only for offenses committed in their presence or for offenses immediately reported to them by witnesses. All other arrests required a warrant. Constables also needed a warrant to raise a hue and cry, which was the colonial equivalent of raising a posse. A hue and cry could issue on the constable's own authority only when no magistrate was available to authorize one.[17] These requirements were designed to keep police power accountable and under judicial control.

Overzealous constables sometimes overstepped their authority. This usually involved making summary arrests in cases where a warrant was needed. One Boston constable, described as "a godly man, and zealous against such disorders," took summary action in 1644 and arrested a drunken visitor to Boston in his own lodgings without a warrant. He had not observed the man drinking but made the arrest on information provided by witnesses some time later. The constable put the prisoner in the stocks, from which he was released a short time later by a Frenchman. When informed of this, the constable arrested the Frenchman and clapped him in the stocks before transferring him to jail. He had no personal knowledge of what the Frenchman had done, nor did he have a warrant authorizing the arrest. Since both arrests had been unlawful, the constable was rebuked in court for his "ignorance and misguided zeal." The magistrates took the occasion to issue a cautionary warning on the law of arrests: "The constable may restrain, and, if need be, imprison in the stocks, such as he sees disturbing the peace, but when the affair is ended and the parties departed and in quiet, it is in the office of the magistrate to make inquiry and to punish it, and the persons so wrongfully imprisoned by the constable might have had their action of false imprisonment against him."[18] Defendants whose rights had been violated could thus recover civil damages from the constable regardless of the outcome of the criminal charges against them.

A warrant also had to be obtained before the constable could enter private premises, except in cases where immediate entry had to be made in order to halt an offense in progress. There could be no entry, with or without warrant, on mere suspicion or to search for evidence of suspected wrongdoing. Rhode Island enacted the common-law rule that a man's home was his castle and not to be entered except under warrant issued for cause or in cases where summary entry was specifically authorized by statute.[19] The Puritan colonies had similar safeguards. New Plymouth limited summary entry to offenses actually in progress.[20] Massachusetts and Connecticut adopted essentially the same rules.[21] New Haven discouraged illegal searches by providing for the removal of the offending constable and subjecting him to suit for civil damages.[22] The safest course when in doubt was for constables not to make forced entry without first obtaining a warrant.

Only private premises were protected against summary searches without warrant. Premises licensed as public accommodations such as inns and taverns might be entered at any time and searched for evidence of wrongdoing. The proprietor had waived his right of privacy in return for the privilege of carrying on a regulated business. Not even private premises were completely safe from summary searches. Statutory exceptions allowed searches without warrant for theft, smuggling, and unauthorized religious meetings. Even when a warrant was required, it provided much less protection than today. Whereas modern warrants must specify the purpose and scope of the search, those issued in colonial times were often of the shotgun variety. They gave law officers almost unlimited authority to search anywhere they thought evidence might be discovered.[23]

The numerous duties loaded upon the constables over the years eventually made the office onerous. Massachusetts required them to collect taxes, levy attachments, keep track of strangers, and assist customs officers in smuggling cases. They also had to collect assessments for the salaries of ministers and count the votes in elections for the General Court.[24] These colonywide duties were in addition to the local duties imposed upon them by their towns. Cambridge, among other things, required the constable to keep track of persons carrying firewood, while Salem required its constable to make sure that the local swine were properly ringed.[25] All these assignments were in addition to their duty to enforce the laws and keep the peace.

Constables everywhere evolved from simple police officers into key administrative officials. Connecticut required them to collect taxes, compile voting lists, keep lists of missing farm animals, and certify the claims of bounty-hunters for killing wolves.[26] New Plymouth expected them to collect fines and taxes, report regularly on the condition of highways, and notify the local residents when the next town meeting would be held.[27] These functions were in addition to their general duty to enforce the colony laws and local ordinances. New Haven even gave its constables judicial functions. Together with one or two of the local freemen, a constable could try minor offenses in towns without a magistrate.[28] While Rhode Island's constables had fewer colonywide duties, the local duties imposed by the towns were onerous enough. Providence required them to collect fines and keep order at public meetings, and in Warwick they had to collect excise taxes and confiscate firearms from Indians.[29]

The qualifications for constable became stricter as the responsibilities of the office increased. In the beginning Massachusetts allowed any adult male with an estate worth twenty-five pounds to serve.[30] The property requirement was eventually raised to eighty pounds to ensure that only substantial citizens were chosen.[31] Anyone could originally serve as a constable in New Plymouth if the General Court approved the appointment. But when the selection of constables shifted to the towns, a law was passed providing that only persons worth at least twenty pounds and members of the official church should be eligible to vote in elections for constables.[32] This virtually guaranteed that only substantial citizens would be chosen, though in theory anyone might be elected. Connecticut began by allowing all freemen to participate in the election of constables.[33] The selection later became more exclusive when the property qualification for freemanship was set at twenty pounds.[34] New Haven allowed the towns to set their own standards, though no one might be chosen who was not a member of the Puritan church.[35] Rhode Island left the selection of constables completely to the towns. The only requirement was that the person chosen had to take an oath to enforce the orders of the colony government.[36]

The constable's duties were not only onerous but sometimes distinctly unpleasant. Arrests sometimes required the use of physical force, and the constable had to meddle in the affairs of his neighbors in enforcing the numerous regulatory measures.[37] Nothing connected with the office was likely to enhance a constable's popularity. Not only did he have to collect fines imposed on offenders by the courts, but he also had to preside at public whippings, brandings, and hangings. While the grisly details might be handled by assistants, he still had to be present to make sure that the sentence was carried out.[38] Even a mere supervising role on such occasions could be unpleasant and degrading. There was no way a sentence of branding or mutilation could be carried out without some loss of social standing for the person in charge. Passing such a sentence was one thing; actually carrying it out was quite another.

The constable's duties were so time-consuming that he was left with little time for his own affairs, and the office was financially unrewarding. His only compensation consisted of small fees for the specific services rendered.[39] The fee system ensured greater diligence perhaps than a fixed salary, but the fees were set so low that most qualified persons had no desire to serve. Refusals to serve became so common that laws had to be passed making acceptance of appointment mandatory under penalty of a fine. Massachusetts began by setting the fine at twenty shillings, and Connecticut and New Plymouth set theirs at forty and fifty shillings, respectively.[40] But the penalties proved insufficient to obtain compliance. Substantial citizens preferred to pay these relatively small amounts rather than accept appointment. The fines finally had to be raised to four pounds in New Plymouth and to five in Massachusetts. Getting qualified constables for Boston and Salem was so difficult that fines of up to ten pounds had to be ordered for refusals.[41] New Plymouth conceded the hardship of the assignment by providing that those who accepted appointment could not be called upon again for at least seven years.[42]

Constables who neglected their duties faced fines and possibly civil damages as well. Connecticut set fines at the rate of ten shillings for each failure to perform an official function and made constables personally liable for any resulting loss of public revenue. Thus a constable who failed to collect taxes in full had to make up the difference out of his own pocket.[43] New Plymouth took the same approach to uncollected taxes and made the constables generally liable for civil damages if they neglected their duties.[44] They faced additional penalties for every failure to perform their basic police function to preserve the peace.[45] In Massachusetts, constables who failed to organize a proper watch had to pay a fine to the colony government in addition to whatever penalties might be assessed against them by their towns.[46] Though poorly compensated, they were held strictly accountable for their performance in office.

The constables often worked closely with civil officers known as marshals in carrying out their duties. Although marshals were primarily responsible for enforcing court orders in civil cases, their duties at some points overlapped those of the constables.[47] Constables, for example, routinely assisted marshals when forced entry had to be made to enforce writs of attachment.[48] The marshals themselves had limited police functions in Connecticut and New Haven. They arrested offenders who failed to pay fines and bound them out to service until payment had been made.[49] The constable's responsibilities in these colonies did not extend to collecting fines. Massachusetts authorized marshals to make arrests for religious infractions, and New Plymouth required them to assist in dealing with

Quakers.[50] Towns too small to have both a constable and a marshal usually made the latter responsible for the constable's duties.[51]

Grand jurymen also played a role in law enforcement. In New Plymouth they were charged "to serve the King by inquiring into the abuses and breaches of such wholesome laws and ordinances as tend to the preservation of the peace and good of the subject."[52] Their oath of office bound them to report any offenses that came to their attention during the term in which they were impaneled. Connecticut imposed the same reporting duty, originally to the General Court, and later to the local courts with jurisdiction to try the offense. Their specific mandate was to report "any breaches of laws or orders or any other misdemeanors they know of in this jurisdiction."[53] In Massachusetts they had to appear at least once a year before their respective county courts to disclose "all misdemeanors they shall know or hear to be committed by any person." But they were not bound to disclose anything that violated "any necessary tie of conscience."[54] This allowed them to distinguish between offenses observed in the public sphere from those discovered because of their privileged position in relation to the offender. To report the secret shortcomings of close relatives would strain the bonds of trust sustaining family relations. It was more important to protect such ties than to punish secret offenses.

The duty of grand jurymen went beyond reporting offenses that came to their attention. They also had a duty to investigate suspected wrongdoing and to question anyone whose behavior seemed suspicious. A person questioned by a grand juryman could expect further scrutiny from the constable or magistrates if unable to give a satisfactory explanation.[55] The effectiveness of the system can be gauged from the long lists of grand jury presentments for all sorts of deviant and criminal misconduct. Very little escaped the attention of grand jurymen, least of all the shortcomings of public officials. A town failing to provide stocks or a whipping post for the punishment of offenders would likely itself become the subject of a grand jury presentment.[56]

Most grand jurymen could count on the trust and support of their fellow citizens. Unlike grand jurymen in England, they were not appointed by sheriffs, who often packed the panel with their friends and supporters. The selection process in New England produced fairer and more independent grand juries. They were chosen in Massachusetts at town meetings, an arrangement guaranteeing strong community support.[57] In Connecticut they were appointed by the county courts, and every town in the county had to be represented on the panel.[58] The provision for local representation

reduced the possibility that some offenses would go unreported and reinforced confidence in the fairness of grand jury findings.

The grand jury system worked somewhat differently in Rhode Island.
The members of the panel did not usually perform investigative functions
or file criminal charges with the court. Their primary responsibility was to
review criminal complaints filed by others.[59] They functioned in much the
same way as English grand juries in the seventeenth century. In England
the grand jury's original investigative functions had been assumed by
sheriffs and constables who enforced the laws on a full-time basis. After the
sheriff or constable gathered and presented the evidence, the grand jury
decided whether it justified indicting and bringing the accused to trial. The
Puritan colonies turned back the clock and restored to grand juries some of
their early common-law investigative responsibilities. They not only passed
on the merits of charges brought by others, but in many cases brought the
charges themselves.[60]

Massachusetts constructed the most extensive police network in New
England. Besides constables, marshals, and grand jurymen, tithingmen
were appointed to report anything that might be overlooked by the others.
In England the tithingman was an official responsible for supervising a
tithing, a political subdivision consisting of ten families of freeholders.[61]
The system was adopted by Massachusetts in 1677 as part of a last-ditch
effort to enforce its regulatory measures more effectively.[62] Each neighborhood in each town was to appoint a tithingman to oversee the morals of ten
neighboring families. Tithingmen had a special duty to report Sabbath
violations, and they were also expected to arrest drunkards when the
constable was not available. With one of them for every ten families, not
much was likely to escape their attention. Watertown alone had fifteen
tithingmen by 1679, and the number increased proportionately as the
population grew.[63] In theory, the system gave every town and village an
almost ubiquitous police presence.

But tithingmen in practice turned out to be less than effective law
enforcers. They were expected to be the neighborhood censors of private
morality, an unenviable task for any public official. The system did not fail
immediately, but actually began on a note of official enthusiasm. The
magistrates welcomed the prospect of tighter law enforcement, and in some
places presentments for morals offenses increased dramatically for a time.[64]
But the system was doomed to failure in the long run. Most neighbors were
unwilling to inform on one another and compromise their everyday relationships (see chapter 3). The system died a gradual death as fewer and

fewer persons proved willing to take on such a burdensome task. By the end of the century the office of tithingman had either become a dead letter or been turned into a system for reporting liquor offenses.[65]

Ordinary citizens were expected to play an active role in colonial law enforcement. Anyone who refused a constable's request for help faced fines and other penalties.[66] The law required every male over the age of sixteen to participate in hues and cries for the apprehension of offenders. English law made whole towns liable for local robberies if the perpetrator was not found and brought to justice.[67] The townspeople were presumed to be in collusion with the culprit, and they therefore had to reimburse the victim for failing to punish the crime.[68] Rhode Island adopted a modified version of the English statute. The town had to reimburse the victim if town officials had been negligent in failing to apprehend the culprit. But collusion was not presumed, and an honest effort to do justice absolved the town of all responsibility.[69] No other colony adopted even a modified plan of victim compensation. Fines might be imposed on individuals for failure to cooperate in the investigation, but the community at large was not held responsible.[70]

Fugitives from justice could not rest easily just because they had escaped to another colony. If they remained in New England, they were not beyond the reach of the law. The extradition provisions of the New England Confederation, to which every colony except Rhode Island belonged, guaranteed their return to the colony from which they had fled.[71] In 1644 New Plymouth returned two adulterers to Massachusetts for trial and execution although Plymouth law did not make capital punishment mandatory for adultery.[72] Fugitives from the Puritan colonies were not safe even in Rhode Island unless they had fled to escape religious persecution. Ordinary offenders faced extradition as they would have in the Puritan colonies.[73] The process itself was simple and direct. A fugitive from Massachusetts who was apprehended in Connecticut would be passed along from one constable to another until finally back in Massachusetts. The Massachusetts constables then took over and passed him from town to town until he reached the place having jurisdiction to try him.[74]

Police protection in the colonial towns was the responsibility of ordinary citizens who performed local guard duty known as watch and ward. Persons on watch did guard duty after sunset, and those on ward covered the daytime hours. All males between ages sixteen and sixty had to take turns at both or pay fines for each rotation missed. The constables were responsible for making the assignments and for reporting absences and derelictions of duty to the magistrates. Massachusetts required every town to maintain a watch from May through September, by which time the onset of cold weather was expected to keep people off the streets at night. The towns could extend the watch into the winter months, but they could not end it earlier than October.[75] The local authorities managed the details, subject only to the statutory requirement that only qualified persons should be assigned to duty.[76]

Similar arrangements for watch and ward were adopted in Connecticut. The constables had responsibility for setting rotations and making sure that everyone obliged to serve performed his turn of duty. The only detail mandated by statute was that at least two men should be assigned to ward in every town. Anyone who had to be out of town when scheduled for duty could hire a substitute or make up the rotation upon returning.[77] Those assigned to the watch would report to the constable who would assign them their posts for the night. For a watchman to leave his post unattended was a serious offense punishable by fine. Half went to the constable for reporting him, and half went to a fund for the benefit of the watch.[78]

New Haven legislated the details of watch and ward somewhat more closely. The towns had much less flexibility in handling the arrangements than in Massachusetts and Connecticut. Local exemptions from service could not be granted without the approval of the General Court. While it was up to the constables to compile duty rosters and assign rotations, statutes mandated how many men had to be assigned to particular duties. Refusal to serve or neglect of duty brought severe penalties. Fines were prescribed for routine delinquencies, but exemplary punishments were authorized for derelictions compromising the public safety.[79] Far more than any other colony, New Haven turned watch and ward into a system of military service.

New Plymouth and Rhode Island took the opposite approach, leaving watch and ward almost completely to the towns. In the beginning New Plymouth hired guards instead of making the duty a civic obligation.[80] But this was expensive and probably left some neighborhoods unprotected. In 1643 the Plymouth town government made service in watch and ward compulsory, and the following year the General Court required the other towns to do the same.[81] The details of organizing and managing the system were left to the towns. The only exception was during King Philip's War, when watch and ward temporarily became part of the military system.[82] Local control was also the rule in politically decentralized Rhode Island. The towns made their own security arrangements long before a central government emerged to set colonywide standards.[83]

Watch and ward gave every town the sort of visible police presence that deterred crime and kept the streets safe around the clock. Like modern police, the constables were geared to respond to crime rather than prevent it, so the safety of a particular neighborhood was really up to the residents who lived in it. The precedents for communal responsibility went back to Anglo-Saxon times, when hundredmen were fined for failing to join in the search for cattle missing from another hundred.[84] The same spirit pervaded law enforcement in early New England. Citizens who served in watch and ward provided the community with much more security than a system of paid professional police could possibly have provided. Paying for such security would have been beyond the means of colonial government. The system worked only because New Englanders took personal responsibility for keeping their communities safe.

Given the importance of watch and ward, the granting of exemptions was a hotly debated issue. Massachusetts originally left it up to the towns to decide who should serve, but abuses became so common that the General Court finally set colonywide standards. The only outright exemptions granted were to clergymen, civil officials, and militia officers. Any additional exemptions granted by the towns had to be approved by the General Court.[85] Connecticut granted both partial and full exemptions from service. Militia sergeants were excused from ward duty completely but had to serve every other rotation of the watch. Citizens whose professions or occupations served the public sometimes got conditional exemptions. Thomas Lord, a physician, got one by agreeing to practice medicine at Hartford under a fee schedule approved by the General Court. A similar arrangement was made with Jasper Gun.[86] New Haven granted full exemptions to clergymen, civil and military officials, physicians, schoolmasters, millers, and sailors.[87] Rhode Island set no colonywide standards but left the towns free to decide who should serve.

Anyone not eligible for an exemption could still avoid service by hiring a substitute. But such arrangements were subject to public regulation. Massachusetts allowed them only if the substitute met standard qualifications.[88] New Plymouth and Connecticut adopted similar rules.[89] Substitution was permitted on the theory that it made no difference whether guard duty was performed as a civic obligation or for money. But the practice invited abuses. Many of the substitutes hired did not meet the statutory standards. The most common abuse was the hiring of youths not old enough to be entrusted with such an important assignment. The Massachusetts General Court found it necessary to order the constables to reject all substitutes under the age of sixteen.[90]

Reinforcing the police network was a Puritan practice known as holy watching. Calvin had used it in Geneva as a means of promoting good Christian living. The idea was for church members to take responsibility for correcting the faults and shortcomings of one another.[91] The system took root in New England from the very beginning. The Reverend John Robinson, pastor of the Leyden congregation, wrote to the Pilgrims: "Let every man repress himself and the whole body in each person, as so many rebels against the common good, all private respects of men's selves, not sorting with the general conveniency." Thomas Hooker believed that true Christians had a duty "to prevent all taint of sin in any member of the society, that either it may never be committed; or if committed, it may be speedily removed, and the spiritual good of the whole preserved." The covenant adopted by the Beverly congregation in 1667 bound church members "to the brotherly watch of fellow members" to keep everyone on the path of righteous living.[92] Every Puritan was his brother's keeper both for his own good and the good of society at large.

Holy watching sharply reduced the amount of privacy that an individual could expect to enjoy. There was mutual spying and moral nit-picking to an extent that would be intolerable today. But privacy at the personal level was then considered much less important than the prevention of sin and criminal misconduct.[93] The Puritan colonies rewarded holy watchers with a share of the fines collected from the offenders they reported.[94] Not to report an offense was itself an offense, and women were punished for not immediately reporting men who sexually abused them.[95] Even Rhode Island, which had no holy watching, rewarded informers by splitting fines with them.[96] Whether out of piety or for profit, informing was everywhere a social reality.

Many of the offenses reported by informers probably otherwise would have gone unpunished. The fornication charges brought against John Pearce in 1673 provide a vivid glimpse of holy watching in Massachusetts. Pearce aroused the suspicions of his neighbors by bringing female friends to his home, and so they kept him under close surveillance. While spying through his window one day, a neighbor observed Pearce in a compromising situation with a female visitor. The neighbor summoned other neighbors to the window, and together they filed charges against Pearce.[97] Another Massachusetts couple landed in court for "lascivious behavior" on charges brought by a neighbor who had seen them kissing. Corroboration was provided by another neighbor who reported that he had once observed the couple tickling one another. The sight so shocked him, he told the court, that he had to turn away and therefore could not testify on what may have followed.[98] With neighbors such as these, not even the most private conduct was safe from scrutiny.

Holy watching sometimes led family members to inform on close relations. In 1634 an unnamed minister felt compelled by conscience to inform the Massachusetts magistrates about "some seditious speeches" made to him by his son in private. The father's zeal embarrassed even the magistrates. Winthrop notes that they decided not to act on the information, "being loath to have the father come in as a public accuser of his own son." They put off taking action until other witnesses came forward or the son could be prosecuted on charges not requiring his father's testimony.[99] Protecting close family ties had a higher priority than punishing secret offenses that had not caused any actual harm.

Charges brought by family members sometimes backfired with unexpected consequences. In 1663 Rebecca Bishop reported Henry Greenland to the Massachusetts authorities for allegedly making sexual advances to her married daughter Mary in her husband's absence. She brought the charges when John Emery, the grand juryman for Ipswich, refused to do so. Emery advised her that no harm had been done and that he would dissuade Greenland, a physician much esteemed by the community, from further improprieties. But Rebecca wanted Greenland to be punished, having been assured by her daughter that his advances were unwelcome and that she had done nothing to encourage him. But the facts proved otherwise. Witnesses testified that Mary sometimes had to be warned "not to carry herself so lovingly and fondly toward Mr. Greenland." It also came out that she had invited Greenland to her house and had lied in saying that he came uninvited. The upshot was that the court fined Mary for her "miscarriages" and made her husband responsible for her future good behavior. A complaint filed partly to protect her reputation in the end left it in tatters.[100]

Informing for profit was the mercenary first cousin of holy watching and an important factor in law enforcement in every colony. It even had the gloss of piety and the sanction of religion, which taught that God would judge New England harshly if it permitted sin to go unpunished. Indeed, anyone who tolerated wrongdoing shared in the guilt of the offender. Informing became an integral part of law enforcement. Without it, many offenses would probably have escaped detection.[101] There was no way, for example, that constables or watchmen could detect card-playing in private homes. Massachusetts rewarded players with immunity for turning in the others so that they might be punished for offenses that otherwise would not have come to light.[102] Connecticut made the head of the household responsible for any gambling on the premises whether he participated or not.[103] The only way to avoid liability was to report the offense and claim a share of the fine for informing. Given the choice between paying fines themselves or benefiting from fines paid by others, most citizens probably preferred the latter.

The duty to inform extended to persons who had themselves been victims of the offense. In 1638 John Bickerstaffe was sent to the Boston whipping post for fornication with Alice Burwood. Although the evidence suggests that Alice was more victim than accomplice, she was sentenced to be whipped "for yielding to Bickerstaffe without crying out, and concealing it 9 or 10 days." Similarly, a Connecticut servant girl who had been sexually abused was punished "for concealing it so long." Any delay in reporting a sexual offense could turn the tables on the victim. When Blanch Hull reported an assault to the Plymouth authorities in 1656, she was prosecuted for not crying out in time.[104] Delay raised the implication of complicity and turned the victim into a likely accomplice or possibly a false accuser.

Despite its importance in law enforcement, informing gradually became socially disreputable. As in England, the term *informer* became synonymous with *liar* and *villain*.[105] Informing for profit incurred the most opprobrium, but even holy watching came under a cloud. The Puritans were ambivalent about the nature of the religious duty to inform. Thomas Hooker made a distinction between the need to inform against church members and the nonelect. Church members were bound to inform against one another only if the delinquent failed to mend his ways. William Ames, who authored the standard handbook on Puritan ethics, had doubts about the morality of informing. He wrote that "no man is bound to reveal a secret crime of another, of which no ill report went before. For he, whose offense is hidden, has he as yet right to preserve his fame, that it should not rashly be laid open."[106] Even Puritan law recognized an inchoate right of privacy. Massachusetts excused magistrates, grand jurymen, and public officials from revealing private crimes when conscience bound them to secrecy.[107] Connecticut made similar exceptions to the duty to inform.[108] The effect of all this was to undermine and raise doubts about what in theory should have been a moral imperative.

The reach of the police network did not make New England authoritarian in the modern sense. Grand jurymen were not constantly on the lookout for offenses, nor were most constables likely to inquire too closely into the private affairs of their neighbors. Indeed, willingness to look the other way, particularly in minor matters, led Massachusetts in 1675 to order fines for grand jurymen who failed to enforce the apparel laws.[109] The waning of popular support for the official morality inevitably made strict enforcement difficult. Most New Englanders had an earthy attitude toward sex, and the tolerance of moderate immorality was probably closer to social reality than Puritan moralists cared to admit. Puritan church records indicate that disciplinary proceedings for sexual indiscretions were fairly routine.[110] The failure of the tithingmen on the grass-roots level demonstrates how difficult it must have been to enforce the official morality. Though such cases continued to fill the court dockets well into the eighteenth century, by the late seventeenth century enforcement had become less effective in the area of private morals.[111]

The decline of Puritanism itself paralleled the problems of law enforcement in late seventeenth-century New England. As individuals became less intensely Puritan and more worldly in their attitude toward life, church membership declined. The influx of new immigrants and the emergence of business and commercial elites abetted the process. Law enforcers increasingly found the problems of maintaining basic law and order difficult enough without trying to implement unpopular morals regulations. To enforce the letter of the regulations might upset the delicate balance of personal relationships upon which everyday life depended.[112] The order of colonial life could survive occasional drunkenness, Sabbath violations, profane language, and minor sexual indiscretions. It was less likely to survive heavy-handed enforcement of nit-picking measures out of step with popular mores.[113]

Long before their fall from grace, New Englanders had a commitment to liberty more compelling than the official morality. Even the most zealous holy watchers prized personal freedom too highly to become conscious instruments of an overreaching state. Like the pious minister who informed on his son, they spied more to save the sinner than to exalt the state. Nor did persons who informed on neighbors regard themselves as meddlers interfering in matters that were none of their business. People who helped guard their neighborhoods on watch and ward were naturally alert to wrongdoing wherever it occurred. The cost to privacy was high, but there were also benefits in the form of safe streets and personal security. Neighbors were as ready to assist and defend one another as to pry into personal lives. Perhaps even more important, official law enforcers did not pose a threat to liberty. Local accountability and rotation in office made it unlikely that their police powers would be abused. The constable who enforced the

71

laws one year knew that he would be out of office the next, and that any high-handedness would likely complicate his return to private life. Power subject to such constraints was naturally geared to moderation, giving New Englanders the happy paradox of a society where life, liberty, and property were equally protected.

Many commonwealths subsist without true religion and
much mercy; but without justice, no commonwealth can
long subsist; and it is this, of the three, the
most immediate and proper work of the magistrate's
office, to see true justice executed.—Hugh Peter (1651)

5 The Judicial System

Judicial functions in the early settlements were not separate from the other business of government. Justice was dispensed by executive and legislative bodies that in some cases passed the measure covering the offense.[1] In some colonies this concentration of power was the result of charter provisions, while in others it was incidental to their political development. The Massachusetts charter, for example, gave all powers of government to the Court of Assistants, a sort of executive council, and to the General Court, the highest governing body in the colony.[2] The Assistants Court consisted of the governor, deputy governor, and twelve Assistants (all of whom were referred to as magistrates), and the General Court included both the deputies elected by the towns and the members of the Assistants Court. So the latter was a separate court for some purposes and part of the General Court for others. Although both courts had concurrent jurisdiction to try all cases, from the outset most of the judicial details of government were assumed by the Court of Assistants.[3] They met more frequently than the General Court, and their prestige ideally suited them for the administration of justice.[4] By the 1640s the judicial functions of the General Court had shifted almost completely to the Assistants and to other courts created by the General Court.[5]

Individual Assistants sitting alone performed most of the judicial functions of English justices of the peace. They presided at arraignments, took depositions, and decided whether the evidence justified further proceedings. An Assistant sitting alone had authority to try minor offenses without a jury, though he could not order corporal punishment without calling in another Assistant. Assistants who overstepped their authority were themselves subject to censure and other penalties. Richard Saltonstall, one of the leading Assistants, was fined in 1630 by the full Assistants Court for ordering whippings on his own authority.[6] While much of their authority came from the charter, the way in which the Assistants discharged their duties was governed by statutes passed by the General Court.

Although the General Court became essentially a legislative body, it also performed judicial functions. Appeals were brought to it from the Assistants Court when there was disagreement between the Assistants and the jury or among the Assistants themselves. If convinced that justice had not been done, the General Court might order a new trial or reverse the decision and render judgment itself.[7] Lower courts could certify questions of law to the General Court and obtain clarification before proceeding with the case. This obviated the need for a later appeal to the General Court on the issue. The General Court also had original trial jurisdiction, and the jurisdiction was exercised in politically important cases. It tried and convicted Anne Hutchinson and John Wheelwright during the antinomian controversy.[8] Although trial jurisdiction was turned over to the Assistants Court and to other local courts after 1642, the General Court never relinquished its judicial functions completely. It always retained its appellate jurisdiction as the highest court of appeals in the colony.[9]

The General Court itself created the local courts to which it delegated most of its trial jurisdiction. In 1636 it set up Inferior Quarterly Courts for Boston, Cambridge, Ipswich, and Salem for the trial of cases not serious enough for the Court of Assistants. The Assistants Court thereafter tried only crimes punishable by banishment, dismemberment, and death. The Assistants also had jurisdiction to hear appeals from defendants convicted in the Inferior Courts.[10] The latter became county courts in 1643 when county government was established.[11] These courts performed numerous administrative functions in addition to their judicial responsibilities. They appointed officials for the laying out of highways, managing the house of correction, and administering public trusts. They also confirmed the nomination of officers for the militia, assessed charges for the repair of bridges, and regulated licensed businesses.[12] There were eventually seven county courts altogether, including two for the annexed settlements in Maine and New Hampshire, and they all played a key role in local government.[13]

Each of the county courts had a five-member bench, with at least three judges needed for a quorum. One of them had to be an Assistant, but the others might be Commissioners (also known as Associates) selected by the freemen of the county and confirmed by the General Court.[14] The composition of the Maine and New Hampshire courts was somewhat different. Both lacked resident Assistants, so outside Assistants had to be assigned when they were in session. Since the assignment was considered onerous, the General Court usually sent them Commissioners instead of Assistants. These Commissioners Courts had less jurisdiction than regular county courts presided over by Assistants. Their jurisdiction was limited in part by the reluctance of the General Court to delegate too much judicial power to the annexed settlements. These courts tried cases without a jury, and their jurisdiction in criminal cases was limited to offenses punishable by no more than a twenty-shilling fine.[15]

Below the county courts were town courts for the trial of minor offenses and misdemeanors.[16] They were presided over by resident Assistants or by Commissioners appointed by the General Court.[17] Town courts presided over by Assistants had more power than those entrusted to Commissioners. An Assistant could remand accused persons to jail, but a Commissioner could only order the posting of bail. For nonbailable offenses, the accused had to be brought before an Assistant or remanded to a higher court.[18] If tried before a Commissioner, a defendant might not be sentenced to more than ten lashes or fined more than forty shillings.[19] If tried before an Assistant, he might be more severely punished. Anyone convicted in a town court, whether by an Assistant or Commissioner, had a right of appeal to the county court.[20]

In 1639 a Strangers Court was set up to expedite the trial of nonresidents when the regular courts were not in session. The Court consisted of three Assistants and might be called into session at any time.[21] Its jurisdiction was limited to cases triable in the county courts.[22] More serious cases had to await the next session of the Assistants Court. Since its purpose was to expedite the administration of justice, defendants who invoked its jurisdiction had no right of appeal. They got speedier justice but had to give up a right available in the regular courts. Some of its critics considered the Strangers Court costly and redundant, but it worked well enough to last for more than three decades.[23] Until abolished in 1672, it provided nonresident defendants with what amounted to justice on demand.[24]

A special local court, the Quarterly Court of Boston, was set up in 1639 to share the heavy work load of the local Inferior Quarterly Court.[25] What became of this court is not clear, but it apparently lasted only a brief time. None of its records have survived, and no mention of it appears in later legislation dealing with the courts. Since it duplicated the functions of the Inferior Quarterly Court, it was probably discontinued when the latter became the Suffolk County Court a few years later.[26] Boston got another special court in 1651 for the trial of cases not serious enough for the County

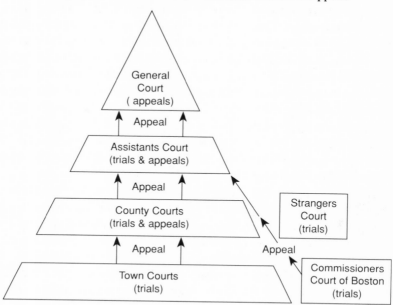

Figure 1   Massachusetts Jurisdiction and Flow of Appeals

Court. Presided over by Commissioners appointed by the General Court, it had jurisdiction over offenses punishable by no more than forty-shilling fines. Defendants convicted in the Commissioners Court had a right of appeal to the Assistants Court.[27] Appeal was directly to the Assistants rather than to the County Court, mainly because it had been set up to relieve the work load of the latter. Originally established on a trial basis for only part of Boston, the Commissioners Court worked so well that it became a permanent part of the system.[28] In 1674 its jurisdiction was extended over the entire town.[29]

By mid-seventeenth century Massachusetts had four distinct levels of judicial administration. The system was pyramidal, as shown in Figure 1, and specialized from top to bottom. The base of the system consisted of town courts for the trial of minor offenses and infractions of local ordinances. Next came the county courts and the Strangers Court for the trial of offenses too serious for the town courts. Then came the Assistants Court for the trial of crimes punishable by banishment, dismemberment, and death. Finally, at the apex of the system was the General Court, the highest court of appeal.[30] Except in the Strangers Court, there was a right of appeal at every level. The *Body of Liberties* adopted in 1641 granted a direct right of appeal to the General Court from any court in the colony.[31] Such appeals ended in 1648 when the *Laws and Liberties* regularized appellate procedure.[32] Appeals thereafter could be brought only from town courts to the county courts, from the county courts to the Assistants Court, and from the Assistants to the General Court.[33] There was a right of appeal to the court at the next higher level, but no right of appeal beyond that level. One appeal was considered sufficient to correct trial errors and prevent miscarriages of justice; anything more would have caused unreasonable delays and logjams in the administration of justice. While the General Court could review any case on petition after an appeal had failed, the review was discretionary and not something defendants could claim as a matter of right.[34]

Massachusetts recognized no right of appeal beyond its borders. Because the colony's charter did not mention appeals to the king, the Massachusetts authorities denied that such a right existed.[35] In 1632 Thomas Knower was punished with the bilboes (a shackling device) for threatening to appeal a conviction to England.[36] Five years later John Wheelwright attempted to appeal his sentence of banishment to the king but was informed that this was not possible because the charter gave the Massachusetts courts authority to try all cases without recourse to England. In 1646 Dr. Robert Child and six other petitioners were summoned before the General Court for sending the Court a remonstrance urging reforms unpalatable to the Puritan regime. They refused to acknowledge the Court's jurisdiction and prepared an appeal to the parliamentary commissioners in England. But the Court refused to allow the appeal, citing the terms of the charter as grounds for refusing. Not only was their petition denied, but the petitioners were found guilty of subversion and heavily fined.[37]

Alarmed by the Child affair, the General Court dispatched Edward Winslow to England to mend fences with the Commissioners for Foreign Plantations. Winslow carried a petition urging Parliament to accept the principle that there should be no appeals from the decisions of the Massachusetts courts. The Commissioners responded favorably, declaring that "we intended not thereby to encourage any appeals from your justice, nor to restrain the bounds of your jurisdiction." While this did not prevent others from attempting appeals to England, it did provide a gloss of legitimacy for the fines imposed on those who persisted in doing so. The Massachusetts government assumed that it had prevailed on the issue. A petition of thanks was sent to Parliament in 1651 for stopping appeals from the colony.[38]

But the issue was far from settled, because whatever Parliament had conceded did not cover appeals to the king, only to Parliament. This made no difference during the 1650s when there was no king, but it became a serious problem when the Interregnum ended. After the Restoration, various petitions against the Massachusetts government came before the Privy Council. One of the petitioners was Samuel Maverick, a bitter opponent of the Puritan regime and the only freeman in the colony who was not a church member. Maverick urged the council to bring Massachusetts under closer English control. He had signed the Child remonstrance, and he cited the affair as an example of arbitrary conduct by the colony government. He recommended revocation of the Massachusetts charter unless the ruling elite agreed to appeals to England on just and reasonable grounds.[39]

Maverick's petition coincided with the goals of the crown with regard to a wide range of problems which had arisen in the colonies during the Interregnum. In 1664 the king issued a commission to Maverick and three other commissioners granting them broad and varied powers in the New England colonies. Among other things, they were authorized to hear appeals and settle disputes.[40] Assuming that this gave them judicial powers, the commissioners set aside the sentence imposed by a Massachusetts court on John Porter, Jr., who was convicted of abusing his parents (see chapter 3). A public uproar ensued, and the General Court warned that the reopening of settled cases would cause civil turmoil and enable offenders already punished to bring civil proceedings against the officials who punished them.[41] The Court claimed that the intrusion of the commission into judicial matters violated the colony's charter. Brushing these objections aside, the commissioners announced that they would sit as a court of appeals in the case brought by Thomas Deane and others against the Massachusetts government. But when the General Court forbade them to proceed, the commissioners abandoned the project and referred the matter to the king. The home government, however, had more pressing problems, so no immediate action was taken against Massachusetts. A reckoning would come later, but for the present, judicial autonomy had been preserved.[42]

For several years the Assistants and the deputies in the General Court disagreed sharply on how the Court should handle its judicial functions. Although they met together, the Assistants and the deputies voted separately, giving each group what amounted to a veto over the decisions of the other. Concurrent majorities were needed for all actions by the General Court. This caused no problems with regard to legislative matters, but the deputies questioned its propriety at judicial sessions where the Assistants could use their veto to reject appeals from their own decisions in the Court of Assistants. Such use of the veto not only negated the defendant's right to an impartial review, but raised questions about the fairness of the system.[43]

The issue came to a head in the celebrated case of Goody Sherman's lost sow. The sow had apparently strayed away, and Sherman charged that the animal had been misappropriated by Robert Keayne, a prominent Boston merchant. In 1640 she sued Keayne in the Inferior Quarterly Court, but the decision went against her. Keayne not only won but was awarded heavy damages in his countersuit for slander. Two years later Sherman tried to revive the case by filing an original petition with the General Court. The Court would have ruled in her favor if the Assistants had not used their veto to prevent reversal of the Inferior Quarterly Court's decision.[44] This precipitated a sharp debate over the propriety of the Assistants' veto in judicial matters. Critics of the veto pointed out that defendants who had been treated unjustly by the Assistants in the lower courts would have no possibility of redress if the same Assistants could veto their appeal in the General Court.[45] The right of appeal granted to them by statute would thus be rendered illusory.

The debate went on until 1649, when it was finally ended by compromise. The Assistants and deputies agreed that deadlocks arising between them when voting separately should be resolved by a majority of the Court voting together. Uncertainty as to whether the arrangement covered legislation or only judicature led to another agreement in 1652 limiting it to the latter.[46] The General Court thus became bicameral in political and legislative matters but unicameral in its judicial functions. The change improved the administration of justice by guaranteeing impartial appeals. The Assistants also benefited because the compromise ended a debate that might have undermined their position in government. They came out of the affair with their political prerogatives intact and with no loss of prestige as a governing elite.[47]

New Plymouth had a somewhat different judicial development. All governing power, including judicature, was originally in the hands of a General Court and Court of Assistants. The latter was a sort of executive council which assisted the governor when the General Court was not in session. The Assistants had no veto in the General Court, but they nevertheless had formidable powers. They were particularly important during the early years, when the General Court met only to deal with matters of great importance. Between sessions, the governor and Assistants were in complete charge of the business of government.[48] Besides performing executive and administrative functions, they also served as a judicial court of un-limited jurisdiction.[49]

In 1636 the first step toward judicial specialization was taken when the General Court authorized the individual Assistants to try minor cases in the manner of justices of the peace. They were also to preside at arraignments of more serious offenders and decide whether the evidence warranted referring the case to the full Assistants Court for trial. The jurisdiction of individual Assistants to try cases was uneven and haphazard. While a single Assistant could try a defendant for lying, he could not try him for idleness without calling in a second Assistant.[50] The governing statute determined how the offense would be tried, so the Assistants' jurisdiction varied from one minor offense to another.

For the first two decades the full Assistants Court met only when called into session by the governor. This changed in 1641, when the General Court ordered the Assistants to hold regular monthly meetings to deal with the growing volume of judicial business. A majority of the Assistants had to be present for important cases, though it was up to them to determine which cases were important. Individual Assistants still had authority to try minor cases, but defendants had the right to a jury trial whether tried by an individual Assistant or the full Assistants Court. In an apparent effort to expedite things, jury trial was suspended in 1660 for certain minor offenses. But the experiment proved so unpopular that it was almost immediately abandoned. The right of jury trial was fully restored the following year in all criminal cases.[51]

In 1666 the General Court completely reorganized the justice system by taking over most of the judicial functions of the Assistants Court. The latter no longer held regular monthly meetings but convened only at the call of the governor. This marked a step backward to the judicial arrangements in effect before 1641. To deal with its new responsibilities, the General Court scheduled three regular judicial sessions each year and provided for the calling of special sessions for the trial of important cases. The transfer of jurisdiction from the Assistants affected only the full Assistants Court; the individual Assistants continued to try minor offenses as justices of the peace. Assumption of judicial power by the General Court broadened the popular base of judicature by giving the deputies, the representatives of the people, a direct role in the administration of justice. That the new arrangements reduced the importance of the Assistants was underscored by cancellation of their exemption from taxation.[52]

The new system ran counter to the normal tendency toward greater specialization in the administration of justice. The growing legislative work load of the General Court made the assumption of additional judicial functions highly unusual. It also meant that defendants convicted of serious crimes would no longer have the right of appeal to a higher court. Since the General Court was the highest court in the colony, its decisions were final and unappealable. The system was ill conceived in theory and lasted only five years in practice. In 1671 the General Court turned over all its judicial functions to the Court of Assistants. The transfer was complete. The Assistants got even more power than before and thereafter became the highest trial and appellate court in the colony. There was no right of appeal from the Assistants Court to the General Court.[53] The Assistants thus got the judicial monopoly denied to their Massachusetts counterparts. What probably made this politically acceptable was that the authority of the Plymouth Assistants came not from disputed claims of charter powers but from the General Court, which might rescind it at any time.

Even more sweeping judicial changes came in 1685, when most of the trial functions of the Assistants Court were transferred to newly created county courts. Presided over by the Assistants of the respective counties, these courts met twice yearly for the trial of all but the most serious cases and to hear appeals from the town courts. The trial jurisdiction of the Assistants Court was thereafter confined to offenses punishable by banishment, dismemberment, and death.[54] Petty offenses and violations of local ordinances were triable in town courts presided over by individual Assistants, Associates appointed by the General Court, or by local selectmen. There was a right of appeal from the town courts to the county courts and from the county courts to the Assistants Court, which was the highest judicial court in the colony.

Another judicial reorganization in 1686 gave New Plymouth a justice system almost identical to the one in Massachusetts. At its base, were town courts for the trial of petty cases; then came county courts for the trial of more serious offenses; and finally the Assistants Court for the trial of crimes punishable by banishment, dismemberment, and death. Defendants tried in the town and county courts had the right of appeal to the next judicial level. New Plymouth differed from Massachusetts only in not providing for appeals from the Assistants Court. The decisions of individual Assistants who presided over the town courts could be appealed to the county courts, but the decisions of the full Assistants Court were final.[55]

Justice in Connecticut was first administered by commissioners appointed by Massachusetts to oversee the new settlements.[56] But this ar-

Figure 2   New Plymouth Judiciary in 1686

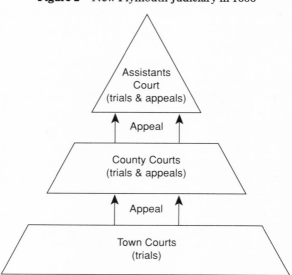

rangement ended in 1637 when the first General Court met at Hartford to take over the colony's public business.[57] The General Court proceeded to delegate its judicial functions to a committee of magistrates collectively known as the Particular Court, so called because it handled particular cases, whereas the General Court attended to general public business. While none of its records before 1639 are available, the Particular Court apparently tried cases too serious for trial in the town courts. Essentially a subdivision of the General Court, it performed only those functions delegated to it by the full Court.[58]

In 1643 the Particular Court emerged from the shadow of the General Court and became a separate institution with the same trial jurisdiction as the General Court. It thereafter met four times yearly for judicial sessions at which the governor and two other magistrates constituted a quorum. The Particular Court tried the most serious cases, including capital crimes, and defendants tried there had a right of appeal to the General Court. But appeals were vitiated by what amounted to a magistrates' veto in the General Court. Separate voting by the deputies and magistrates enabled the latter to prevent the reversal of cases decided by them in the Particular Court.[59]

Figure 3   Connecticut Judiciary, 1650

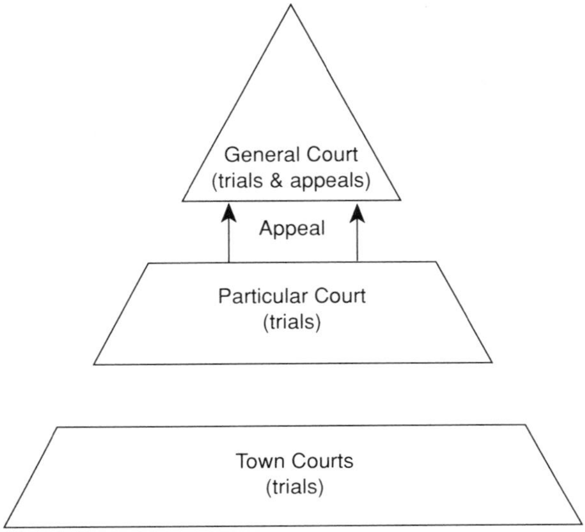

The town courts in Connecticut were presided over by individual magistrates with jurisdiction to try minor offenses.[60] Some were presided over by commissioners appointed by the General Court for towns without a resident magistrate. The magistrates and commissioners performed functions similar to those of justices of the peace. They presided at arraignments, took depositions, and authorized hues and cries. But their trial jurisdiction did not go beyond petty offenses and violations of local ordinances. Since the offenses tried were not serious, there was no right of appeal from their decisions. However, this did not prevent the General Court from reviewing town cases as a matter of discretion.[61] The system closely resembled arrangements in Massachusetts before the creation of county courts in the 1640s.

New Haven Colony established a similar justice system under the Fundamental Order of 1643. Its base consisted of Plantation Courts presided over by a resident magistrate or by a judge chosen by the freemen in towns without a magistrate. These courts had jurisdiction to try minor offenses and violations of local ordinances. At the next level was the Court of Magistrates, which met twice yearly at New Haven to try more serious cases and to hear appeals from the Plantation Courts. Finally, there was the

General Court, the highest governing body, with unlimited jurisdiction to try cases and hear appeals. Defendants could appeal to the General Court from any court in the colony.[62]

Cases tried in the Plantation Courts and in the Court of Magistrates were decided by majority vote of the judges. Those tried in the General Court were decided by concurrent majorities of the magistrates and deputies voting separately. There was no provision for jury trial at any level, probably because the ultra-Puritans who settled New Haven found no precedent for it in Scripture. But something akin to jury trial emerged in 1645, when the local deputies got the right to sit as judges with the magistrates in the Plantation Courts.[63] This participation by the people's representatives gave the process a broader popular base. Since the deputies already had an equal voice with the magistrates in the General Court, there was popular input at the top as well as at the bottom of the system.

But because the deputies and magistrates voted separately in the General Court, appeals to the Court could be vetoed by the magistrates. Like their counterparts in Connecticut, the latter could prevent the reversal of cases decided by them in the lower courts.[64] That this caused none of the controversy that the issue provoked in Massachusetts suggests that the magistrates used their power with restraint. Besides, their authority came not from a colony charter but from the General Court, and could be taken away at any time. As in New Plymouth and Connecticut, the magistrates had no prerogatives which could be claimed as a matter of constitutional right. Their political accountability made it unlikely that they would behave unreasonably.

New Haven's law code of 1656 made significant changes in judicial organization. The governor and deputy governor got authority to call special sessions of the Court of Magistrates for the trial of important cases. They were also authorized to cast a tie-breaking vote in case of deadlock in the Plantation Courts or the Court of Magistrates. A Strangers Court on the model of the one set up in Massachusetts was established for the trial of nonresidents not wanting to wait for the next session of the Plantation Courts.[65] The Strangers Court had the same jurisdiction as a Plantation Court, and the more serious offenses not triable there had to await the next session of the Court of Magistrates. Defendants using the Strangers Court had no right of appeal to a higher court. The New Haven system, in most respects, followed the Massachusetts model. The only structural difference was the absence of intermediary county courts between the Plantation Courts and the Court of Magistrates.

Figure 4   New Haven Colony Judiciary, 1656

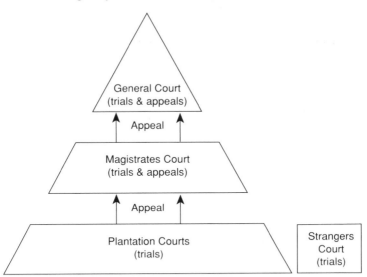

The new system gave individual magistrates authority to try minor offenses when the Plantation Courts were not in session. It also authorized the local deputies to convene courts in towns without a resident magistrate. The penalties imposed on offenders by individual magistrates or deputies could not exceed those authorized for the regular Plantation Courts. These arrangements were designed to speed up the local administration of justice and prevent backlogs from developing when the regular courts were not in session. Even the constables were recruited to perform limited judicial functions. A person charged with cursing could be tried by the constable together with one of the local freemen if no magistrate or deputy was available.[66] Defendants retained the right of appeal from these courts to the next judicial level.

Traveling to New Haven for the trial of serious offenses by the Court of Magistrates could be burdensome to defendants and witnesses. In 1664 another reorganization addressed that problem by turning the Court of Magistrates into a circuit court. Its jurisdiction remained the same, but sessions were thereafter held throughout the colony. This made it easier to get witnesses and evidence to court. The arrangement bridged the gap between the local and central administration of justice much as the county courts did in Massachusetts and New Plymouth. Established just before the union with Connecticut, the new system marked the final stage in New Haven's separate judicial development.[67]

Connecticut's courts had to be completely reorganized after the merger with New Haven under the 1662 charter. The Particular Court was replaced by a Court of Assistants to try offenses punishable by banishment, dismemberment, and death. The new court met twice yearly at Hartford, with jury trial available for defendants tried before it. County courts were also set up to try cases not serious enough for the Assistants Court. The courts met twice yearly, though special sessions might be convened at the call of the local Assistants. Ordinarily, three Assistants were needed for sessions of the county courts, but one Assistant and two Commissioners appointed by the General Court could also try cases.[68] Offenses not serious enough for the county courts were triable in town courts presided over by individual Assistants or Commissioners. There was a right of appeal from the town courts to the county courts, from the county courts to the Assistants Court, and from the Assistants Court to the General Court. Although no one had a right to more than one appeal, the General Court had discretionary power to set aside convictions after an appeal to a lower court had failed.[69] Except for the omission of a Strangers Court, the new system closely followed the Massachusetts model. The need for a Strangers Court was obviated by the provision for special sessions of the county courts.

Rhode Island had justice systems at the town level a decade before colony government was established. The Providence settlers began by handling judicial matters at town meetings in the course of other public business. In 1640 provision was made for the arbitration of civil disputes, but nothing was done to separate criminal cases from the ordinary business of government.[70] Warwick did not even have a regular town meeting to deal with judicial matters. The settlers were reluctant to create formal institutions of government without approval from England. They wanted to do nothing that might jeopardize their chances of gaining recognition as a separate jurisdiction. All public business, including judicial functions, therefore, was handled informally by groups of private citizens.[71]

Portsmouth set up a more formal system of government and judicature. The town meeting, the highest governing body, appointed a judge and council of elders to manage public affairs. They took care of executive and judicial matters and reported back regularly to the town meeting. Their judicial mandate authorized them to try minor cases sitting alone and to impanel juries for the trial of serious offenses. When settlers from Portsmouth founded Newport in 1639, they brought this system with them. The

Figure 5   Connecticut Judiciary, 1673

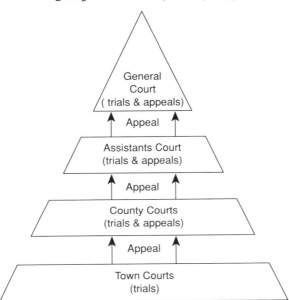

town meeting delegated executive and judicial functions to a judge and council of elders. When sitting as a court, the judge and elders decided all cases by majority vote.[72]

In 1640 Newport and Portsmouth united under a federal form of government. Provision was made for a governor, deputy governor, and assistants who performed judicial as well as executive functions. Sitting alone, they could try minor cases; sitting together, they constituted a Particular Court for the trial of the most serious cases. The Particular Court met alternately at Newport and Portsmouth, and defendants in both towns had the right to be tried by jury.[73] The judicial system was much more advanced than the arrangements made by Providence and Warwick. The latter had no system at all, and the former tried cases at town meetings, where politics must have complicated judicial proceedings.[74]

In 1647 when central government was established, Rhode Island finally got a uniform justice system. A General Court of Trials was established with colonywide jurisdiction to try serious offenses and to hear appeals from the town courts. Because of the emphasis on local self-government, the new court functioned as a circuit court, moving from town to town for

Figure 6   Rhode Island Judiciary, 1663

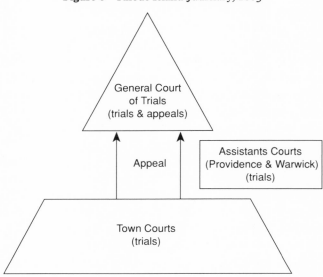

the trial of offenses where they occurred.[75] The principal officers of the host town had the right to sit with the judges and provide them counsel and advice. Their advisory function was upgraded in 1650, when they were granted an equal vote with the judges.[76] This concession to decentralized government broadened the base of popular support and increased local confidence in the fairness of the system.

Lines were not sharply drawn between the cases triable in the General Court of Trials and those triable in the town courts. This was partly because any obvious reduction in the jurisdiction of the local courts would have been fiercely resisted.[77] The only real change in the operation of the town courts was that the judges of the General Court of Trials had authority to try minor offenses in their own towns when the full Court was not in session. This created what amounted to a dual system of judicature at the town level. But the key concession to local autonomy was that serious cases had to be tried by the General Court locally, where the host privilege could influence the outcome.[78] This made it possible for the same local judges who tried cases in the town courts to cast what might be the deciding votes in the General Court of Trials.[79]

In 1663 a new charter from the king gave Rhode Island a more centralized justice system.[80] The General Court of Trials ceased being a circuit court and thereafter held all its sessions at Newport. This put an end to the host town privilege and reduced local influence on the outcome of local cases.[81] The Court held sessions twice yearly, though special sessions might also be called for the trial of important cases.[82] Because the trip to Newport was difficult for people on the mainland, Assistants Courts were set up for Providence and Warwick. Both were subdivisions of the General Court of Trials and therefore not under local control. But since local juries were used, local sentiment was amply represented in their proceedings.[83]

On balance, these changes significantly reduced the power of the towns in judicial matters. The jurisdiction and independence of the General Court of Trials grew at the expense of the town courts. Decisions of the town courts could now be appealed to the General Court of Trials even when the issues decided were completely local. Growth of confidence in the central government made these changes politically acceptable.[84] By the 1660s local self-government had come to be perceived as less important than the charter rights which were best protected by an effective colony government.[85]

New Hampshire had no courts of its own before separating from Massachusetts in 1679. When the separation came, it had almost no impact on the administration of justice, except with regard to appeals. The charter granted broad judicial powers to an Assembly, which was also the highest lawmaking body, and to an Inferior Court, which consisted of the provincial president and his council. The Inferior Court was a circuit court of unlimited jurisdiction. It met at Dover, Hampton, and Portsmouth on a rotating basis. Individual members of the Inferior Court, sitting alone, had jurisdiction to try cases not serious enough for the full Court. Whether tried by an individual member or by the full Court, defendants had a right of appeal to the Assembly. They also had something not yet available to other New Englanders: the right of appeal to England.[86] That right was a harbinger of even more sweeping changes in store for the region.

No person in this colony shall be taken or imprisoned
or . . . otherwise molested or destroyed but by the lawful
judgment of his peers, or by some known
law, and according to the letter of it, ratified and
confirmed by the major part of the General Assembly.
—Rhode Island Laws (1647)

6   Legal Due Process

Court proceedings began with a preliminary hearing to determine whether the evidence justified holding the accused for trial. The hearing was held before some judicial officer following the arrest or filing of charges. The latter usually came first unless the circumstances justified a summary arrest (see chapter 4). If charges were filed first, a court order in the form of a summons or arrest warrant would be issued requiring the appearance of the accused to answer the charges against him. The summons was simple and straightforward by seventeenth-century English common-law standards. The New England colonies abandoned the complicated English writ system for bringing defendants before the courts and substituted direct orders instead. The hearing itself was also uncomplicated. The accusers would be heard, witnesses would testify, and the accused would be questioned with the understanding that anything he said might be used against him. The purpose was to sort out the facts to determine whether to proceed with the case or simply dismiss the charges. Only if the evidence seemed plausible would the case be remanded for trial.

Not every case remanded for trial necessarily came to trial. A felony charge had to be followed by a grand jury indictment listing the charges against the accused. The indictment was drafted by officers of the court and submitted to the grand jury, which then determined whether the counts listed were supported by credible evidence.[1] After hearing the witnesses and reviewing the record of the preliminary hearing, the grand jury either endorsed the indictment as a *billa vera* (true bill) or rejected it with a finding of *ignoramus* (We do not know). The latter usually meant dismissal of the charges against the accused.[2] If the grand jury voted to indict, the form of the indictment could be crucially important, because the accused could be

90

convicted only of offenses alleged in the document. In 1665 a witchcraft conviction was overturned in Connecticut on the ground that the guilty verdict went beyond the charges in the indictment.[3] Even if the evidence supported the verdict, there could be no conviction for offenses not listed in the indictment on which the defendant was tried.[4]

Grand jury indictments were needed only for felony prosecutions. The device, which dated from the twelfth century when it was used to bring powerful wrongdoers to justice, evolved over the centuries into a safeguard against arbitrary prosecutions. No one could be brought to trial for a serious offense unless the grand jury first determined that the evidence warranted a trial. For lesser offenses the filing of an information or criminal complaint was usually sufficient. If it was found at the preliminary hearing that the information was supported by convincing evidence, the accused would be brought to trial without any intervening grand jury action. Although much more flexible and convenient than the indictment, the information could be used only to prosecute offenses less than felonies.[5]

Petty offenses and infractions of local ordinances were disposed of in summary proceedings not much different from a preliminary hearing. These proceedings resembled those conducted in England by justices of the peace, who tried numerous misdemeanors without juries. Although the common law originally required jury trials for all offenders, Parliament over the years dispensed with juries for a vast number of petty offenses.[6] The justice would hear the complaint, examine the witnesses, question the accused, and decide the case on his own authority.[7] The New England colonies made similar arrangements. Summary proceedings before judges were authorized for such offenses as cursing, swearing, idleness, lying, drunkenness, petty theft, smoking violations, illegal dancing, and other regulatory infractions. These were offenses for which grand jury action and jury trial would have occasioned endless delays.

While adopting the substance of common-law safeguards, the New England colonies discarded the technicalities. Massachusetts showed its scorn for technicalities by providing that no judicial finding should be abated or reversed "upon any kind of circumstantial errors or mistakes, if the person and the cause be rightly understood and intended by the court." The General Court did not enact the special pleas of *autrefois acquit* and *autrefois convict* for double jeopardy but simply ordered that no one should be tried twice for the same crime.[8] The complicated writs for bringing defendants before the courts were also abandoned. After all other writs had failed, English courts would issue an order of outlawry against the accused.

This authorized the forfeiture of personal property for minor offenses and allowed anyone to kill the accused in case of felonies.[9] Massachusetts scrapped all this for the rule that persons who ignored three summonses to appear would be in contempt of court. If the offense called for the death penalty, the property of the accused would be forfeited and his failure to appear would count as one witness against him.[10] The technical formalities of the common law were not permitted to interfere with the efficient administration of justice.

Procedural simplicity was not all a matter of conscious design. It also reflected lack of information about English trial practices. While substantive English law was available in handbooks, the manuals available on procedure were oversimplified and usually out of date. The two most important handbooks on procedure were William Lambarde's *Eirenarcha*, first published in 1581, and Michael Dalton's more current *The Country Justice* (see chapter 1). Despite numerous revisions, neither was ever really updated to reflect important changes in criminal practice in the seventeenth century. Rules of evidence had begun to emerge in England that went unnoted in the handbooks available in the colonies.[11] So it was up to colonial lawmakers and judges to devise procedures on their own.

Criminal trials in the seventeenth century typically pitted the defendant in a no-holds-barred confrontation with his accusers. The only rule limiting the admissibility of evidence was that the accusing witnesses had to testify in open court so that the defendant had a fair opportunity for cross-examination and rebuttal.[12] While accusatory depositions were admissible under special circumstances, defendants generally had the right to confront all witnesses against them. Massachusetts and Connecticut allowed accusatory depositions only in noncapital cases, and only if the witnesses lived more than ten miles away or could not appear for medical reasons. But no exception was made for offenses punishable by death. Witnesses had to appear in court for their testimony to count against the defendant.[13] Only New Haven allowed depositions in capital cases, but only if the deposition was given in the presence of the defendant.[14] This gave him the opportunity to confront and question the witness directly.

Responsibility for prosecuting the case was usually up to the defendant's accusers. When the function of the medieval trial jury shifted from providing evidence against the accused to weighing the evidence presented by others, no provision was made for public prosecutors to take over the jury's original accusatory functions. The persons bringing the charges usually had to manage the prosecution themselves. This was not considered onerous in the early days of the common law, because felony prosecutions were originally begun by appeals brought by ordinary citizens rather than by grand jury action. Since trials were not complicated with procedural technicalities, accusers could handle their side of the case without much difficulty. After the jury had been selected, the presiding judge would read aloud the indictment on which the defendant would be tried. The accusers then told their story, called witnesses, and presented any other evidence relevant to the case. The defendant then had the opportunity to deny the charges, though not under oath, call his witnesses, and try to refute in any way he could the evidence against him. The judges participated actively in the proceedings, questioning witnesses on both sides and commenting on the evidence. The emphasis throughout was on making the case clear and comprehensible to the jury.[15]

The law presumed the defendant to be not guilty, putting the burden of proof squarely on the prosecution. The accused had to prove nothing or even defend himself beyond pleading not guilty to the charges against him. But as a practical matter it would have been highly imprudent for him not to answer questions by the judges. While he could not be compelled to answer, his refusal would almost certainly prejudice the jury against him.[16] Anything less than complete candor would be viewed as evidence of guilt. The pressure on the accused to answer ensured that nothing really important was kept from the jury. But it also exposed defendants to damaging questions and badgering by hostile judges.[17]

One factor keeping trials simple and straightforward was the rule denying counsel to defendants in felony cases. The origins of the rule are far from clear and for the most part defy rational analysis. Coke regarded it as a logical corollary of the defendant's presumption of innocence. The guilt of the accused had to be so obvious, he reasoned, that no defense would be possible; if not obvious, no defense would be necessary. In any case, the defendant's rights would be protected by the judge, who would see to it that the proceedings were fair and within the letter of the law.[18]

Though plausible, Coke's explanation fails on two counts. First, it assumes a greater burden of proof than the prosecution in fact had to carry. Second, it ignores the fact that judges in Tudor and Stuart England were more interested in punishing wrongdoing than in protecting the defendant's rights. The rule probably had more to do with history than logic. Denial of counsel probably originated when all felonies were treasons, in which case the security of the state was in jeopardy, necessitating a hard line in dealing with the accused. As other crimes came to be labeled felonies, the rule against counsel, though no longer needed for reasons of state security, was applied to them as well because of the confusion of treason with all forms of felony.[19] The rule itself probably did not seem high-handed or arbitrary in medieval times. The right to appoint counsel was originally a royal privilege, not some ancient folk-right rooted in tradition. The king of necessity had to appoint representatives to carry on his numerous law-suits.[20] The privilege that he asserted for himself could be extended or denied to others, and he chose to deny it in felony cases. This rule settled into the bedrock of the English common law and was brought to America by the settlers.

The rule against counsel did not apply in misdemeanor cases, and, again, the reason was mainly historical. Misdemeanors were absorbed into the criminal law from the civil actions for trespass, and defendants in such actions had a right to counsel that dated back at least to the early thirteenth century.[21] English common-law practice not only permitted the use of counsel in civil and misdemeanor cases, but even provided for assignment of counsel when defendants were indigent. In some cases, counsel was actually required. Persons accused of important misdemeanors in the Court of Star Chamber had to have their answers signed by counsel. No defense could be made unless the defendant's counsel assumed responsibility for the statements. A defendant was presumed to have admitted the charge if he submitted an answer not endorsed by counsel.[22] Counsel was barred only in felony cases, and even here there was an exception. Felony defendants could employ counsel to raise technical objections to the indictment. But once the trial began, the accused had to take over and manage his own defense.[23]

Without making technical distinctions between felonies and misdemeanors, the New England colonies permitted essentially the same limited use of counsel. Connecticut allowed defendants to employ counsel to argue technical points of law too complicated for the average layman. But counsel could not dispute the facts of the case. Only the defendant could question the evidence and present arguments in his own behalf. Getting the law straight might require assistance, but getting the facts straight only required telling the truth. This seems to have been the underlying assumption in making the distinction. An attorney who attempted to argue the facts under the pretext of arguing the law was subject to fine and possible disbarment.[24]

Colonial distrust of lawyers limited their use far more than in England. The Puritan colonies originally barred representation by counsel in civil as well as criminal cases. There was widespread apprehension that lawyers would use their technical skills to find loopholes in the laws and defeat the ends of justice.[25] During the first decade of settlement Massachusetts required the parties to a legal proceeding to speak for themselves, though they were free to seek advice from the magistrates before the case came to trial. Such consultations risked prejudicing the magistrate, but the practice was justified on the ground that litigants would otherwise consult lawyers, an even worse evil.[26] In 1641 a tentative right to counsel was recognized in Article 26 of the *Body of Liberties* authorizing the use of unpaid attorneys.[27] Nathaniel Ward, the principal draftsman of the code, regarded private consultations with magistrates as so prejudicial that unpaid attorneys might be a lesser evil.[28] When the *Laws and Liberties* dropped the ban on compensation seven years later, the stage was set for the emergence of a professional bar. Further impetus came in 1649 when the General Court forbade the magistrates to give advice in cases they were likely to try.[29] Thereafter any litigant with a knotty problem had no choice but to hire counsel.

The quality of legal representation available in early New England was spotty at best. Most attorneys had little or no legal training. The first trained attorney in Massachusetts was Thomas Lechford, an English solicitor who arrived in Boston in 1638. While Winthrop, Bellingham, Humfry, and several other magistrates had been students of law in England, on this side of the Atlantic they did not practice professionally. Lechford was the first professional attorney, and almost from the beginning he was distrusted by those in power. His profession made him suspect, and his unorthodox religious views added to his problems. Antinomianism had so traumatized the Puritan establishment that even minor deviations from strict orthodoxy raised hackles. Lechford made the mistake of showing the draft of a proposed book to Deputy Governor Thomas Dudley, who promptly accused him of heresy. In 1639 he was barred from practicing law for attempting to sway jurors out of court, the equivalent of jury-tampering. But when he confessed his fault in a petition for relief, the General Court lifted the ban and allowed him to resume practice. Lechford's credentials should have guaranteed his professional success, but he was anything but successful. The hostility of the governing elite cast a long shadow, and he was barely able to make a living. Lechford returned to England two years later, thoroughly embittered by his experience.[30]

Lechford attributed his difficulties in Massachusetts to his efforts to promote the common law against the preference of the Puritan establishment for the rule of Scripture. Despite the hostility of the establishment,

Lechford probably influenced legal developments in the colony. It was at his urging that the General Court passed a law in 1639 requiring all judicial judgments and decrees to be recorded. Recording was a necessary precondition for implementing the common-law rule of *stare decisis*. There was no way judges could follow case precedents until they had a body of recorded decisions. The recording system urged by Lechford made that possible. He also helped to edit and transcribe the *Body of Liberties*, and so may have had something to do with the Article 26 provision authorizing the use of unpaid attorneys.[31] If he had been orthodox in religion and less controversial, Lechford might have made a name for himself in Massachusetts and played a leading role in public life.

The absence of trained attorneys left the field to incompetents and pettifoggers likely to cause their clients more harm than good. No one who practiced law before the Suffolk County Court, the most important county court in Massachusetts, had any formal training.[32] Given the deplorable state of the profession, the denial of counsel probably did not put offenders at a serious disadvantage. In 1656 the General Court warned practitioners to exercise self-restraint and curb their "many and tedious discourses and pleading." Their pleas were limited to just an hour, and those who took longer were fined.[33] In 1663 attorneys were disqualified from sitting as deputies in the General Court.[34] They were barred to prevent conflicts of interest. It would have been improper for lawyers with a professional interest in the outcome of cases they had handled to review appeals during judicial sessions of the Court.

Connecticut and Rhode Island permitted the use of paid attorneys for civil litigations from the beginning. Many of Connecticut's founders were trained lawyers, and this may have given the profession an aura of respectability.[35] Rhode Island's close adherence to the common law favored legal practitioners. The laws adopted in 1647 not only guaranteed the right to counsel in civil cases but provided for the appointment of public attorneys for parties unable to retain counsel.[36] This closely followed the English practice of assigning counsel to indigent defendants, a practice dating from medieval times.[37] The public attorneys were elected by their respective towns, and they were directed "not to use any manner of deceit to beguile either court or party." Any breach of ethical standards could bring disbarment.[38] Although primarily officers of their town courts, the public attorneys could represent litigants anywhere in the colony. They were the seventeenth-century equivalent of modern legal aid attorneys and public defenders.[39] No other colony went so far in protecting the rights of indigents with legal problems.

Rhode Island also permitted counsel for felony defendants to argue technical questions of law. Noting that laymen lacked "wisdom and knowledge of the law," the Assembly in 1669 authorized every defendant "to procure an attorney to plead any point of law that may make for the clearing of his innocency."[40] While the attorney might argue only the law of the case, he was not limited to pleading only technical defects in the indictment. Any issue of law could be raised, even issues intertwined with the facts of the case. This was a considerable improvement over English practice, which limited the use of counsel to issues concerning the indictment. Not until 1695 and 1837, respectively, did treason and felony defendants obtain the right to counsel in England.[41]

Public prosecutors were used in only a handful of cases in the seventeenth century.[42] While Rhode Island made some moves in that direction, criminal prosecutions never became exclusively a public function. In 1650 the Assembly appointed William Dyre to the office of attorney general with a mandate to prosecute offenders anywhere in the colony. While his primary responsibility was to prosecute in the General Court of Trials, he could also bring prosecutions in the town courts.[43] The office became permanent in 1677 under a law for the public prosecution of criminal cases.[44] But public prosecution was not made the only form of prosecution. Nothing prevented private citizens from starting criminal proceedings if the attorney general failed or refused to prosecute a case.

Massachusetts and Connecticut seldom used public prosecutors. In 1662 the Connecticut General Court appointed William Pitkin to prosecute several offenders, and two years later reappointed him "to implead any delinquents in the colony."[45] In 1670 Richard Callicott was appointed to represent the Suffolk County Court in cases appealed from it to the Massachusetts Assistants Court. Callicott was not appointed to prosecute offenders, just to oppose appeals brought by convicted defendants, and his appointment was only for a single session of the Assistants Court.[46] Massachusetts did not have a trial prosecutor until 1679, when Anthony Checkley was appointed attorney general to manage the prosecution of Elizabeth Morse for witchcraft. The reason for his appointment is unclear, but it may have been because discord among Morse's accusers made private management of the case impossible. Checkley got a guilty verdict, but the court set the conviction aside on the ground of insufficient evidence.[47] Checkley's tenure as attorney general expired with the case.

The right to bail was better protected in the colonies than in England. English bail rules were complicated by statutes giving judges almost unlimited discretion.[48] Every New England colony recognized bail as a basic right except in capital cases or for offenses requiring preventive detention. Heresy, for example, was made nonbailable in Massachusetts to prevent the accused from proselytizing.[49] Bail rules were similar in New Plymouth and Connecticut.[50] While New Haven and Rhode Island did not guarantee bail by statute, the courts in both colonies granted it routinely in noncapital cases. New Haven courts frequently released defendants on their own recognizance.[51] Practical considerations favored the granting of bail. Most jails were not adequate for the confinement of everyone awaiting trial, and the extradition arrangements of the New England Confederation made defendants less likely to flee. Rhode Island encouraged its sergeant general to grant bail by allowing him a fee when he accepted it and no fee at all if he refused it.[52]

The New England colonies also strengthened the rule against double jeopardy. No exceptions were made of the sort made in England to the principle that an accused could be tried only once for the same offense. In 1641 Massachusetts banned multiple prosecutions unconditionally, and the ban was reiterated in every subsequent revision and codification of the laws.[53] Connecticut also enacted statutory guarantees, though the principle was so basic that legislative action was not really needed.[54] Courts everywhere recognized it as essential to the civilized administration of justice and for the protection of individual liberty from an overreaching state. Apart from some questionable witchcraft prosecutions, which may have bent if not broken the rule, no colony prosecuted anyone more than once for the same offense (see chapter 8).

Accused persons had to be brought to trial within a reasonable time. The Massachusetts statute of limitations on criminal cases provided that if proceedings did not begin within a year of the alleged offense, they would be barred forever.[55] New Plymouth and Connecticut set the same time limits.[56] The statutes began to run from the commission of the crime, not from its discovery or the filing of criminal charges. The purpose of the limitations was to protect people against harassment for offenses long past and to ease the work load of the courts. The only offenses not subject to time limitations were those punishable by death. Capital cases carried too much moral freight to be dismissed just because of the passage of time. They were also far fewer than minor ones and therefore unlikely to create judicial logjams. Accusers were also less likely to bring false charges in such cases, because every colony made perjury to take life a capital offense (see Appendix A).

Perhaps the most fundamental procedural guarantee in the seventeenth century was the right of the defendant to be tried by jury. This was an ancient common-law right that emerged in the early thirteenth century. Trial had previously been mainly by ordeal, but the abolition of ordeals by the Fourth Lateran Council in 1215 made it necessary to find some other method of trying defendants. The abolition of the ordeal caused moral and legal disarray, because responsibility for putting men to death could no longer be put on God. For several years no trials were held because no method existed to try defendants. Persons accused of grave crimes and considered dangerous were imprisoned without trial. In the decade that followed, the judges seem to have solved the problem by themselves. Using the grand jury as a model, they impaneled trial juries to determine the guilt or innocence of the accused.[57] The new method of trial, originally a judicial expedient, evolved over the centuries into a basic constitutional right. Its historical justification was the protection it afforded against the death penalty and the tyranny of judges. The courage and independence of trial jurors came to be relied upon to protect life and liberty against the growing power of the state.[58]

The right of the accused to be tried by jury was recognized in New England from the beginning. In 1623 jury trial was guaranteed in New Plymouth by an order of the General Court that all cases were to be decided by "twelve honest men to be impaneled . . . upon their oath." Subsequent statutes provided for the trial of minor offenses by judges without juries, but jury trial remained the only way of trying serious crimes.[59] Unless the trial took place in the General Court, in which case the deputies took the place of jurors, Massachusetts provided for jury trial in all felony prosecutions.[60] How minor offenses were tried depended upon the governing statute, but the most common practice was to try them before judges without juries.[61] To impanel a jury for every misdemeanor would have been costly and time-consuming. Since the common-law right to be tried by jury developed in the context of serious cases, excepting minor offenses from jury trial did not vitiate the basic right. But serious crimes had to be tried by jury unless the defendant expressly waived the right.[62]

Rhode Island had jury trial at the town level even before it had colony government. Juries were impaneled at Portsmouth in 1639 and again in 1640 for the joint courts established with Newport.[63] The colony laws adopted in 1647 guaranteed defendants the right to be tried by jury, and standards were set for the selection of jurors. Only persons with an estate worth at least twenty pounds could be impaneled for the trial of minor offenses, and at least forty pounds for serious cases.[64] Despite the colony's commitment to democratic government, juries were so essential to the orderly administration of justice that only substantial citizens were eligible to serve.

Connecticut had jury trial in civil cases long before it was guaranteed by statute for criminal defendants.[65] Not until 1673 was the right expressly granted, and even then only for offenses punishable by banishment, dismemberment, or death.[66] But this does not mean that jury trial was previously unavailable, only that it was not available as a statutory right. Both the Particular Court and later the Assistants Court impaneled juries for serious cases on their own authority.[67] Why the right was not included in the statutes can only be guessed at. It may have been omitted through legislative oversight or perhaps because it was taken for granted. But lawyers played such a prominent role in public life that the latter seems more likely.

Only New Haven made no provision for jury trial, not even in capital cases. Most of the criminal law was based on Scripture, and there were no precedents in Scripture for jury trial. Besides, if the magistrates could be trusted to rule on questions of law, there was no reason to doubt that they would weigh the evidence fairly. Leaving everything to the magistrates probably seemed preferable to trial by jury. They were selected for qualities of mind and character much higher than any practical standard of jury selection. Moreover, public accountability for their actions constrained them to be fair. Whatever the reasoning, New Haven was the only colony to try all offenders by judges without juries.[68]

Defendants tried by jury had the right to challenge prospective jurors. Parliament created the right under a statute passed in 1352 allowing the accused to challenge a member of the trial jury on the ground that he had served on the grand jury bringing the charges.[69] Jury challenges evolved into a regular part of jury selection in England and the colonies. Massachusetts allowed defendants unlimited challenges for cause, which meant challenges based on the bias or incompetence of prospective jurors.[70] But no provision was made for peremptory challenges for which the defendant did not need any explanation. Rhode Island allowed unlimited challenges for cause plus twenty peremptory challenges in capital cases. This was also the number of peremptory challenges allowed in England for crimes punishable by death.[71] New Plymouth allowed unlimited challenges for cause and eight peremptory challenges in capital cases. The peremptory challenges were later increased to twenty, bringing the colony into line with English practice.[72] Because Connecticut had no laws on jury selection, no provision was made for challenges of any sort. But nothing prevented defendants from objecting to biased jurors or prevented the court from removing them as a matter of judicial discretion. For the court to ignore a challenge for cause would have been incompatible with the defendant's right to a fair trial.

Juries had three options in reaching a verdict. They could convict or acquit the defendant completely or find him guilty of some lesser offense. Murder charges might result in an assault or manslaughter conviction, or rape charges might lead to a conviction for lascivious misconduct. Jury trial came to be regarded as a safeguard for defendants partly because juries could ameliorate the harshness of the law. Jury modification of the law was historically inseparable from the development of jury trial. When the trial jury replaced the ordeal in the thirteenth century, it assumed part of the discretionary power of the grand jury bringing the charges. That assumption of discretion was natural, because for about a century the same people often served on both juries. The overlapping membership went out of practice in the fourteenth century, and the accused thereafter faced two separate panels. But the tradition of discretion survived the separation.[73] Trial jurors, after all, were originally official witnesses rather than the triers of the facts. They came to court more to speak than to listen and regarded themselves as the ultimate authorities on what the outcome should be.[74] They also felt free to bring in verdicts that were often at variance with the letter of the law.

The medieval assumptions underlying trial by ordeal probably also had something to do with trial jury discretion. The ordeal was an appeal to God, and the outcome was a moral statement as well as a legal judgment. It covered not only whether the accused had done the things charged but also whether he was morally culpable and deserved to be punished. The judgment of God took into account *mens rea,* that is, whether the defendant had criminal intent, a mitigating factor ignored by medieval secular law. When the jury replaced the ordeal and took over the judicial functions of God, it took over His discretion as well. God was not bound by the letter of man-made laws. He could be merciful and acquit the defendant if there were extenuating circumstances. The trial jury, standing in the place of God, assumed the right to do the same.[75]

The medieval tradition of jury discretion survived into the seventeenth century. It was probably stronger in the colonies than in England because the pressure of the crown and royal judges to convict was not a factor in jury deliberations. Even in England, except in treason cases where the security of the state was involved, juries usually weighed the evidence in the light of the defendant's reputation and their own views of what would be a just outcome.[76] The right of jurors to ignore the letter of the law was openly defended in the seventeenth century. The Levellers rejected the fact-versus-law distinction between the functions of judges and jurors. After John Lilburne's trial in 1649 a theory rapidly developed of total jury control of the law, analogous to lay control of the interpretation of Scripture. In his 1653 trial Lilburne advanced a radical theory of jury nullification if the jurors found a particular statute violative of fundamental English law. The right of juries to bring in verdicts without fear of reprisals became part of the Leveller program.[77]

But English juries were not completely free of judicial reprisals until *Bushel's Case* in 1671. For refusing to vote for the conviction of William Penn and William Mead for preaching to an unlawful assembly, several jurors were fined for what the court took to be outright jury nullification of the law. The jurors had responded to Penn's argument that they were judges of the law and acquitted him contrary to the evidence. Edward Bushel, one of the jurors, was imprisoned at Newgate for refusing to pay his fine. He sued out a writ of habeas corpus in the Court of Common Pleas, claiming that the fine had no basis in law and that he was, therefore, being held unlawfully.

Bushel's suit, in which three of his fellow jurors joined, brought to a head the debate over the fining of intransigent jurors. Chief Justice John Vaughan, after consulting with other royal judges, ruled in favor of Bushel.[78] He reasoned that law did not exist in the abstract but grew out of the facts of the case. Because of the impossibility of ascertaining completely objective facts, it was wrong to second-guess the jurors' findings. Their job was to ascertain fact and apply the law to it. The process was too complex, Vaughan concluded, to justify penalizing jurors for their verdicts.[79] The ruling was a total victory for jury nullification.

Massachusetts and New Plymouth tried to resolve the law-versus-fact issue by providing for special verdicts. Unlike general verdicts which either acquitted or convicted the defendant, the special verdict determined only the facts of the case, leaving it up to the judges to decide whether the facts determined made the defendant legally guilty of the offense charged.[80] This did not give the judges a completely free hand to take over the case. Massachusetts allowed convictions after a special verdict only with the concurrence of the jury. If there was disagreement between bench and jury, the case went to the General Court for resolution.[81]

By the seventeenth century trial juries were supposed to consider only the evidence presented in open court. Jurors not only lost their medieval role as official witnesses, but had a duty to avoid outside influences that might bias their judgment. Massachusetts created an exception that allowed jurors to consult in court with anyone they thought might assist them in reaching a verdict.[82] What sort of consultation the lawmakers had in mind is not clear, but it probably covered consultations with clergymen on questions of conscience.[83] In any case, it opened up jury deliberations to matters not in evidence and which the defendant had not had an opportunity to refute. No other colony authorized the practice. Jurors in Rhode Island were prohibited by statute to consider anything not in the trial record. The only exception was that jurors might take into account personal knowledge of witnesses in weighing their credibility.[84]

The guarantees of jury trial by no means meant that every case would be tried by jury. The right applied only in serious cases and even then might be waived if the defendant preferred trial by the bench instead. As a practical matter, trial by jury was the exception rather than the rule. Most offenses, serious as well as minor, were tried by magistrates unassisted by juries. One study has turned up only four jury trials for noncapital crimes in Massachusetts before 1660.[85] The difficulty of impaneling juries in the early years when the population was sparse and scattered must have put pressure on defendants to expedite things by waiving the right. Such pressure would have been compelling in cases where evidence of guilt was so overwhelming that judicial leniency was the defendant's best hope. Most cases probably fell into this category, thus obviating the need for jury trial. Still, defendants who insisted on jury trial in serious cases had an absolute right to be tried by jury regardless of the difficulties involved or the weight of evidence against them.

But even absolute rights often succumbed to judicial pressure for more summary proceedings. John M. Murrin makes a convincing case that before 1660 this routinely happened, and that the availability of jury trial had more to do with religious orthodoxy than with statutory guarantees. His study of the court records reveals an unmistakable bias against jury trial, and the bias clearly correlates with the sway of Puritanism. In ultra-Puritan New Haven, the magistrates meted out justice in all criminal cases, and in Massachusetts and Connecticut, juries were usually impaneled only for offenses punishable by death. The magistrates in these colonies showed a clear preference for summary justice along Old Testament lines. In New Plymouth, which practiced a more easygoing brand of Puritanism, jury trial was more common, but not so common as to be taken for granted as an automatic right. Only heterodox Rhode Island fully protected the right to be tried by jury. Scriptural models were never in vogue, and the colony courts closely followed English trial practices with regard to juries. But for the rest of early New England, the right of jury trial may have been more illusory than real.[86]

Every colony had a cutoff age on the criminal accountability of children. Those too young to comprehend the wrongfulness of their actions clearly lacked the criminal intent needed to justify a conviction. English law barred the prosecution of anyone under the age of seven, and there is no evidence that the rule was not followed in New England. Some colonies went even further in protecting youthful offenders. Connecticut and Massachusetts made ages fifteen and sixteen, respectively, the cutoff ages for the death penalty in arson cases.[87] Massachusetts, New Plymouth, and New Haven made sodomy a noncapital offense for defendants under the age of fourteen, and Connecticut set the cutoff age at fifteen.[88] Rhode Island did not prosecute persons under the age of fourteen for burglary, a capital crime, but tried them instead for the noncapital offense of larceny.[89]

Mentally impaired persons theoretically had a blanket exemption from prosecution if they could not understand the unlawfulness of their actions. Not being capable of criminal intent, they could not be held accountable for their wrongdoing. Both England and the colonies followed the rule that no one should be punished for something beyond his comprehension and control. Without moral culpability, there could be no criminal liability.[90] Massachusetts granted idiots and distracted persons statutory exemption from prosecution, but unfortunately provided no guidelines for identifying such persons.[91] The Connecticut statute was equally vague, and New Haven made "sufficient understanding" the talisman of accountability.[92] Rhode Island's burglary statute exempted "fools and madmen" from capital punishment, though the extent to which a burglar had to be foolish or mad was not made clear.[93]

Persons obviously insane were simply not brought to trial, so there were no formal pleadings or sanity hearings. The courts had considerable discretion in determining whether the accused was competent and triable. Fornication charges against one Massachusetts defendant were dismissed on the ground that she was "a distempered crazy woman," which was hardly a precise definition of her state of mind.[94] Craziness itself was not always enough to save a defendant.[95] Dorothy Talbye and Mary Parsons murdered their children while obviously deranged, yet Massachusetts sent them both to the gallows.[96] Not even Talbye's long record of mental disturbance could dissuade the court from condemning her.[97] The court in both cases seems to have confused mental incapacity with lack of criminal intent. Though they killed their children because of psychotic compulsions, both women understood the nature and criminality of their actions. This understanding, not their delusional motivations, was the standard by which they were judged. But the same standard also saved lives. In 1682 an Indian convicted of rape in New Plymouth escaped the gallows when the court ruled that Indians were too morally debased to comprehend the wickedness of the crime.[98]

The courts dealt with insanity essentially the way medical science defined the condition. Physicians in the seventeenth century did not recognize the broad range of functional psychoses and compulsions treated by modern psychiatry.[99] They recognized only forms of insanity involving defects of the rational or cognitive faculties. Mental disease was simply a matter of intellectual disability, with no allowance made for emotional dysfunction. Defendants aware of what was going on were considered competent to stand trial regardless of their actual mental state. Dorothy Talbye, for example, understood the charges against her, answered all questions rationally, and showed no outward signs of intellectual dysfunction. That she was subject to insane delusions made no legal difference. By the standards of the age she was sane and legally accountable for her actions.[100]

Mercy Brown of Wallingford only narrowly missed going to the Connecticut gallows under circumstances similar to the Talbye case. She killed her adult son, and her trial in 1691 was the first recorded instance of anything like an insanity defense going to a jury. The only issue at the trial was the defendant's state of mind at the time of the killing, and the jury had great difficulty reaching a verdict. But in the end the jurors found her guilty, leaving it to the Assistants Court to pass sentence. The Assistants delayed, however, and an appeal was brought on her behalf to the General Court. The appeal apparently succeeded, because sentence was not passed. But the Assistants for a time remained uncertain what to do. Finally, after delaying for two years, they declared her to be "distracted" and remanded her to the custody of the New Haven magistrates for confinement.[101] The failure of the courts to clear her outright on grounds of insanity underscores the difficulty of the defense.

No safeguard was more important than the privilege against compulsory self-incrimination. The privilege was much less comprehensive in colonial times than it is today. From the middle of the sixteenth century to the middle of the nineteenth, defendants in England went through preliminary examinations at which they were expected to answer questions put to them by the presiding magistrate. The accused was not warned that he need not answer; indeed, if he did not answer, it would be entered in the record and reported to the jury if the case came to trial. The jurors would then be free to infer the worst from his refusal to cooperate. The original privilege against self-incrimination probably related to compulsory oaths, not to the unsworn statements made by the accused to examining magistrates.[102]

If the privilege did originate with sworn statements, it was probably not originally for the benefit of the accused. Oaths by the accused carried so much weight in the early years of the common law that they were barred to keep the focus of the trial on the evidence. Defendants were barred from testifying under oath either for or against themselves.[103] Every New England colony adopted the common-law rule against sworn testimony by the accused. The only exception related to illegal sales of liquor to Indians. A white accused by Indians of selling them liquor could clear himself by swearing that the charges were false. This amounted to trial by oath, a common-law anomaly, but it applied only if Indians were the only witnesses available.[104] The exculpatory oath could not be taken if the accusing witnesses were white.

The Puritans loathed incrimination by compulsory oaths as intrusions into the privacy of conscience. They brought to the colonies bitter memories of the ex officio oaths administered by the prerogative courts of England. The judges of Star Chamber and the Court of High Commission claimed the right to administer oaths by virtue of their office. The device became an effective means of forcing suspected religious dissenters to incriminate themselves. Suspects confronted with the oath had to choose between refusing to be sworn, in which case they faced imprisonment for contempt, or taking the oath and falsely denying the charges against them. The latter was more to be feared by devout Puritans than the consequences of telling the truth. Abolition of the hated ex officio oath was one of the main goals of Puritan law reform in England.[105]

In 1637 the ex officio oath surfaced as an issue in Massachusetts when the General Court summoned the antinomian minister John Wheelwright for questioning about an allegedly seditious sermon. When Wheelwright insisted on knowing who had accused him and exactly what charges had been made against him, he was informed that these formalities would be dispensed with because the questions concerned a sermon that he freely acknowledged preaching. The Court then announced that it would proceed "ex officio" to determine whether the sermon was seditious. This caused an uproar among Wheelwright's supporters, who charged that the Court intended to force him to incriminate himself in the manner of the Court of High Commission. Taken aback by the charge, the Court reassured him that nothing of the sort was intended, that no oaths would be administered, and that the words "ex officio" had been used only to describe the official nature of the inquiry.[106] After Wheelwright consented to be questioned, the Court asked him about a matter not related to the sermon, and he refused to answer. There was another outburst, and his supporters charged that the Court sought to ensnare him by making him accuse himself. The incident leaves no doubt about the acute sensitivity of New Englanders on the issue of compulsory self-incrimination.[107]

The *Body of Liberties* adopted by Massachusetts in 1641 banned ex officio oaths. Public officials were precluded from administering oaths not expressly authorized by the statutes prescribing their official duties.[108] Connecticut adopted a similar ban in 1673, though such precautions were really not necessary.[109] Compulsory oaths were so universally reviled that no public official in his right mind would try to administer one. Besides, the ex officio oath was a device of the English prerogative courts, and there were no prerogative courts in New England. With the abolition of Star Chamber and High Commission, the process ended in England as well.[110]

The use of torture was even more repugnant than the psychological pressure of compulsory oaths. The idea of punishment before conviction was alien to the common law and prohibited by a key provision of Magna Carta.[111] Although authorized by the Privy Council or the monarch in more than eighty cases between 1540 and 1640, torture had no legal or judicial basis. It was employed not only in treason cases but also in cases of murder, robbery, embezzlement, and other ordinary crimes. Sir Edward Coke, who boasted in his legal commentaries that English law did not countenance torture, was himself delegated to examine suspects under torture. But Coke never claimed that torture was not used; he only insisted that it had no legal standing. The use of torture was always ad hoc and not part of the legal system.[112]

Coke was right about the extralegal character of torture. The great majority of cases for which torture warrants were issued involved crimes against the state: sedition, treason, and organized religious dissent. Moreover, it was used not so much to convict the accused as to extort information from him about accomplices and hidden aspects of the crime. Torture virtually disappeared after 1600, even as an extralegel process. Only seven cases were recorded during the reigns of James I and Charles I, and all seven involved state crimes. Although the threat of torture was used as late as 1662 to obtain a treason confession from Thomas Tonge, no actual use of torture after 1640 has been uncovered.[113] The last recorded use of torture to investigate an ordinary crime occurred in 1597. Since its demise preceded the clamor over compulsory self-incrimination, it seems reasonable to conclude that the privilege related to compulsory oaths, not to torture. The latter was always extraordinary, and its use rested on the sovereign immunity of the crown from prosecution. All the commissions ordering torture specifically granted immunity to the officers who carried out the order. Without immunity, the torturers themselves would have been exposed to civil and criminal penalties.[114]

The exclusion of torture from the common law has been attributed by Professor John H. Langbein to the rise of the trial jury in thirteenth-century England. When the Fourth Lateran Council abolished ordeals in 1215, it destroyed a whole system of proof that had given the medieval justice system the stamp of divine approval. A new system of proof had to be devised that approximated the certainty of divine justice. On the continent, the ordeal was replaced by judicial torture to obtain the sort of hidden evidence that would have been known to God. To convict on evidence that was merely persuasive was not enough; Roman canon-law standards of proof required certainty of guilt. English law did not take this route primarily because a substitute for certainty emerged in the form of the trial jury. Jury trial had already become an option in exceptional situations for defendants who wished to avoid the ordeals. It now became the regular mode of proof in serious criminal cases, filling the gap left by the abolition of ordeals. Since proof would be by jurors with direct knowledge of the case, torture was not needed, as it was on the continent, to dig out the facts. Besides, the jury retained some of the inscrutability of trial by ordeal in the unpredictability of its verdicts. The collective judgment of the jury, unanimous and without rationale, seemed more like the voice of God than the uncertain findings of continental jurists.[115] It would be safe to say that torture played no role in common-law development primarily because it was not needed.

The exclusion of torture from English law was a source of national pride by the seventeenth century. Coke cited it in his *Third Institute*, noting "there is no one opinion in our books, or judicial record . . . for the maintenance of tortures or torments."[116] That tradition became a bedrock principle of New England law. In 1641 Massachusetts prohibited torture to obtain confessions, though allowing it after a capital conviction to force the culprit to reveal the names of accomplices.[117] But this was something of an aberration not found anywhere else in New England. No other colony authorized torture for any purpose, either before conviction or afterward. Connecticut prohibited it absolutely and unconditionally.[118] As a practical matter, it was not used even in Massachusetts, at least not before the Salem witch panic worked havoc with the orderly administration of justice.[119]

The only legitimate purpose for which physical force might be used was to compel the accused to plead to the charges against him. The case could not be tried until a formal plea had been entered. This was because trial by jury had originally been at the option of the defendant, and the consensual formalities continued to be observed even after it became the regular form of criminal proceedings. Because jury trial was theoretically by choice, the right to refuse it was difficult to take away. For a time there was uncertainty about what to do with criminals who refused to plead, thus avoiding jury trial and punishment for their wrongdoing. In 1275 Parliament passed a statute directing that notorious offenders be kept in *prison forte et dure* (prison hard and strong) unless they entered a plea.[120] Practice somehow transformed the phrase into *peine forte et dure* (punishment hard and strong), and finally into judicial torture. By the sixteenth century, this took the barbarous form of placing the accused between boards and piling on weights until he entered a plea or expired.[121]

Compelling the accused to plead was not considered compulsory self-incrimination. The process was not designed to extort a confession but to force a plea so that the case could proceed. The law did not care whether the plea was guilty or not guilty, only that the trial should begin. English felons whose guilt was obvious sometimes chose to die by pressing rather than plead and face certain conviction. This was because a prisoner who died under *peine forte et dure* died unconvicted, so his property could not be forfeited to the crown and his family left destitute.[122] The practice was not abolished until 1772 by legislation which provided for automatic conviction if the accused did not plead. Finally, the law was changed in 1827 to provide for a plea of not guilty if the defendant failed to enter one.[123]

Although no one died of pressing before 1692, the process existed in New England from the beginning. In 1638 when Dorothy Talbye stood mute at her arraignment for killing her child, she was warned by the court that unless she responded to the indictment she would be pressed to death. She thereupon entered a guilty plea and died on the gallows.[124] In 1692 Giles Corey pleaded not guilty to witchcraft but refused to consent to jury trial, which was a procedural formality for the case to be tried. He had seen juries convict everyone charged with witchcraft and realized that his fate was sealed. So he died under weights but at least managed to save his property from forfeiture.[125] According to Robert Calef's account of the pressing, Corey's tongue "being pressed out of his mouth, the sheriff with his cane forced it in again, when he was dying."[126] The grisly spectacle was never repeated. Corey was the only New Englander to die under *peine forte et dure*.

No safeguard counted more or saved more lives than the two-witness rule. This was the scriptural rule adopted by the Puritan colonies that no one could be sentenced to death on purely circumstantial evidence (see chapter 2). Proof of guilt had to be established by two or more eyewitnesses testifying to the same facts and thus corroborating one another. One witness might suffice under certain circumstances, but no one could be condemned on circumstantial evidence alone.[127] The rule made the difference between life and death in many cases, for many offenses were not likely to be committed in the presence of witnesses. In 1637, before the rule was adopted, Massachusetts sent William Schooler to the gallows for murder on purely circumstantial evidence.[128] If tried five years later when the rule was in force, Schooler could not have been sentenced to death.[129] The rule was sometimes bent in witchcraft cases, but witchcraft was an area of law riddled with exceptions and aberrations (see chapter 8). However, for ordinary crimes the rule was clear: no eyewitnesses, no capital convictions.

Persons accused of capital crimes for which no witnesses were available could only be punished for lesser offenses. A Massachusetts adultery prosecution in 1667 illustrates how difficult it was to get a capital conviction even when witnesses were available. The witnesses in this case testified that they had seen the defendants in bed together, but they could not swear that they had actually seen them engage in sexual intercourse. So there was insufficient evidence for a capital conviction. Being in bed together was strong circumstantial evidence of adultery, but circumstantial evidence was not enough. The defendants could be convicted only of "adulterous behavior," a less serious offense not punishable by death.[130] Rape, like adultery, seldom had witnesses, and two Massachusetts men apparently escaped the gallows in 1643 because their victim was the only witness against them. Both were found guilty of "filthy dalliance" and sentenced to whippings.[131] In 1657 the two-witness rule saved John Ferris from the New Haven gallows for bestiality with a mare. Because only one witness had observed the offense, Ferris could only be convicted of attempted bestiality and severely whipped.[132]

Nothing in the two-witness rule protected defendants against perjury.

Matthew Giles, a New Hampshire resident, discovered this in 1662 when his wife Elizabeth falsely accused him of sodomy with their servant boy. She had coached the boy to back up her story and thus send her husband to the gallows. The plot might have succeeded except for doubts about Elizabeth's credibility. She had a reputation for lying, and the boy was known to be under her influence. When closely questioned by the authorities, the boy broke down and admitted that the charges were false. So the tables suddenly turned, and the accusers went to the whipping post for lying.[133] They actually got off lightly, because perjury to take life was itself a capital crime.[134] The plotters apparently had not made their accusations under oath and therefore could not be prosecuted for the offense.

The two-witness rule operated only if the accused denied the charges against him. If he pleaded guilty, nothing had to be proved. The court only had to pass sentence against him. An admission of guilt by the defendant was considered the best evidence of guilt. While a defendant might falsely deny the charges against him, it was highly improbable that he would falsely admit them. Even a repudiated confession could send the accused to the gallows if supported by convincing evidence. It then became a question of deciding whether the confession was more credible than the repudiation. The two-witness rule protected defendants against circumstantial evidence, but not against their own admissions. The latter could send them to the gallows whether eyewitness testimony was available or not.

A 1642 bestiality case in New Haven illustrates the devastating consequences of a repudiated confession. The accused, George Spencer, had worked as a servant for a man whose sow subsequently gave birth to a deformed piglet, described in the records as "a prodigious monster." Unfortunately for Spencer, some people saw a striking resemblance between him and the piglet. Spencer, like the piglet, had only one eye, and the eye he did have, like the piglet's, was "whitish and deformed." Rumors soon circulated that the deformed piglet was a sign from God that an abominable crime had been committed. The rumors seemed credible to many because of Spencer's bad reputation as "a profane, lying, scoffing and lewd spirit." The suspect was arrested and jailed on bestiality charges.[135]

Spencer denied the charges and would have been safe from conviction if he had stuck by his denials. Bestiality was a capital crime requiring eyewitness testimony, and there were no witnesses against him. He continued to deny the crime until visited in prison by one of the magistrates, who told him that confession and repentance would bring mercy and forgiveness. So he confessed and repeated the confession when visited by several other magistrates, confessing to additional offenses as well, such as lying and profaning the Sabbath. But instead of wiping the slate clean, the admissions became the principal evidence against him. When Spencer learned, too late, that the forgiveness promised would come only in the hereafter, he repudiated his confession and declared that he had made it only to please the magistrates. But the damage had been done, and it proved fatal. The credibility of the confession became the key issue at his trial and opened the door for the admission of circumstantial evidence tending to corroborate it. The corroboration, which included his access to the sow and his resemblance to the piglet, would have been legally insufficient to convict him without the confession.[136] But as proof of the credibility of the confession, it was enough to send him to the gallows.

New Haven had an almost identical bestiality case five years later, but with different results because the accused refused to incriminate himself. Another deformed piglet was born, and suspicion this time centered on Thomas Hogg, a disreputable character thought by some to resemble the piglet. Hogg, who was already awaiting trial for lying, stealing, and indecent exposure, might easily have gone to the gallows. The circumstantial evidence against him convinced the authorities of his guilt. A confrontation was arranged at which he had to touch the sow so that its responses could be observed. The record notes that at his touch "there appeared to be a working of lust in the sow." But still he would not confess, and without a confession, there could be no conviction without witnesses. The authorities finally gave up and tried him only on the noncapital charges already pending. Hogg was back in court the following year for failing to report for guard duty.[137]

The Hogg and Spencer cases turned out differently because of the two-witness rule. Hogg had the benefit of the rule while Spencer did not. By admitting nothing, Hogg kept the rule in effect to prevent the circumstantial evidence from convicting him. His resemblance to the piglet and the "working of lust in the sow" would have been evidence enough to corroborate any repudiated confession. If Spencer had been as resolute and less trustful, he too would have escaped the gallows. The sort of guile used to incriminate him was completely legal. Tricking the accused into making a confession was quite different from forcing him to make one. Such tactics had been long used in England to dupe defendants into confessing.[138]

Common-law anachronisms such as benefit of clergy never took root in New England. The device entered English law in the twelfth century to accommodate the claims of church authorities that clerics should not be subject to trial in the secular courts. The test of clerical status was the ability to read, which was appropriate in an era when literacy was almost a clerical monopoly. The privilege was gradually extended to literate laymen in order to commute the death penalty then in force for a wide range of minor felonies. Laymen could claim clergy only once, and to prevent a second claim a statute passed in 1490 provided that persons other than real priests who claimed it were to be burned on the brawn of the left thumb with a *T* (thief) or an *M* (manslayer). The brand enabled court officers to detect those who had claimed the privilege previously.[139]

Benefit of clergy evolved over the years into a legal fiction that saved countless defendants from the gallows.[140] Even the ignorant and uneducated could invoke its protection, for it was only necessary to read or recite from memory the first verse of Psalm 51, known as the "neck psalm," to escape the gallows. Since the verse was always the same, anyone with a modicum of literacy or coaching could qualify. The privilege split the felony laws of England into "clergyable" and "nonclergyable" offenses. The latter were serious crimes for which the privilege could not be claimed. The statutes limiting the privilege were the main reason for the development of distinctions between murder and manslaughter, robbery and larceny, burglary and housebreaking. Manslaughter, for example, was a clergyable crime, while murder was nonclergyable; both were capital offenses, but only the latter was actually punished by death.[141] In 1706 Parliament extended clergy to the invincibly illiterate by abolishing the reading test, and in 1779, when judges were authorized to impose fines or whippings for minor felonies, it went out of use completely.[142]

While benefit of clergy entered the legal system of the southern colonies, it never really took hold in New England. For one thing, Puritans were not likely to write a medieval Catholic device into their laws, particularly straightforward laws based on the revealed word of God. For another, any device that allowed offenders to escape punishment must have seemed arbitrary and immoral. Besides, there were no minor felonies for which offenders had to be rescued from the gallows. Only the most serious offenses called for the death penalty, so there was no conflict between law and conscience. Benefit of clergy did not appear in Massachusetts until 1686, during the Dominion period. The abrogation of the colony laws had put larceny on the capital list, leading Chief Justice Joseph Dudley to grant clergy to several larceny defendants.[143] Rhode Island, which closely followed English practice, was the only colony where benefit of clergy may have had a statutory basis. The laws adopted in 1647 made murder, robbery, arson, sodomy, and bestiality capital crimes "without remedy," which was the legal term for "without benefit of clergy."[144] This seems to imply that for other crimes clergy was available, though the court records provide no instances of its use.

New England trial practices were generally more enlightened and progressive than those of England. The admission of accusatory depositions, a practice routine in English courts, was severely restricted to safeguard the defendant's right of rebuttal.[145] The right to bail was protected in the colonies by statutes limiting the discretion of judges. Whole categories of offenses for which bail was denied in England were bailable in Massachusetts.[146] The colonial rule against double jeopardy afforded greater protection than the English rule. English law made it a complete defense only in capital cases and did not prevent second prosecutions for minor offenses.[147] The Massachusetts version made it an ironclad defense for every crime and misdemeanor.[148]

Jury trial in New England was generally free of the judicial badgering and intimidation found in England. Before *Bushel's Case* in 1671, English jurors were subject to fines and other penalties for bringing in verdicts that displeased the judges.[149] Judicial power was more evenly balanced between bench and jury in New England. Disagreements between judges and jurors were resolved in Massachusetts by the General Court, where the participation of the deputies acted as a brake on the power of the magistrates.[150] Although New Plymouth punished jurors for personal misconduct during the trial, they could not be punished for how they decided the case.[151] Jurors nowhere could be forced to bring in guilty verdicts or punished for not following the instructions of the court. Trial juries modified the law routinely, bringing in acquittals or convictions for lesser offenses than warranted by the law and the evidence.

But the most important feature of the Massachusetts system was that the defendant's rights were spelled out in readily ascertainable statutes. Nothing really important was left to the discretion of the judges. This minimized the judicial high-handedness typical of court proceedings in England. Statutes, not judicial whim or discretion, determined whether an offense was bailable, where and when the accused would be tried, and the sort of evidence or testimony needed to convict him. Rights that really counted were protected against the awesome power of the state. This represented a quantum leap forward in the civilized administration of justice.

Nor shall any true gentleman nor any man equal to a
gentleman be punished with whipping unless his crime be
very shameful and his course of life vicious
and profligate.—Massachusetts Laws (1641)

7   Unequal Protection of the Law

Seventeenth-century due process of law did not mean equal protection of law. Judicial fairness required only that everyone should get a fair hearing, not that everyone should be treated exactly the same. The age did not subscribe to modern notions that differences in social and economic circumstances do not count. Such differences were taken into account, so that people stood with the law as they stood in relation to one another in society. Servants had different duties to their masters than masters to their servants; husbands and wives had different duties to one another and to their children; and children had different obligations to their parents than to society in general. Such things as age, sex, race, and class not only defined a person's social standing but his standing before the law as well. To ignore such differences would have been unrealistic and in some cases actually unjust.

The New England Puritans gave short shrift to opponents of church and state. In the 1630s Massachusetts banished antinomians for sedition, and during the following decade expelled Anabaptists as purveyors of heresy.[1] The turn of the Quakers came in the 1650s, when they entered New England in force to challenge the Puritan hegemony.[2] The Salem minister John Higginson spoke for the establishment in denouncing their doctrines as "a stinking vapor from hell" that would poison the air of New England if tolerated.[3] But they would not be tolerated, because every Puritan colony took measures to suppress them.[4] New Plymouth provided for the preventive detention of Quakers, expelled them from the colony, and whipped them if they returned.[5] New Haven permitted them to enter on business for short periods, but any Quaker who attempted to proselytize was subject to arrest, whipping, and deportation.[6] Massachusetts, which attracted Quaker missionaries in droves, ordered whipping, branding, mutilation, and finally death for those who returned after deportation.[7] The anti-Quaker measures taken would earn Massachusetts the distinction of being the only English colony to execute people for religious offenses.[8]

Puritan attempts to exclude Quakers put severe strains on legal due process. When the first missionaries arrived in Boston in 1656, they were summarily arrested and thrown into jail to prevent them from preaching. Since no law then in force authorized such treatment, their detention violated the guarantee against arbitrary imprisonment.[9] The General Court rationalized what was done on the ground that they were jailed not to punish them but to prevent them from spreading heresy until they could be deported.[10] Preventive detention, the theory went, had nothing to do with the guarantee against punishment before conviction. This was pure casuistry, of course, but the best the Court could do to legitimize the summary detention. The ruling provided a precedent for dealing with other dissidents who challenged the Puritan establishment.[11]

The repression extended to resident Quakers as well as to newcomers. In 1656 Massachusetts fined and banished Nicholas Upshall, a former selectman and one of the founders of the Dorchester church, for joining and publicly defending the sect. Although Upshall was widely respected, the authorities could not tolerate his defense of Quakers nor his criticism of the measures taken against them. When Upshall violated the order of banishment by returning to Boston, he was confined to jail. But this proved embarrassing to the government when numerous sympathizers flocked to the jail to express their support. The General Court finally paroled him to the custody of John Caper, a deputy from Dorchester, to get him out of the public eye. He was warned to live quietly and have no further contacts with Quakers or he would be imprisoned for life on Castle Island in Boston harbor.[12] Upshall caused no more trouble, and the authorities thereafter left him alone.[13] His beliefs had not been the issue, only his defense of Quakers and questioning of the measures taken against them.

The anti-Quaker measures taken by Massachusetts were challenged by Quakers as contrary to the laws of England. They argued that there was no precedent in English law for executing Quakers who returned in violation of orders of banishment. This was a serious charge, because the colony's charter expressly prohibited measures contrary to English law. It was the sort of charge likely to make trouble with a home government that had turned hostile to Puritans after the Restoration. The General Court took the challenge so seriously that it prepared a detailed defense of its actions. It justified imposing the death penalty on returning Quakers on the ground that the death penalty had been ordered by Parliament for Jesuits who entered England.[14] The analogy had a hollow ring, though it scored political points by conceding the supremacy of English law. A better argument would have been that the measures in question supplemented rather than violated English law. The charter provision did not require an English precedent for every colonial law, only that colonial law should not be contrary to English law. Since no English law expressly protected Quakers, the measures taken hardly amounted to charter violations.

The treatment of ordinary offenders contrasted sharply with the treatment of political and religious offenders. The law was more indulgent toward those who did not challenge the church-state establishment. The treatment of youthful offenders, for example, was lenient and humane by seventeenth-century standards. They were treated differently from adult offenders, probably on the theory that they were better candidates for rehabilitation. While this did not square with the Puritan belief in predestination, it did not prevent lawmakers from hoping for the best. The cutoff age on the death penalty ranged from fourteen to sixteen according to the offense, except for murder, which was punished everywhere according to adult standards.[15] But for other capital crimes, every colony took into account the age of the offender.[16]

Giving the young a break did not mean taking them out of the regular justice system completely. They were tried by the regular courts under the same rules applicable to adult offenders. It could not have been otherwise in an age that judged everyone by the same moral standards.[17] There was then no generational gap to justify separate standards for the young. Links between the generations were strong, and young people fully entered the adult world by the age of sixteen, the age at which young males had to serve in the militia and take turns at watch and ward.[18] That young people were treated more leniently did not mean that society winked at their offenses. It meant only that the young were often given a second chance to mend their ways. Those who did not make the most of it soon discovered the mistake of confusing leniency with license.

The law also took gender into account and treated females differently from male offenders. Some New England capital laws were not even made applicable to women, perhaps because they were considered incapable of such offenses. Massachusetts and Connecticut made only males punishable under the statutes against idolatry, perjury, and sodomy.[19] Connecticut eventually made women equally punishable, but Massachusetts retained its double standard through several law revisions.[20] The reason may have been

117

that male lawmakers assumed these to be essentially male offenses. This was true of sodomy under English law and Scripture, but not of idolatry and perjury. Such gender distinctions reflected prevailing preconceptions about the propensities and capabilities of women.

The double standard figured prominently in sex offenses. Prostitutes, for example, were treated more harshly than their clients because they sinned for gain, while their clients sinned out of human weakness.[21] Married women were also at a disadvantage to married men in the definition of adultery. The law made the adultery of the married woman punishable but not that of the married man. A married woman who had an extramarital affair was guilty of adultery regardless of the marital status of her partner, but a married man was guilty only if he became involved with a married woman.[22] An offense committed with an unmarried woman would be punished, but only as fornication, not adultery.[23] Marital fidelity was insisted upon for women to protect the husband's family line from spurious progeny. But if adultery law tilted against married women, it also favored unmarried ones. A single woman could not be prosecuted for adultery with a married man, but a single man could be prosecuted for adultery with a married woman.

The risk of pregnancy made it more likely that women would be punished for extramarital affairs. Any unmarried woman who became pregnant was automatically guilty of fornication, whether her male partner could be identified or not.[24] The man might escape punishment completely unless she identified him. Unwed mothers sometimes stood trial and suffered punishment alone, while the men responsible went unpunished. Even if the woman cooperated and identified the man, he might not be convicted on her word alone without corroboration. She might lie in order to mitigate her own punishment, likely to be more severe if she refused to cooperate, or to shield the real culprit. But even testimony insufficient for a fornication conviction might be enough to hold the putative father civilly liable for support payments.[25] This had almost as high a public priority as convicting the accused on criminal charges.

Fear of disgrace and punishment caused some women to conceal their pregnancy and do away with the child at birth. If the body was later discovered, they could plausibly contend that the infant had been born dead and its body concealed to avoid punishment for fornication. The two-witness rule made infanticide almost impossible to prove, and before 1691 no woman who did not confess was sent to the gallows for it. In 1624 Parliament dealt with the problem in England by passing a law making concealment of an illegitimate child's death presumptive evidence of murder. The presumption could be rebutted by the testimony of a witness to the birth that the child had been born dead.[26] But the English rule was not adopted in New England until the 1690s. Until then, the killing of newborns remained an almost unprovable crime.

Although the witchcraft statutes made no explicit gender distinctions, the law was stacked against women in such cases. Prosecutions correlate so closely with sex that the offense can fairly be called a gender-related crime. A few men were prosecuted, but the overwhelming majority of defendants were women. Fourteen of the sixteen defendants executed before the Salem trials were women, and the only males executed were implicated because they were married to convicted witches. The folklore of witchcraft targeted women for suspicion. It was believed that Satan lusted for the bodies of his followers, and so was more likely to recruit women than men. Male chauvinism was another factor. Women were thought to be the weaker sex spiritually as well as physically, and so more likely than men to succumb to temptation. This sort of misogyny could prove lethal to women when witchcraft was suspected (see chapter 9).

The law treated women approximately the way male-dominated society perceived them. They were viewed as breeders and housekeepers whose purpose in life was to assist and make things easier for men. Denial of education cut most women off from cultural and intellectual life and helped reinforce invidious stereotypes. The stereotypes were caricatures really, depicting women as mindless prattlers, given to railing and scolding. Those who refused to play the role and sought intellectual satisfaction were ridiculed and accused of pride or perversity. Equally invidious was the stereotype of women as temptresses who enticed men into sin, just as Eve had tempted Adam in the Garden of Eden. One of the reasons adultery was considered more heinous for the woman, apart from the risk of bastards, was because an adulterous woman betrayed the loyalty she owed her husband. English law gave husbands a property interest in the chastity of their wives and allowed them to recover civil damages against the wife's partner in adultery.[27] But wives could not bring similar actions if their husbands went astray. English wives had no standing to bring suit without spousal consent because of the legal fiction that a married couple was one person.[28]

Conditions for women were somewhat better in New England, though not dramatically better. They still lived in a society where sexist stereotypes prevailed.[29] Males alone could qualify for freemanship and participate in public affairs.[30] Female inferiority was taken for granted as an incontestable fact of life. John Winthrop, one of the best minds in Massachusetts, actually thought that intellectual pursuits could drive a woman mad. He attributed the mental breakdown suffered by the wife of Governor Edward Hopkins of Connecticut to excessive reading.[31] Some women who tried to take a more active role in Puritan religious life were derided by the Puritan historian Edward Johnson as "silly women laden with diverse lusts and phantastical madness."[32] When a woman of superior mind and character like Anne Hutchinson appeared on the scene, the sexist establishment lost no time in banishing her to the wilderness. Hutchinson's expulsion from Massachusetts may have had less to do with heresy than with her refusal to conform to female stereotypes.

The law made explicit allowance for the social standing of offenders in prescribing penalties. Massachusetts provided that no "true gentleman" should be whipped for a minor offense unless his life was "vicious and profligate." Numerous provisions for the payment of fines in lieu of corporal punishments wrote class standing directly into the criminal laws.[33] Since Puritan society sorted people out by rank and class, it seemed perfectly reasonable that the justice system should do the same. Persons at the top paid higher taxes and assumed greater public responsibilities than those at the bottom of society. Their privileges had been earned by their superior contributions to the community. Moreover, their standards were higher and stricter. If a member of the elite went astray, the embarrassment of a court appearance and fine would usually be enough to ensure that the offense would not be repeated.

The lower classes got comparatively harsher treatment than those at the top. Disobedient servants were punished like common criminals, often with whippings besides extended periods of service.[34] Susan Cole's "rebellious carriage" cost her a term at hard labor in the Connecticut house of correction.[35] A servant absent without leave could expect an automatic increase in his term of indenture.[36] Masters, on the other hand, got off lightly for offenses against servants. In 1649 William Wilkes was let off by a New Haven court with no criminal penalties at all for assaulting his servant with a hammer. The court merely took two months off the servant's term of indenture.[37] In 1682 a Massachusetts court let William Fowles off with a mere reprimand for hanging his servant by the heels like a beast for slaughter.[38] If the tables had been turned in these cases, the penalties imposed would probably have been different.

Class justice took into account the social standing of both the offender and the victim. The most serious offenses were those by an unrespectable person against a respectable party, and the least serious were those by a respectable party against an unrespectable party.[39] A study by M. P. Baumgartner of the records of the New Haven town court from 1639 to 1665 reveals the extent to which the court protected the local elite. Most of the identifiable criminal complaints were brought by upper-class persons who comprised only a minority of the population. Moreover, the overwhelming majority of criminal defendants were persons of low standing. In nearly three-fourths of the cases, a person of high status brought a person of low status into court. The next most frequent complaints were those made by low-status persons against other low-status persons. While ready enough to accuse one another, few low-status persons accused those above them. The least likely complaints were those by high-status people against others of high status. The top of society tended to be more cohesive than the bottom in the filing of criminal charges. Most complaints were directed downward, toward persons of lower social standing.[40]

The conviction rate in New Haven also correlated with social status. High-status people were more likely to be acquitted than those lower in standing. Statistically, the chance of acquittal was about five times as great for a defendant of high social standing as for a low-status person. Although the defendant's status itself was a reliable predictor of the outcome of the case, the source of the complaint predicted it even more accurately. When the complaint issued from a high-status person against a low-status defendant, only 1 percent ended in acquittal, with 7 percent referred to a higher court, and the rest resulting in convictions. This contrasts sharply with the outcome of cases where both the complainant and accused were of low standing. Defendants won acquittal in 11 percent of the cases, more than ten times the rate as in cases begun by members of the upper class. Of the high-status defendants accused by their social equals, all were found guilty. But of those complained against by a low-status person, three were acquitted, one case went to a higher court, and only one was convicted. Not only were high-status persons more likely to be successful in their complaints, but they were also more likely to be acquitted when complained against than those beneath them in social standing.[41]

The punishments meted out by the New Haven court also varied with the social status of the accused. Punishments of humiliation were almost always reserved for persons of low social standing. No one of high or even middle-class status was sentenced to the stocks or compelled to wear locks, signs, or halters. But such sentences were imposed on about 10 percent of the low-status defendants convicted. Upper-class defendants, if convicted, were required to post peace bonds, make restitution in cases of theft, and undergo miscellaneous penalties almost never applied to those at the bottom. The imposition of fines and corporal punishments corresponded closely with the class of the offender. Sentences of whipping were disproportionately imposed on low-status offenders, and fines were more often exacted from those higher on the social ladder. The magistrates used their sentencing discretion in such a way that the likelihood of a whipping correlated inversely with the rank of the offender.[42] Gentlemen in New Haven, as in Massachusetts, seldom went to the whipping post.

The cases also make clear that criminal justice at New Haven was highly geared to social control. The system operated to protect the social and economic elite by holding the lower ranks of society to a strict standard of accountability. Standards were less strict for outsiders whose temporary residence did not threaten local power relationships. The court treated strangers as high-status persons regardless of their status at home. In fact, they were treated even better than members of the resident upper class. Their acquittal rate was higher than for any group in New Haven. They had an acquittal rate of 25 percent, as against 15 percent for high-rank residents, and only 3 percent for low-rank residents. When convicted, their punishment was no harsher than that of high-rank residents.[43] Since they had no permanent place in local society, making an example of them served no purpose.

Fear may have been a factor in the treatment of servants. While most entered the servant class voluntarily to pay for their passage to New England, many had the status imposed upon them by circumstances beyond their control. Some were paupers and vagrants bound to service to keep them off the public dole, and a few were thieves sold into service to make good what they had stolen.[44] Still others were prisoners of war from Ireland and Scotland condemned to servitude in the colonies. Although the policy of transporting criminals did not begin in earnest until Parliament passed the Transportation Act of 1718, several thousand criminals, malcontents, and prisoners of war were banished in the latter half of the seventeenth century.[45] During the 1650s more than four hundred Scottish prisoners from the English civil war were sold as servants in Boston for terms ranging from six to eight years.[46] The Irish prisoners brought over caused the most anxiety because of their known hatred of the English nation.[47] They were so feared that the General Court imposed a prohibitive duty of fifty pounds on every Irish prisoner brought into Massachusetts.[48]

Court records show that servants as a class were probably no better or worse than other groups in society. Most of their offenses involved sexual misconduct and petty theft, but nothing really serious enough to threaten society. However, the Scots and Irish were viewed differently because of fears that their national grievances might explode into violence. But most did not remain in New England long enough to cause trouble. The bulk of the prisoners brought to Boston were purchased by traders for resale in other colonies.[49] Still, those who remained were regarded with suspicion, and even isolated incidents would be blown up out of all proportion (see chapter 9). Every violent incident lowered the threshold of fear about servants generally.

Really the most dangerous group of all from the standpoint of public safety were the native American Indians whose lands the settlers occupied. The English in large measure shared the assumptions of Western culture about the inferiority of non-Europeans and the right of Christians and Christianity to world hegemony. They brought these assumptions to New England, making peaceful relations with the natives virtually impossible. Roger Williams was one of the few Englishmen to challenge these assumptions and uphold the rights of the Indians. The Indians had legal title to the land, he asserted, and from them alone could valid title be obtained. The charter of Massachusetts from the king was worthless in this regard, for the king could not grant what did not belong to him. This theory called every land title in Massachusetts into question and raised doubts about the legitimacy of the Puritan state.[50] Williams's expulsion from the colony in 1636 ended all discussion of Indian rights and foreclosed the possibility of amity between the two races.

Two schools of thought exist regarding the treatment of the New England Indians. One is moral, the other historical. The latter holds that the settlers made a good-faith effort to treat the natives fairly, but that cultural differences between the two races made permanent accommodation impossible.[51] The moral approach holds that European racial assumptions poisoned relations from the beginning and made conflict inevitable.[52] Colonial law served as a tool for promoting the interests of the settlers at the expense of the natives.[53] The cultural bias embedded in the laws made evenhanded dealings with the natives impossible.[54]

The reality of relations with the Indians probably lies somewhere in between. Certainly outrages were committed against them, but whether they were aberrations or deliberate policy is less certain. Moreover, outrages were a two-way street, and the Indians committed more than a few against the settlers. Relations between whites and Indians were complicated by the fact that some Indians lived under the white man's laws while others did not. Those belonging to self-governing tribes were accountable only for offenses against whites. What they did among themselves was settled according to tribal customs and traditions. Only Indians who had abandoned tribal life to live in the white man's world were subject to white law completely.[55] They were held, at least in theory, to the same standard of conduct as everyone else in the community.

In the beginning, relations with the tribes took the form of diplomatic exchanges between independent nations seeking to resolve mutual problems. The English made no sweeping claims to legal title to Indian lands. Rather, the colony government negotiated through bribery, threats, or persuasion purchase of the lands needed for a growing population. As the settlers grew in numbers and power, the bargaining power of the tribes began to dissolve. The power shift was gradual, but its progress was as inexorable as the rising tide. The settlers used their growing preponderance to force one concession after another. Indian freedom and independence gradually slipped away, and the natives of New England came more and more under white control.[56]

Bringing tribal Indians before the white man's courts could be difficult as well as dangerous.[57] In 1644 the New Haven authorities seized several Indians as hostages to force the surrender of Indians suspected of murdering a white. To have allowed violence against whites to go unpunished would have put every settler and settlement at risk. While Indians accused of such crimes generally got a fair hearing, the punishments meted out were often different from those imposed on white offenders. In 1639 an Indian convicted of murder was decapitated at New Haven and his head set on a pole to impress Indian visitors with the consequences of killing whites. Five years later, another Indian was beheaded at New Haven for murdering a white. The execution was a grisly affair requiring five strokes to separate the culprit from his head. New Plymouth beheaded an Indian for complicity in a murder at the conclusion of King Philip's War in 1676, but this was an extreme measure related to the war and not part of the regular justice system.[58]

Cultural differences made much of the white man's law incomprehensible to the natives. They were expected to adjust to ways different from their own, and the adjustment was never easy. Whites who broke the law at least knew that what they were doing was wrong, an insight often unavailable to Indian offenders.[59] The Massachusetts lawmakers recognized the problem and ordered Indians to assemble in the settlements each year for a reading and explanation of the laws.[60] Even if they could not understand every detail and nuance, they would at least come away with a general idea of what was expected of them. New Plymouth held similar assemblies at which the attendance of the natives was compulsory.[61] While these efforts doubtless did some good, it would be fatuous to assume that they more than touched the surface of the problem.

Most of the laws specifically relating to Indians do not seem to have been framed to oppress them, but rather to guarantee them a modicum of fair treatment. Without such legal safeguards, their situation would have been far worse from every standpoint. The racial hostility of some settlers was so intense that institutional protection was needed. If the Puritan political system had been more democratic and responsive to public opinion, the Indians would have gotten even shorter shrift. The white man's law created a form of racial détente that reassured whites while it also protected the natives. Offenses by whites against Indians were punished by the same laws that punished Indians for crimes against whites. The legal safeguards never worked perfectly, but even imperfect safeguards were better than none at all.

However high-minded their intent, some of the efforts to bring Indians within the white cultural orbit were high-handed and deplorable. The Massachusetts laws banning powwows and the worship of false gods had the practical effect of outlawing the religious observances of the natives.[62] New Plymouth and Connecticut went even further down the road of forced assimilation. Both required Indians living within the pale of settlement to observe all the Sabbath regulations prescribed for whites.[63] They were obliged to conform whether they were Christians or not. The pressure to conform was so great that only Indians leading tribal lives managed to keep their customs and beliefs intact.[64]

Laws originally designed to protect the natives also eventually provided the means for their despoilment. The statutes prohibiting the settlers from purchasing Indian lands are a clear example.[65] While they temporarily kept tribal lands in Indian hands, they also asserted governmental control over all land acquisitions and distributions. There was never any intention that Indian lands should remain in Indian hands permanently. The only issue was the method by which they should be expropriated by whites. The

Puritans assumed that the Indians had no right to the lands they occupied because their method of possession was not recognized by English law. Title to all the land in Massachusetts, the theory went, passed to the Massachusetts Bay Company under the charter granted by the crown, and it was up to the General Court to extinguish Indian claims and distribute the land among the settlers. For individuals or even towns to deal directly with the natives would reduce the importance of the General Court and weaken the central government. If the Indians had to be compensated for the land, compensation would come from the government and not from private purchasers. No one could obtain valid land titles from Indians, because Indians had no valid titles to sell. What it came down to really was that key laws supposed to protect Indian interests actually promoted the political goals of whites.[66]

In 1676 tribal life and Indian self-government ended in New England amid the calamity of King Philip's War. When the killing finally stopped, Massachusetts assigned the survivors to four "plantations" completely subject to the white man's laws. They were really detention centers from which no one might leave without permission, and those who attempted to do so were jailed until they agreed to return.[67] These plantations resembled the Indian reservations of the late nineteenth century, though on a smaller scale and with less calculated brutality. But conditions on them were nevertheless bad, particularly with regard to personal freedom. Not even blacks, at least not those who were not slaves, had to accept such constraints. Free blacks could generally live and work where they pleased and faced few restrictions based on race.[68] Only Indians had to live under conditions amounting to a racial quarantine.

The plantation Indians had only partial control of their own affairs.[69] They elected their own constables and judges, but the laws under which they lived were passed by whites in the General Court. They were not even fully trusted to administer justice in their own plantation courts. Indian judges had jurisdiction to try minor offenses, but white judges had to be called in to sit with them for the trial of serious cases. These mixed courts of Indians and whites had the same jurisdiction as the regular county courts.[70] They also heard appeals in cases tried by Indian judges sitting alone. But they had no jurisdiction over capital cases. These were tried at Boston by the Assistants Court. The Assistants also heard appeals from the mixed plantation courts.[71]

Connecticut established similar enclaves for the Indian survivors. They were confined to "Indian towns" with limited rights of self-government.

Indians might not leave their assigned towns without obtaining permission. Although law enforcement was in the hands of Indian officers, the laws they enforced were made by whites.[72] But the inhabitants controlled their own justice system without much outside interference. Trials were presided over by Indian judges with jurisdiction over a wide range of offenses. Only offenses calling for the death penalty had to be tried by whites in the Assistants Court at Hartford.[73] Capital cases were considered too important to be left to Indians, who might apply the white man's laws incorrectly.[74]

Indians tried in the white man's courts had the benefit of the same safeguards available to white defendants.[75] The rules were sometimes even bent to ensure that they got a fair hearing. New Plymouth allowed Indian witnesses to testify without taking the oath required of white witnesses. To insist on such meaningless formalities might inhibit or confuse the witness. The important thing was to get the defendant's side of the case before the jury. Jurors were bound to give the unsworn testimony of Indians the same weight accorded the sworn testimony of white witnesses.[76] Rhode Island took similar precautions to ensure the fair consideration of Indian testimony. Juries were instructed not to discount the testimony of Indian witnesses on racial grounds alone.[77] While such measures may have helped marginally, most jurors probably found it difficult to overcome their prejudices. That they had to be admonished to do so underscores the difficulty of the task.

Mixed juries of whites and Indians were sometimes impaneled for the trial of Indian defendants. In 1673 a mixed Rhode Island jury tried an Indian charged with killing a fellow Indian.[78] Mixed juries were also impaneled in Massachusetts and New Plymouth to try Indian defendants. In 1674 a Massachusetts jury of six whites and six Indians convicted an Indian named Tom of raping an Indian woman.[79] But the verdict noted that Tom, like many Indians, probably did not understand the white man's law against rape. So he escaped the gallows and was bound instead to a term of penal servitude.[80] In 1675 a mixed jury in New Plymouth tried three Indians accused of killing a fellow Indian.[81] The presence of Indians on these panels ensured that Indian defendants would not be judged by the white man's standards alone.

Even all-white juries could usually be counted on to take cultural differences into account. Indians convicted of rape seldom got the death penalty, because rape was a less serious crime among the natives.[82] Thus Indians might get off with a whipping for offenses likely to cost a white his life. Although tried in 1685 on a murder indictment for beating his wife to death, an Indian named Joseph was convicted by a mixed Massachusetts jury of "barbarous cruelty," a noncapital offense.[83] Since wife-beating was common among Indians, the jury apparently reasoned that the killing had been unintentional and should not be punished with death. Cultural differences could be a mitigating factor even in punishing crimes against whites. In 1669 a Massachusetts Indian named John got off with a whipping for fatally striking a white woman while he was drunk. He got ten lashes for the assault and another ten for being drunk.[84] Drunkenness would not have been an acceptable defense for a white, but the effect of alcohol on Indian behavior was known to be too devastating not to be taken into account.

Despite efforts to administer justice fairly, innate prejudices must have been difficult to overcome in cases involving Indians. "Beastly-minded and mannered creatures" was the way one Connecticut official described the natives.[85] While Indian jurors were impaneled for the trial of Indians, no Indian was ever impaneled for the trial of a white. And while their testimony was admissible against white defendants, it generally carried less weight with judges and jurors than the testimony of whites. Massachusetts permitted any white accused by Indians of illegal liquor sales to clear himself simply by taking an oath that the charges were false.[86] No matter how many Indians accused him, the case would be dismissed. This is a telling commentary on the assumed credibility of Indians. The need for laws urging jurors to weigh Indian testimony fairly suggests a normal predisposition to do the opposite.[87]

Hostility toward Indians abounded in everyday relations. In Massachusetts the inhabitants of Watertown voted to bar the natives from fishing within the town limits.[88] Salem passed an ordinance forbidding Indians to enter without permission and excluding them completely after sunset.[89] Groton barred Indians from settling within the town limits, and severe penalties were prescribed for those who defied the order.[90] The plantations and enclaves set up for the natives after King Philip's War really marked the final stage of a long-standing policy of racial separation. But not even separation sufficed to end white apprehensions. In 1685 New Plymouth put all its enclaves under tight surveillance. Informers were employed to report any offenses or deviant behavior to the white authorities.[91] Such racial distrust would have undermined even the most conscientious efforts made to administer justice fairly.

The fair administration of justice was further complicated by provisions singling Indians out for special penalties. An Indian convicted of drunkenness did not have the option that whites had of paying a fine in lieu of corporal punishment.[92] While Rhode Island authorized fines for Indians in such cases, judges still had discretion to order corporal punishments instead.[93] Indian servants who ran away faced stiffer penalties than those imposed on whites. New Plymouth punished white runaways at the discretion of the court, thus making allowance for mitigating circumstances. But Indians in such cases faced mandatory whippings.[94] Indian runaways in Connecticut might be sold into permanent slavery, while whites were subject only to limited extensions of service.[95]

Indians convicted of theft faced harsher penalties, particularly if unable to make restitution. Connecticut authorized the sale of Indian thieves into slavery outside the colony in order to repay what had been stolen.[96] Whites guilty of similar offenses could be bound only to temporary service until the theft had been repaid. In New Plymouth the courts had authority to turn Indians over to the injured party until quadruple restitution had been made.[97] If necessary, they might be sold into permanent slavery in order to make good the loss. In 1685 a New Plymouth Indian was sold into permanent bondage to raise the amount stolen.[98] Rhode Island enacted similarly harsh measures to ensure restitution. Indians guilty of theft might be enslaved for life, while whites unable to make restitution faced only temporary loss of freedom.[99]

The profound irony of Indian crime is that most of the crimes committed by Indians were crimes brought to New England by the settlers. Before settlement began, the tribes were internally more peaceful than most of European society. Violence among them generally took the form of intertribal wars rather than intratribal violence. Ties of kinship bound tribal members closely together, and fewer crimes were recognized by Indian custom than by European law. Before the settlers arrived, offenses involving sex, Sabbath-breaking, and other victimless crimes did not exist in New England. There was no drunkenness among Indians until alcohol arrived with the settlers. The most common offenses for which Indians were punished and stereotyped were products of English law and Puritan morality. They had less to do with Indian criminality than with the clash of alien cultures.[100]

The blacks of New England also faced racial prejudice, but the problem was less serious than the bias dividing whites and Indians. Both slaves and free blacks lived and worked among whites as part of colonial society.[101] While retaining much of their African heritage, some of which they passed along to whites, blacks adapted readily to European ways and customs.[102] They were not only more assimilable than Indians, but there were fewer of them to be assimilated. New England probably had fewer than one thousand blacks by the end of the seventeenth century, not enough to threaten the whites or cause racial anxiety.[103] While the law was not entirely color-blind, blacks faced much less discrimination than Indians. If free, they could own horses, carry firearms, purchase liquor, move from place to place, and enjoy other rights denied to Indians.[104]

Whether slave or free, New England blacks were tried in the same courts and under the same laws as white defendants.[105] This was not the case in the other English colonies of the seventeenth century. Separate courts and laws for blacks were the rule everywhere, not just in the South but in the Middle Colonies as well.[106] Nor were blacks treated more harshly than whites or singled out for special punishments. In a case of interracial fornication a Massachusetts court let the black male defendant off more lightly than his white female partner because the evidence showed that she had enticed him into the offense.[107] The courts seem to have meted out penalties impartially regardless of the race of the offender.[108] Not even the killing of a white by a black threw the justice system out of joint. If there were extenuating circumstances, the defendant would be punished not for murder but for some lesser offense not calling for the death penalty.[109] While it would be wrong to conclude that there was no bias, New England blacks faced less of it than blacks in other regions.[110]

Now against these witches the justices of the peace may not
always expect direct evidence, seeing all their works are of
darkness, and no witnesses present with
them to accuse them.—Michael Dalton (1618)

8 The Devil and the Law

The most widely feared and socially disruptive crime of all was witchcraft. Suspicions of witchcraft could turn neighbor against neighbor, sowing seeds of distrust that might last for generations. Nothing could be taken for granted when witchcraft was suspected, not even the bonds of friendship or the closest family relations. The malice of Satan was everywhere and anyone might succumb to his temptations. Once the forces of darkness gained a foothold, evil would spread like a plague and poison the wellsprings of spiritual life. Even skeptics of the supernatural recognized that witchcraft could tear a community apart. While scoffing at the notion that witches could cause real harm, Thomas Hobbes endorsed punishing them "for the false belief they have that they can do such mischief, joined with their purpose to do it if they can."[1] Even if they had no supernatural power, they were a malicious antisocial element.

Witchcraft was the sort of crime against which ordinary precautions were useless. Its practitioners attacked their victims with spells and magic, and the effects were often indistinguishable from natural phenomena. An accident or some unexpected misfortune might be just a matter of bad luck, but there was always the possibility that it might be caused by witchcraft. People of the seventeenth century assumed that everything had an explanation, and what could not be explained rationally was routinely attributed to the supernatural. An accident suffered after an argument or altercation might well have a sinister aspect. Nothing was too farfetched or implausible when witchcraft was suspected. Satan's power was a palpable force, as ubiquitous as sin, and something to be feared by every sensible person.

The belief in witchcraft was an assumption of the age, a corollary of the belief in God and a dualistic universe of matter and spirit. Isaac Newton and Francis Bacon took the existence of the supernatural for granted, and

131

Robert Boyle, the father of modern chemistry, thought it a good idea for miners to be on the lookout for demons when they tunneled beneath the surface of the earth. Theologians of every doctrinal stripe taught that Satan sought to capture the souls of men and establish dominion over the world. The witches were Satan's followers, his willing accomplices who in return for power and favors helped to prepare the way for the triumph of evil. Their mission was to cause harm and confusion, undermine faith in God, and win new recruits for the forces of darkness. Unless detected and rooted out, they would spread their moral rot until God's law was overthrown and the world finally belonged to the devil.[2]

The laws against witchcraft usually distinguished harmless folk practices from those involving the powers of darkness. Lawmakers generally adopted the distinction made by English law between so-called black magic, the satanic variety, and the "white magic" involved in fortune-telling, charms, and other harmless superstitions. New Plymouth made demonic contacts the crux of the crime by prohibiting "solemn compaction or conversing with the devil by way of witchcraft, conjuration, or the like."[3] Massachusetts and Connecticut passed similar laws making dealings with any "familiar spirit" punishable by death.[4] The New Haven and Rhode Island statutes prohibited witchcraft without focusing on demonic contacts.[5] Since Rhode Island had no witchcraft prosecutions, the omission did not matter. Nor did it matter in New Haven, where witchcraft indictments routinely alleged such contacts.

While the statutes made invoking the devil a capital offense, they were not clear about whether uninvited contacts were covered. Would a prosecution be justified if the devil just appeared and engaged a person in conversation? The answer probably depended upon whether an effort was made to break off the contact. Not to do so could be regarded as criminal complicity and sufficiently culpable to justify a prosecution. If future contacts were not discouraged, the likelihood of prosecution would be even greater. And accepting favors from the devil would almost certainly result in a conviction. Mary Johnson, a Connecticut servant, was convicted in part for supposedly accepting help from the devil with her household chores. Although he first appeared uninvited, her acceptance of favors made her legally guilty of witchcraft.[6]

What made witchcraft so different from other crimes was that the harm allegedly done by the witch was less important than the means employed to effect it. Most of the harm attributed to witches, if effected by other means, would have called for no more than fines or civil damages. The offenses alleged against witches included causing livestock to sicken, puddings to shrink, and beer to turn sour. One of the accusations against Margaret Jones, the first witch executed by Massachusetts, was that she had caused people to vomit. Causing someone to vomit was not itself a capital crime, but it became one if effected by witchcraft.[7] The form of the misconduct was not important except as proof that the accused was in league with Satan. The source of the mischief, not the mischief itself, called for the death penalty.

Because it was secret and difficult to prove, witchcraft could not be prosecuted like an ordinary offense. Suspicion alone could trigger legal proceedings, though much more was needed to get a conviction. Much of the evidence admissible at a witch trial would have been considered irrelevant in ordinary cases. Absence from the scene of the crime was no defense, for witches supposedly had the power to project their spectral presence across space while their physical bodies remained elsewhere. The suspect's character and even events that occurred many years in the past and not relating to the alleged offense counted as evidence. Still, witches could not be prosecuted for general wrongdoing but only for specific misdeeds against particular people. If no one complained about a specific act of witchcraft, no formal charges could be brought against the suspect.[8]

Guidelines for dealing with suspected witches were spelled out in Michael Dalton's legal handbook *The Country Justice.* Dalton stressed the importance of body searches for evidence of demonic contacts. The devil supposedly assigned familiar spirits to assist witches in the practice of witchcraft, and the familiars sucked blood from the witch through secret teats.[9] Blood was believed to be the carrier of the human spirit through which Satan gradually consumed the souls of his followers.[10] A witch's body might also carry "devil's marks" put there by Satan for purposes of identification. So a body search would be the first thing ordered at the preliminary hearing.[11] Male suspects were examined by committees of men, and females by committees of women. The findings would then be filed with the court in the form of a deposition that would be used as evidence if the case came to trial.[12]

Body searches were unreliable for obvious reasons. Even fairly expert examiners had difficulty distinguishing suspicious-looking growths from warts, lesions, and other physical abnormalities. They might disagree among themselves, or a second search might produce completely different findings. The first examination of Margaret Jones revealed "an apparent teat in her secret parts as fresh as if it had been newly sucked." But a second search showed that the supposed teat had withered while another had grown on the other side.[13] The discovery of suspicious growths was not proof of witchcraft, but it was evidence to be considered with other evidence if the case came to trial. On the other hand, the failure of a body search to turn up anything would probably bring a dismissal if the other evidence was weak.[14]

Connecticut had an official checklist for screening suspects. The first thing considered was the suspect's reputation and standing in the community. It was assumed that a witch's total depravity could not be concealed completely but would reveal itself at some point in ordinary social relations. Whether the suspect had recently quarreled with the supposed victim was also considered important. A quarrel followed by a sudden unexplained injury created a presumption that witchcraft was involved. Whether a relative or close friend of the accused had ever been convicted of witchcraft also counted. The checklist noted that witchcraft "may be learned and conveyed from man to man and oft it falleth out that a witch dying leaveth some of the aforesaid heirs of her witchcraft."[15] The possibility of guilt by association probably made it difficult for the suspect to organize an effective defense. Witnesses would likely hesitate to testify for the accused for fear of being tarred with the same brush.

Evidence could be obtained by confronting the suspect with the supposed victims of witchcraft. The accused might be required to touch them, and the results would be carefully noted. These confrontations could be very damaging to the suspect regardless of what happened. If the victim's condition improved, it might be assumed that the spell causing the affliction had returned to the witch. If things got worse, the suspect would almost certainly be blamed. The confrontation between Margaret Jones and her accusers counted heavily against her. Winthrop noted that "Many persons (men, women, and children) whom she stroked or touched . . . were taken with deafness or vomiting or other violent pains or sickness."[16] The same sort of evidence nearly sent Elizabeth Morse to the Massachusetts gallows. Witnesses reported that she "stroked Goodwife Ordway's child over the head when it was sick, and the child died." Even if the child had recovered, she still might have been suspected.[17] The best that a suspect could hope for was no reaction at all from the victim.

Suspects detained in jail were watched closely for anything that might incriminate them. The notorious English witch-hunter Matthew Hopkins recommended close watching, and the recommendation was followed in Massachusetts. It was not used, as Hopkins had used it, to extort confessions from suspects by forced sleeplessness, but only to keep track of their behavior.[18] The General Court ordered the jailers to keep a strict watch over Margaret Jones every night of her detention.[19] What they observed was startling, to say the least. According to Winthrop's account,

> There was seen in her arms, she sitting on the floor, and her clothes pulled up, etc., a little child which ran from her into another room, and the officer following it, it was vanished. The child was seen in two other places, to which she had relation; and one maid that saw it, fell sick upon it.[20]

The report by itself would have been enough to send her to the gallows.

But what are we to make of the report? Did the watchers lie or suffer a shared hallucination? The child they allegedly saw was apparently a familiar sucking the teat Jones reportedly had "in her secret parts." This would explain why her clothes were pulled up when they were first observed together. What the watchers really saw, if they saw anything, was probably influenced by what they had been told to look for and therefore expected to see. Observations made by candlelight in a shadowy jail would hardly be reliable even if unbiased minds were brought to the task. Possibly they saw nothing and fabricated everything to speed the suspected witch to the gallows. But whatever they saw or fabricated, no one questioned the credibility of their report. It only confirmed what people already believed about the behavior of witches.

Not everything was grist for the mills at a witchcraft trial. Evidence based on the so-called water test was rejected by the courts as superstitious and unreliable. Popular belief held that witches would float because their dealings with the devil made them too light to sink. It was also believed that water, supposedly a pure element, would reject anyone corrupted by the practice of witchcraft. Although inadmissible as evidence, the water test had strong support among ordinary people as a means of discovering witches. In 1663 two suspected witches were seized by their Connecticut neighbors, bound hand and foot, and thrown into the water. The mob's suspicions were confirmed when both floated to the surface, though the results had no standing as evidence. But the suspects, as soon as they were dry, lost no time leaving the colony rather than await legal developments or the possible return of the mob.[21]

The courts also rejected the popular belief that witches could not weep or recite the Lord's Prayer correctly. The folklore of witchcraft held that witches became so used to saying the prayer backward in their spells and incantations that they could not get it right if put to the test. Their inability to weep was attributed to the hardness of heart that resulted from dealings with Satan.[22] But such tests had no standing as evidence. They resembled too closely the old medieval method of trial by ordeal to be reliable.

While crying had no standing as evidence, defendants who did cry at their trials seem to have fared better than those who reacted with rage and indignation. Margaret Jones displayed such anger and belligerence, at times railing against the judges and jurors trying her, that she probably hurt her own case.[23] On the other hand, Elizabeth Morse may have saved herself by shedding copious tears throughout her trial. The judges were so impressed by her humble, tearful defense that they reprieved and finally released her despite a jury verdict of guilty.[24]

What made a witch trial so different from other criminal trials was the admissibility of spectral evidence. This came in the form of testimony that the defendant had appeared in spirit form to the witness in the course of practicing witchcraft. Witches were believed to have the power to project their spirit across space in order to harass victims while their physical body remained somewhere else. They were also thought to be able to assume various shapes and forms, animal usually, in harassing their victims. The main problem with spectral evidence was that there was no way to determine whether the apparition described by the witness was that of the real witch. It was always possible that the witch might assume the form of an innocent person in order to avoid detection and cause confusion. Accepting spectral evidence at face value meant trusting in the honesty of witches.[25] That was considered so imprudent prior to the Salem trials that the courts generally required corroborating evidence for a conviction. Cases based on spectral evidence alone almost invariably resulted in dismissals or acquittals.[26]

Every effort was made to get confessions from suspected witches. Although physical force was not employed, at least not before the Salem trials, the psychological pressure on the suspect to confess must have been tremendous. Friends and relatives would be brought in to urge complete candor, and the ministers would counsel the suspect that to die unrepentant meant eternal damnation. This may have been sufficient to convince mentally unstable suspects that they were actually guilty.[27] Some of the witchcraft confessions were obvious products of deranged imaginations. Mary Johnson, a confessed Connecticut witch, claimed that the devil had assisted her with household chores in return for sexual favors. Rebecca Greensmith, another Connecticut witch, confessed that the devil first appeared to her in the form of a fawn and "had frequently carnal knowledge of her." She also claimed that she had once attended a conclave of witches at which one of the witches arrived late "flying amongst them in the shape of a crow."[28] Whatever we may think of such claims today, they confirmed what the seventeenth century took for granted about the nature and power of witches.

Suspected witches at least had the benefit of all the legal safeguards available to ordinary defendants. There would first be a preliminary hearing to determine whether the evidence justified further proceedings. If there was sufficient evidence, the case would be referred to the trial court for grand jury action. An indictment would then be drafted listing the specific charges against the accused. If indicted, the accused could be convicted only of things specified in the indictment. In 1665 a jury verdict against Elizabeth Seager was overturned by the Connecticut Court of Assistants on the ground that it went beyond what was charged in the grand jury indictment.[29] Except in New Haven, where all cases were tried without juries, witchcraft defendants had the right to a jury trial. As far as trial safeguards were concerned, there was nothing to distinguish witch trials from other criminal proceedings.

The fact that witchcraft called for the death penalty brought into play the two-witness rule requiring eyewitness testimony (see chapter 2). There can be no doubt that the rule kept down the conviction rate and saved lives. It almost certainly saved Mary Webster from the Massachusetts gallows in 1683. Her neighbors strongly suspected her of witchcraft, and a body search turned up what appeared to be witch marks. But the case against her was still only circumstantial, and without witnesses to specific acts of witchcraft, she had to be acquitted.[30]

While it raised the level of proof needed for a conviction, the two-witness rule did not protect witchcraft defendants to the same extent that it protected ordinary defendants. In ordinary cases, the witnesses had to testify about the same incident and thus corroborate one another. But because witchcraft was a continuing crime and not limited to any particular act, Massachusetts allowed the witnesses to testify about different acts of witchcraft observed separately. One witness could testify about one thing and another about something else, and their combined testimony satisfied the requirements of the rule. Whether this actually met the test became an issue at the trial of Elizabeth Morse, and the Assistants Court ruled that it did.[31] But in Connecticut, at least after 1669, the witnesses had to testify about the same incidents.[32] However, this seems to have made little difference in the outcome of the trials. The conviction rate in Connecticut was about the same as in Massachusetts (see Appendix D).

The two-witness rule was further weakened by the sort of evidence admissible against the defendant. In 1651 Hugh Parsons was convicted in Massachusetts on testimony that would be laughed out of court today. One witness testified that Parsons had stared at a pudding and that it later mysteriously shrank; a second testified that after quarreling with him she had suddenly been afflicted with sharp pains; and a third claimed that after a quarrel with Parsons, an "evil thing" in the shape of a dog appeared and menaced her child.[33] All their testimony amounted at best to bits and pieces of circumstantial evidence. But it nevertheless satisfied the two-witness rule and helped convict Parsons of witchcraft. If a key witness had not recanted, he probably would have gone to the gallows. Nathaniel Greensmith, husband of the confessed witch Rebecca Greensmith, went to the gallows on testimony just as implausible. One witness testified that he had seen the defendant in the woods with "two creatures like dogs" (presumably familiars), and another testified that he had seen him lift a log so heavy that "two men such as he could not have done it" (evidence of supernatural powers). Their combined testimony satisfied the two-witness rule and convinced the jury of Greensmith's guilt.[34]

Even the rule against double jeopardy was bent in witchcraft cases. Since every supposed incident of witchcraft counted as a separate offense, there could be no final and complete exoneration of the defendant. An acquittal did not necessarily end the affair. Several Massachusetts suspects were prosecuted more than once on essentially the same charges. Eunice Cole was haled into court on witchcraft charges in 1656, again in 1673, and a third time in 1681.[35] She was never convicted, but any of the proceedings might have brought her to the gallows. John Godfrey was another perennial defendant. His acquittal in 1659 did not prevent a second prosecution several years later on almost identical charges. Some new evidence was offered, but the second trial was basically a rehash of the first. Even his second acquittal was only grudging, the jury noting that he appeared "suspiciously guilty of witchcraft."[36] Susanna Martin, another Massachusetts suspect, was not so lucky. Witchcraft charges dismissed in 1669 were revived a generation later and sent her to the gallows.[37]

One reason procedural safeguards were relaxed in witchcraft cases was because it would have been almost impossible to obtain convictions under the ordinary rules. Even with the rules relaxed, the difficulty of proving a case resulted in a high acquittal rate (see Appendix D). Because of this, backup charges for lesser offenses were sometimes filed to ensure that the suspect did not get off completely. In 1655 Nicholas Bailey and his wife had to defend themselves not only against witchcraft charges, but against several minor and essentially frivolous charges as well. The upshot was that while there was not enough evidence to convict them of witchcraft, the court convicted Mrs. Bailey of "impudent and notorious lying, endeavoring to make discord among neighbors, and filthy and unclean speeches." These offenses standing alone would have been punished with no more than an admonition or fine. But because the defendants were also suspected of witchcraft, the court sentenced them both to leave town.[38] Backup charges of adultery were filed in Connecticut when Elizabeth Seager was charged with witchcraft in 1663. The witchcraft charges could not be proved, but she was convicted of adultery, which was also a capital crime.[39] Seager escaped execution, however, because Connecticut never enforced its adultery law to the hilt, not even against suspected witches. Seager was back in court two years later on new witchcraft charges.

Defendants acquitted of witchcraft sometimes incurred backhanded penalties in the form of court costs and witness fees. Such penalties were usually imposed when the evidence seemed plausible enough but still not legally sufficient for a conviction. John Godfrey had to pay all his Massachusetts trial costs plus the fees of the witnesses who appeared against him.[40] Caleb Powell was another Massachusetts defendant who had to pay court costs despite his acquittal.[41] The amounts assessed seem to have varied according to how strongly the defendant was suspected. Elizabeth Garlick had to pay only the cost of her transportation to Hartford for trial. The case against her was so weak that the town of Easthampton, which had brought the charges, had to pay for the trial.[42] The tables might be turned completely if the charges proved to be utterly false. In 1673 the Massachusetts Assistants Court assessed full costs against the accusers of Anna Edmunds for falsely accusing her.[43]

The courts had authority to impose such backhanded penalties under laws penalizing defendants adjudged delinquent despite their acquittal on the specific charges brought against them. Delinquency in a witchcraft case meant being strongly suspected regardless of the outcome of the trial.[44] John Godfrey, for example, had a long record of antisocial conduct, so the court reasoned that he should pay for the cost of the trial that he had helped bring upon himself. The same reasoning also applied to Caleb Powell, whose attempts to impress his superstitious neighbors led directly to the charges against him. The court found his behavior so suspicious that he deserved "to bear his own shame and the costs of prosecution."[45]

Court costs were not the only penalties imposed on acquitted defendants. While setting aside a jury verdict against Katherine Harrison in 1669 as legally insufficient, the Connecticut Assistants Court ordered her to leave her hometown of Wethersfield "for her own safety and the contentment of the people who are her neighbors."[46] In acquitting Elizabeth Godman of witchcraft in 1655, a New Haven court ordered her to "forbear going from house to house and carry it orderly in the family where she is."[47] Although acquitted, she lost her personal freedom, though probably in part for her own protection. There was always the chance that fearful people might take things into their own hands and inflict mob justice on the suspected witch.

The disabilities and restrictions imposed on acquitted suspects had precedents in the early common law. The Assize of Northampton promulgated by Henry II in 1176 ordered banishment for persons acquitted of infamous crimes. Trial was then by ordeal, and those cleared by ordeal of "murder, treason, arson, or other disgraceful felony" were nevertheless required to leave England if "of very bad reputation, being publicly and shamefully denounced by the testimony of many lawful men." The "disgraceful" felonies for which acquitted defendants were exiled included all offenses except minor thefts and robberies.[48] The order probably reflected doubts about the reliability of some acquittals, or perhaps assumed that disreputable persons should be removed for the good of the community. This certainly would apply to suspected witches, whose continued presence could keep a community in turmoil.

Some witchcraft suspects owed their lives to judges who overturned guilty verdicts based on weak and unconvincing evidence. The Massachusetts Assistants Court reprieved and later released Elizabeth Morse, despite public clamor for her execution.[49] The Assistants also set aside the conviction of Hugh Parsons and then ordered his release after an inconclusive second trial.[50] The Connecticut Assistants Court saved Elizabeth Seager, a perennial suspect, on the ground that the jury verdict against her went beyond the grand jury indictment.[51] The Assistants also set aside the conviction of Katherine Harrison, although public opinion considered her guilty.[52] These reversals were unpopular and required courage on the part of the judges. The Massachusetts Assistants had to weather a storm of criticism for their handling of the Morse case. The deputies in the General Court charged them with high-handedness for setting aside the jury's verdict.[53] If it had been left to the people or their representatives, these defendants would have gone to the gallows. The refusal of the courts to be swayed by public opinion helped to keep the death toll down. There were fewer witchcraft executions during the first half-century than during the Salem panic of 1692–1693 (see Appendix D).

The judges handled witchcraft accusations routinely, just as they handled ordinary criminal complaints. Nothing was done that might alarm the public or create the impression that things were out of control. However sensational the charges, the proceedings themselves were tedious and dull. Suspects were even released on bail, though there was no right to bail in capital cases.[54] The courts took charge in a way likely to allay public fears and prevent panic, just the reverse of what was later done in the Salem trials. Panic could always erupt when witchcraft was suspected, and the danger of vigilantism could not be ignored. In 1683 a Massachusetts mob dragged Mary Webster from her home and severely beat her for some supposed acts of witchcraft. The water test inflicted by the Connecticut mob on two suspects could easily have turned into a lynching.[55] Such incidents probably would have been more common if the courts had been less responsible in dealing with the problem.

Some accused witches apparently went out of their way to make people suspect them. Why they behaved as they did can only be conjectured, but perhaps it was to play on the fears of their neighbors for personal advantage. An otherwise unimportant person who appeared to have occult powers could easily impress superstitious people. No one wanted to make an enemy of someone possibly in league with the devil.[56] Provoking a witch could bring such terrible reprisals that being suspected of witchcraft could be useful in many situations. It might earn for the suspect a grudging respect and deference. But the deception could turn fatal if things got out of hand. A too-convincing performance could land the bogus witch on the gallows.

Caleb Powell seems to have been a suspect who played this risky game. His claims to knowledge of the occult led William Morse, a superstitious neighbor, to accuse him of witchcraft. Morse's household had been plagued by mysterious happenings: pots rattling on the hearth, brickbats dropping down the chimney, and dishes flying about the house. Powell offered his assistance, advising Morse that the source of the trouble was Morse's young grandson, who lived with his grandparents. He assured Morse that the disturbances would cease if the boy left the house. When the boy moved in with Powell, everything returned to normal just as Powell had predicted.[57] But the respite proved brief. The disturbances began again, even worse than before, when the boy returned to his grandparents. Morse blamed Powell, accusing him of bewitching the house through the medium of the boy. While there was not enough evidence to convict him, Powell was assessed court costs for bringing suspicion upon himself.[58]

John Godfrey was another suspect who apparently played on the fears of his neighbors. He once told some fellow workers that he had made a covenant to serve a mysterious master, and he described the arrangement in terms that made it appear to be a pact with Satan.[59] On another occasion, when refused a job tending oxen, he angrily predicted that one of the animals would be lost and never recovered. When the prediction turned out to be correct, people suspected that the supernatural might be involved. Godfrey seemed determined to create the impression that he was no ordinary person. On observing some sick cattle rumored to be under a spell, he boasted that he would be able to "unwitch" them.[60] The subsequent recovery of the animals had a frightening aspect. If Godfrey could remove spells, he could probably cast them, and perhaps on people as well as animals. Whatever his motives, Godfrey certainly gave people cause to suspect him.[61]

Both Godfrey and Powell must have known that they were playing with fire. Even talking loosely about the occult could have serious consequences. Some foolish remarks about seeing a book of magic and hearing mysterious voices landed John Bradstreet before a Massachusetts court in 1652 on charges of "familiarity with the devil." Although the charges were finally dismissed, Bradstreet was fined for lying and alarming the public.[62] In 1665 John Browne was haled before a New Haven court for allegedly trying to summon the devil. The court accepted his explanation that it had been a prank, but warned him not to repeat such "folly and madness" in the future.[63] The devil, after all, might take the summons seriously.

Most witchcraft suspects tended to have aggressive, belligerent personalities. This alone might have been enough to target them for suspicion, because combativeness was thought to reflect inner malice, an assumed characteristic of witches. The Reverend John Davenport once warned his New Haven congregation that a belligerent, discontented mind was "a fit subject for the devil to work upon."[64] John Godfrey owed his bad reputation in part to an antagonistic personality that made people dislike and fear him.[65] His quarrels and altercations over the years involved him in over one hundred lawsuits.[66] He seems to have gone out of his way to make enemies, which could be dangerous in a society on the lookout for witches.

Hugh Parsons, another perennial suspect, was almost as abrasive as Godfrey. A sawyer and brickmaker by trade, he had a reputation for overcharging his customers.[67] Parsons also had a quick temper and often threatened people who crossed him. These threats finally backfired when misfortune befell his antagonists.[68] His accusers had all been threatened at one time or another, and they attributed their misfortunes to witchcraft. Parsons probably would have gone to the gallows if a key witness, his wife, had not retracted her testimony against him.[69] The unfortunate woman was apparently deranged, and she later went to the gallows herself for killing their child (see chapter 6).

Anne Hibbens had a reputation for combativeness that finally proved fatal. As the widow of a prominent Boston merchant and magistrate, her social position alone should have shielded her from suspicion. But her truculence turned everyone against her. She was censured for causing antagonism among church members and finally expelled from church membership.[70] Her extreme belligerence led directly to the witchcraft charges against her. Observing two of her neighbors talking, she correctly guessed that they were talking about her. When she confronted them with an accurate account of what had been said, the astonished women denounced her to the authorities as a witch. Their testimony provided the key evidence that sent her to the gallows.[71]

Their bizarre behavior suggests that some suspects may have suffered from mental disorders. Professor John P. Demos makes a convincing case that John Godfrey's extreme belligerence was a form of neurotic compensation for acute psychic distress.[72] Everything about him suggests that he was a highly unstable person. The same furies seem to have afflicted Hugh Parsons and Anne Hibbens, both of whom apparently suffered from a compulsion to make enemies. Hibbens managed to make herself so unpopular that in the end it literally killed her. The Assistants in the General Court considered the case against her weak and wanted to set aside the jury verdict. But they were prevented from doing so by the deputies who voted to uphold her conviction.[73] If public opinion had not run so strongly against her, she would not have gone to the gallows.

Evidence of insanity appears unmistakably in some of the witchcraft confessions. Mary Johnson and Rebecca Greensmith made admissions that today would land both of them in psychiatric wards. But the seventeenth century regarded stories of sexual relations with devils as plausible. The belief that the devil had sexual relations with witches was part of the folklore of witchcraft. Satan's lust partly explained his preference for female followers and why most witchcraft defendants were women. Given these assumptions, there was no reason not to believe the stories told by Greensmith and Johnson.

Some of the supposed victims of witchcraft appear to have been as unbalanced as the supposed witches. Rebecca Greensmith was accused by

Ann Cole, a young woman who apparently suffered from convulsive hysteria. During her seizures and hallucinations she spoke in strange voices believed to be the voices of demons who possessed her. She named Greensmith during one of these seizures as the person responsible for her afflictions. When questioned, Greensmith at first denied the charge; but she changed her story and confessed when Cole's statement was read to her. One possible explanation for her reversal is mental derangement. Greensmith seems to have been more than slightly unbalanced herself, and she may have become locked with Cole in mutually complementing delusions. One believed herself bewitched, and the other found psychic relief in assuming the role of the witch.[74] That Cole's symptoms vanished when her supposed tormentor was executed tends to support the hypothesis.[75] The hysteria that may have been brought on by fear of witches ended with the death of the supposed witch.

A similar case in Massachusetts fortunately did not end on the gallows. The supposed victim was Elizabeth Knapp, a sixteen-year-old servant who suffered from seizures and hallucinated about being tormented by witches. She lived in the household of Samuel Willard, the Groton minister, who took a close interest in the case. Her symptoms were serious and alarming. During the seizures Elizabeth's tongue would curve back in her mouth and become rigid, while her body thrashed about so violently that several strong men were needed to restrain her. She ranted about witches and devils, screaming on one occasion that she was being strangled by a witch with the head of a woman and the body of a dog. Demons apparently possessed her, causing her to speak in strange voices and shout blasphemies against God. She also made animal noises, barking like a dog and bleating like a calf. The seizures were so realistic that everyone assumed that she was in the grip of demonic forces.[76]

Elizabeth made her first accusations about a month after the seizures began. She first accused a neighbor, a woman highly regarded for her piety, of bewitching her.[77] The charge was met with disbelief, partly because of the woman's reputation, but also because the demons thought to possess Elizabeth might have deceived her into accusing an innocent person. The accused woman went to the Willard household to confront Elizabeth directly. She arrived in the middle of a seizure, and although Elizabeth's eyes seemed to be closed, the girl had no difficulty recognizing her visitor by touch. The accused woman requested permission to pray, and her piety and obvious concern for the girl impressed everyone. Perhaps taking her cue from the general mood, Elizabeth retracted the accusation, explaining that the devil had tricked her into making the charge.[78] This undermined her general credibility, because if the devil could deceive her once, why not a second time? She accused a second woman about a month later, but enough discrepancies were spotted in her story to clear the woman. Although her seizures continued, Elizabeth made no further accusations.[79]

Most of the credit for preventing the affair from claiming lives belongs to Willard. He took charge at the outset, kept an open mind, and spotted the discrepancies that cleared the second woman. If the Cole case had been handled with the same good sense, Rebecca Greensmith might not have gone to the gallows. There were differences, of course, the principal one being that Greensmith was the sort of person likely to be suspected of witchcraft. The records describe her as a "lewd and ignorant woman," just the sort likely to be involved in witchcraft.[80] So no one was particularly surprised when Cole accused her, and her confession left no doubt about her guilt. If the women accused by Elizabeth Knapp had also confessed, the outcome probably would have been the same.

The problem was that mental pathology of this sort went largely unrecognized by medical science in the seventeenth century. All mental disorders were viewed as intellectual impairments involving a breakdown of the rational and cognitive processes. If the ability to reason remained intact, a person's mental competency went unquestioned.[81] Ann Cole and Elizabeth Knapp gave rational accounts of their experiences and showed no signs of intellectual impairment. Nor was there reason to doubt the sanity of Mary Johnson or Rebecca Greensmith. Neither showed signs of intellectual dysfunction. Although their confessions appear incredible today, they were credible by the standards of the seventeenth century. The things they confessed were thought possible, so there was no reason to question their sanity.[82]

The witch trials conducted in the pre-Salem period were essentially fair and safeguarded the rights of the defendants. No rights were denied simply because the charges involved witchcraft. Indeed, given the probative standards then in force, many of the guilty verdicts were justified by the evidence. That much of the evidence would be laughed out of court today has no bearing on its standing three centuries ago. It was credible and legally sufficient in the seventeenth century, the only fair standard for judging what happened. The guilt of Nathaniel Greensmith, for example, must have seemed obvious to the court that convicted him. His own wife accused him, and two eyewitnesses provided corroboration to satisfy the requirements of the two-witness rule.[83] Even the conviction of Anne Hibbens met every legal requirement.[84] The fact that such defendants could not be convicted today does not mean that modern standards are higher, but only that we no longer believe in witches.

Persons targeted for suspicion sometimes nipped dangerous rumors in the bud by bringing civil suits for slander. When Thomas Mulliner of New Haven accused William Meaker of bewitching his hogs, Meaker sued and recovered damages. The court ordered Mulliner not to repeat the charges and to make public acknowledgment that the accusation was false.[85] Since loose talk about witchcraft could destroy lives as well as reputations, persons who spread such rumors were held strictly accountable. In 1661 a New Plymouth court convicted Dinah Silvester of defamation and ordered her to make a public apology for falsely accusing Goodwife Holmes. Roger Ludlow, a leading Connecticut magistrate, had to pay damages for repeating in private conversation some unproved charges against Mary Staples.[86] Ludlow merely repeated the charges without endorsing them, but even this was slander if the charges could not be proved.

One of the unanswerable questions about witchcraft is whether it was actually practiced in New England. There is really no safe answer one way or the other, but the best guess would probably be a qualified yes. For one thing, New Englanders of every class and background took its practice for granted. For another, the superstition had an inner logic that likely translated into social reality. If God communicated with people through miracles and revelations, why should the devil not do the same? Both were involved in the affairs of mankind, and belief in one went hand in hand with belief in the other. God and Satan had made the earth a battleground in the eternal conflict between good and evil, and mankind had to choose sides. These were not just the beliefs of the ignorant and superstitious, but of sensible and educated people as well. To have doubted them would have called into question the most fundamental assumptions of the age.[87]

What made witchcraft such a formidable superstition was that it had answers for every logical contradiction. The contradictions were as apparent three centuries ago as they are today. Why, for example, did the devil allow witches to be caught, and how, given their supposed powers, could they be jailed and punished like common criminals? Why would a familiar appear in the presence of witnesses, as seemed to happen in the Jones case, and thus provide evidence that might send the witch to the gallows? The answer to all such questions was the justice of God and the malice of Satan. God would not permanently permit evil to go unpunished, and the devil so hated the human race that he sometimes betrayed his own followers.

Satan's promises were not likely to be kept, and he might even help in the discovery of witches in order to get their souls more quickly.[88]

All speculation on whether witchcraft was actually practiced ultimately turns on how the question is framed. If it is a question of whether women actually fornicated with Satan for favors and power, the answer is obviously no. But if it is a question of whether people attempted to invoke the powers of darkness for their own advantage or to pay off grudges, the answer is probably yes. The witchcraft superstition was so deeply rooted in the consciousness of the age that it must have had practitioners. Spells and magic would have had a powerful appeal to persons seeking shortcuts in life. What they could not accomplish by ordinary means might be achieved preternaturally through the power of Satan. Witchcraft turned conventional religion upside down without being essentially different. It had obvious appeal to powerless people overwhelmed and defeated by life.

The belief in predestination probably made witchcraft appealing to New Englanders who despaired of salvation. Persons already damned had nothing to lose in giving their allegiance to Satan. They could have had little regard for the God who had condemned them and no qualms about serving the devil instead. There was little that most people could expect from a God concerned only with the welfare of His elect. That most witches came from the lower ranks of society is no coincidence. The Puritans regarded material success as a sign of salvation, so there was nothing the downtrodden could hope for in this world or the next. One of the paradoxes of Puritanism was that it unintentionally made the devil a source of hope for people who could look to God for nothing.

Anyone contemplating the risks of dealing with Satan could take heart from the low conviction rate (see Appendix D). More witches were executed in a single county in England over a two-year period than in all of New England in the seventeenth century.[89] Credit for keeping the death toll down belongs primarily to a justice system that safeguarded the rights of the accused. But the judges who made the system work also deserve a measure of personal credit. While they believed in the power of witches, they trusted in the processes of law to deal with the threat. Superstition might cloud their judgment in particular cases, but they never abandoned their commitment to the evenhanded administration of justice. A world without justice was more to be feared than all the power of Satan.

While beyond the purview of this study, the Salem trials require at least passing mention. The causes of the tragedy have been debated now for three centuries, with no conclusive results. Cotton Mather thought that the accused were guilty, while his antagonist Robert Calef thought that the charges were humbug. Nor can modern commentators agree on what happened. Paul Boyer and Stephen Nissenbaum attribute the tragedy to social strains in the life of the community, while Marion L. Starkey offers a psychoanalytic explanation. Linnda R. Caporael thinks that a parasitic fungus may have triggered an outbreak of convulsive ergotism causing hallucinations, while Chadwick Hansen brings the debate full circle by concluding that Mather was probably right about some of the accused.[90] There are almost as many explanations of what happened as there were victims of the tragedy.

A striking paradox of the Salem trials is that those who confessed and admitted everything were spared the gallows. This was unheard of in the pre-Salem period when a confession meant almost certain execution. One explanation is that the confessions and repentance of the Salem defendants were thought sufficient to justify leniency. Their submission confounded the devil and made society secure enough to forego the death penalty.[91] The only thing wrong with this reasoning is that it does not square with the usual treatment of confessed witches. Some of the pre-Salem defendants also confessed, but their confessions did not save them from the gallows. The Salem defendants were likely spared not out of leniency but because their confessions were needed to validate the questionable proceedings and to incriminate others. The evidence was so flimsy that cooperative witnesses were needed to get convictions. When it became obvious that confession would bring clemency, the temptation to confess became irresistible. One of the most deplorable aspects of the affair is that those who confessed and falsely accused others were spared, while those who asserted their innocence to the end and falsely accused no one went to the gallows.

Equally deplorable was the almost total breakdown of due process at Salem. The judges who presided at the trials bear most of the blame for what happened. They failed miserably in their responsibilities and ended up presiding over judicial murders. If they had acted with the same good sense and courage as the judges who saved Elizabeth Morse, Hugh Parsons, and Katherine Harrison in the pre-Salem period, the tragedy might have been averted. Samuel Sewall later admitted as much in a public apology for his role in the trials.[92] The pre-Salem judges owed no apologies to their contemporaries or to posterity. Their steadfastness under pressure prevented numerous accusations and rumors of witchcraft from precipitating public panics. If Sewall and the other Salem judges had looked to their example, there would have been no need to apologize for so many needless deaths.

Marvelous it may be to see and consider how some kind of
wickedness did grow and break forth here in a land where
the same was so much witnessed against and
so narrowly looked into and severely punished.
—William Bradford (1642)

9   Patterns of Criminality

The first settlements were tight social networks that discouraged crime and most forms of deviant behavior. The hardships and perils of everyday life made people interdependent, and the limited scale of society made it difficult to deviate from group norms without attracting attention. Good citizenship meant social conformity, signaling that the individual could be trusted as a friend and neighbor. Deviance from the moral consensus was perceived as a form of disloyalty to other members of the group. This closeness of society made it possible to regulate whole areas of private behavior with only a minimum of state coercion.[1] Since group support was so essential for the survival of the individual, most people willingly closed ranks as a matter of self-interest.[2]

Crimes were few in the early settlements, and those that did occur seldom posed a threat to public safety. About 20 percent of the cases tried by the Massachusetts Assistants Court during the first fifteen years involved drinking abuses and illicit sex. The offenses committed ranged from cursing and swearing to rape and murder, but the latter were so infrequent that statistically they appear as aberrations. Thefts were fairly common, but not on a scale serious enough to cause economic problems. Stealing was usually confined to petty pilferage or the misappropriation of livestock, probably because during the early years there was not much to steal. Moreover, thefts almost never involved physical violence. When violence occurred at all, it usually resulted from personal disputes. Not a single burglary or robbery was reported during the entire period.[3] They may have occurred and simply not been recorded, but this seems unlikely in view of the attention given to minor offenses. (See Appendix C.)

The crime records available for the rest of New England generally fit the Massachusetts pattern. Sex and alcohol were the major problems, while property crimes were limited to minor thefts and petty pilferage. The case counts show almost no violence of a criminal nature.[4] A few fights and brawls were recorded, but these almost never resulted in serious injuries. The tight social network prevented most disputes from getting seriously out of hand. Homicides were too few to have any statistical significance. The early settlers lived hard lives in a hostile environment, but they had little reason to fear one another. (See Appendix C.)

By the 1660s the enforcement of social mores increasingly required the coercive intervention of the state. People not only became less responsive to neighborly admonitions, but neighbors became more reluctant to meddle in one another's affairs. In a study of Essex County, Massachusetts, David T. Konig finds a growing indifference over the years to most forms of sexual misconduct. Only 2 of the 534 prosecutions recorded for sexual misconduct resulted from private spying. The bulk of the offenses came to light when women complained of sexual harassment or when an illegitimate birth made the offense impossible to ignore.[5] Some offenses reached the courts in Middlesex County through civil actions brought by the father of the female partner. In 1665 Sergeant Parmenter of Sudbury sued Christopher Bannister of Marlborough for trespass "for defiling his daughter and getting her with child." Robert Proctor, another outraged father, brought suit against Thomas Marrable in 1680 "for defiling his daughter Elizabeth . . . she having by him a bastard child."[6]

Signs of decline in standards of honesty and moral responsibility appear after 1660. Fewer people admitted their sexual offenses, and some fled to escape punishment. Young people also became more difficult to control as family discipline slackened. Fornication and bastardy increased, and by the 1680s marital infidelity reached higher levels than those of the previous generation.[7] The social dynamics behind the case counts are not difficult to understand. The population became more dispersed over the years, and dispersion weakened social controls. There was also a surplus of males in the population and therefore intense competition for sexual partners, marital and otherwise. Between 1671 and 1674, fornication cases were the most numerous category of offenses reported in Essex and Suffolk counties in Massachusetts.[8] The case counts, of course, do not automatically equate with an increase in promiscuity. Many of those prosecuted for sexual immorality showed signs of genuine affection for one another.[9] The circumstances that put their relationship outside the law must have left some to conclude that their conduct was not really immoral.

The weakening of social controls coincided with the Quaker challenge to

Table 1

Witchcraft Cases, Massachusetts and Connecticut, 1650–1679

Years	Massachusetts	Connecticut
1650–59	27	7
1660–69	13	24
1670–79	9	2

the moral consensus. To what extent Quakers contributed to the process cannot be quantified, but they were clearly a force for social destabilization. While their doctrines did not take root, their bold challenge to the status quo helped to undermine group cohesion. Signs of social disorganization appear in the numbers of people who absented themselves from church services, sometimes in such numbers that whole groups were tried and sentenced together.[10] Respect for civil authority also declined, and fights and brawls became more common.[11] People began to shirk their civic obligations, and there was growing reluctance to accept public office. More and more persons turned up in court for infractions of regulatory laws that had previously commanded almost automatic compliance.[12] These trends hardly amounted to a crime wave, but they do indicate that by mid-century the ratio of sinners to saints in the population was clearly on the rise. (See Appendix C.)

Witchcraft reports also became more common, a sure sign of growing distrust and weakening of group cohesion. The first recorded conviction occurred in 1647, and rumors and accusations thereafter became a regular feature of life. (See Appendix D.) Unlike the trend in secular offenses, witchcraft incidents did not increase in neat incremental progressions. Reports show wide swings over the years from place to place. As Table 1 shows, witchcraft cases in Massachusetts during the 1650s outnumbered those in Connecticut. But a sharp reversal occurred during the following decade when incidents declined in Massachusetts and increased in Connecticut. This was followed by another reversal in the 1670s, when witchcraft reports in Massachusetts exceeded those in Connecticut, where incidents almost ceased.[13] These fluctuations are not surprising, for witchcraft was no ordinary crime and therefore not likely to follow ordinary patterns.

Curiously, witchcraft incidents seem to have correlated inversely with crises in the community. This runs counter to the rational expectation that incidents would likely increase when things went seriously wrong. But this did not happen, not even during the worst of the Indian wars when everyone lived with a sense of peril. John P. Demos thinks the explanation may be that the antagonisms behind so many of the accusations were held in check precisely because of the peril and therefore did not surface until the common danger had passed. This would also explain why there were no witchcraft incidents in the early settlements. People who faced common dangers were not likely to turn on one another and weaken group cohesion. The dynamics varied from place to place, but the fear of witches tended to abate during periods of peril, only to revive when the danger had passed.[14] The need to hang together during bad times apparently took precedence over everything else.

Economic growth brought not only prosperity but also new forms of criminal behavior. Bribery, embezzlement, and prostitution were added to the criminal list, and penalties were increased for existing offenses.[15] The social costs of prosperity were high, both for society and the individual. People were more inclined to act selfishly without regard for group opinion and to put private gain over the public interest. The new trends can be discerned in the crime reports in Suffolk County, the business and commercial hub of Massachusetts. Incidents of theft, fighting, and assault increased sharply over previous years. (See Appendix C.)[16] As living standards improved, social cohesion paradoxically deteriorated. The higher standards of material well-being that made people less interdependent set in motion latent forces of social disorganization.

While case counts provide much useful information on crime trends, they are unreliable for quantifying so-called crime rates. They are unreliable because crime rates are not really ascertainable. Case counts quantify only the crimes detected and reported, not the totality of all the crimes committed. Their inherent unreliability is compounded by the colonial practice of trying several offenses together in the same proceeding. This raises questions about how such offenses should be counted, with the answers usually dependent on who does the counting. Should a conviction for lying and stealing count for one offense or for two, and does it matter whether the lie and theft were part of the same incident? On balance, most attempts to quantify crime rates are at best interesting statistical exercises. At worst, they distort the record.

The limited economic sphere of women in the seventeenth century afforded few opportunities to commit economic crimes. The incidence of property crimes by women was insignificant until the 1670s, when the growing wealth of society increased their opportunities. Even then, property crimes remained overwhelmingly male offenses. Similarly, women committed few crimes of violence against the general public. Most of their violence was directed against family members, particularly children, who were the only persons over whom women had much control. All the female convictions for murder before 1660 were for child-killing. This is not to say that women had no lethal instincts, only that they had few opportunities to vent them. With provocation and opportunity, they apparently could be as violent as men. In 1677 following King Philip's War, a group of women attacked and killed two Indian prisoners at Marblehead, Massachusetts. They overpowered the male guards and then used sticks and stones to kill the captives.[17]

But such incidents were too infrequent to have statistical significance. Overall, women accounted for only a small percentage of all the offenses reported. Except for witchcraft, which had a gender bias, they were seldom charged with serious crimes.[18] Theft and assault, for example, were so overwhelmingly male crimes that offenses by women hardly counted.[19] The same was true to a lesser extent of drunkenness, Sabbath-breaking, and regulatory infractions.[20] The number of men charged with lewdness and lascivious behavior exceeded the number of female offenders by a ratio of five to one.[21] No woman was ever charged with bestiality, a crime that sent men to the gallows in every Puritan colony.[22] Only one woman, Sarah Norman, was tried for what seems to have been a lesbian offense. She was sentenced to make a public confession at Yarmouth of her "lewd behavior with Mary Hammon upon a bed." Since only a year before Sarah had been convicted of "unclean practices" with Richard Berry, she apparently kept her sexual options open.[23]

Allowance should be made for the possibility that crimes by women were underreported. The laws were made and enforced by males with stereotypical attitudes about women. They may have seen only what their preconceptions permitted them to see. That only one lesbian offense occurred in all of New England during the seventeenth century is highly unlikely. Females were probably exempted from prosecution under the bestiality statutes because they were considered incapable of such behavior (see chapter 7). Some males, moreover, might have been reluctant to report ordinary sexual offenses by women. Fear of ridicule might have kept down reports of sexual solicitations by women.[24] Men who rejected such overtures might fear making themselves look foolish if they reported them, while those who accepted could not report them without incriminating themselves. Some men may have been obtuse to sexual solicitations, regarding such overtures as a male prerogative. There were so many possibilities for cultural distortion that generalizations based on case counts require extreme caution.

The killing of newborn infants by their unwed mothers was one form of homicide that probably went underreported. This was because the two-witness rule made the crime almost impossible to prove without a confession. Should the body be discovered, the woman could plausibly claim that the child had been born dead and that she had concealed the birth in order to avoid punishment for fornication. Concealment of the death of a bastard did not create a presumption of murder until the 1690s, when the English rule making it a capital crime was adopted. No woman who did not confess was executed during the previous period. The first conviction without a confession came in 1691, when Elizabeth Emmerson was tried on an indictment that incorporated the English statute by reference. It alleged that she had killed her two infants and then "the said two infants did secretly bury contrary to the peace of Our Sovereign Lord & Lady the King and Queen, their Crown & dignity, the Laws of God, and the Laws & Statutes in that case made & provided." No violation of Massachusetts law was alleged, for no Massachusetts law made secret burial a capital crime. Significantly, the jury did not find Elizabeth guilty of murder, but rather "guilty according to the indictment," which invoked English law making the secret burial a capital crime whether she had killed the children or not.[25]

Emmerson's conviction stands in sharp contrast with the outcome of the 1683 trial of Elizabeth Payne for infanticide. Payne, like Emmerson, gave birth secretly, and when the body was discovered, she claimed that the child had been born dead. The indictment charged her with murdering the child "contrary to the peace of our sovereign Lord the king, his crown and dignity, the laws of God, *and of this jurisdiction*" [emphasis added]. The indictment did not allege concealment of the body, because under Massachusetts law concealment was not a capital crime. But concealment was alleged in the Emmerson case because the indictment made English law the governing law of the case. The omission of the words "and of this jurisdiction" from the indictment in the Emmerson case made the difference between life and death. Had Emmerson been tried according to the form of the Payne indictment, she would not have gone to the gallows. Because no witnesses appeared against her, Payne could be convicted only of being "greatly negligent in not calling for help for the preservation of the child's life." Her punishment was twenty lashes, not the death penalty.[26]

Every infanticide indictment before the Emmerson case accused the defendant of murdering the child contrary to the laws of the jurisdiction.[27]

These words were crucially important because the laws of the jurisdiction did not make concealment of the child's body a capital offense. Killing the child was a capital offense, but this required eyewitness testimony. No matter how suspicious the circumstances, a conviction for some lesser offense was the only possible outcome under the "laws of this jurisdiction" form of indictment. Emmerson was hanged because the form of indictment changed in the 1690s as Massachusetts came more into line with English law.

The claim has been made that the two-witness rule did not apply in infanticide cases. Peter C. Hoffer and N. E. H. Hull contend that the circumstantial evidence of concealing the child's death and the defendant's reputation for sexual immorality would be sufficient for a conviction in such cases. They regard the incorporation of the English statute on conceal-ment into Massachusetts law in the 1690s as only a clarification and restate-ment of existing practices. But the only convictions they cite without either witnesses or a confession are the Emmerson case in 1691 and the case of Susanah Andrews in 1696.[28] These cases, however, prove nothing about the earlier period. Both were tried after 1690, when the English law of conceal-ment applied and made capital convictions possible without eyewitness testimony. Women suspected of infanticide were indeed convicted on cir-cumstantial evidence during the earlier period, but not of capital crimes unless they confessed.

When the Massachusetts General Court adopted the English statute on concealment in 1696, the lawmakers made it clear that they were not merely clarifying or restating existing practices. The preface of the law noted how difficult it was to prove a case of infanticide even when the circumstantial evidence was convincing.[29] This was precisely why the 1696 law making concealment a capital crime was enacted. The same problem existed in Connecticut, also because of the two-witness rule. In 1699, despite over-whelming circumstantial evidence against her, Amy Munn was acquitted of murdering her newborn bastard.[30] The verdict outraged public opinion, and the General Assembly responded by enacting the English statute mak-ing concealment presumptive evidence of guilt.[31] Had the law been in force at the time of her trial, Munn would have gone to the gallows.

The only serious crime primarily identified with women was witchcraft. The execution of witches began in 1647 with the hanging of Alice Young at Windsor, Connecticut. Massachusetts sent its first witch, Margaret Jones, to the gallows the following year. During the next four decades, at least six times as many women as men were executed for the crime. Eighteen of the twenty-four defendants prosecuted by Connecticut were women, and four-teen of the twenty-two prosecutions in Massachusetts were against women. All four of the witchcraft complaints filed in New Hampshire and the one trial held in New Plymouth involved women (see Appendix D). Men were nowhere equally at risk when witchcraft was suspected.

An unholy alliance of theology and misogyny targeted women for suspicion. Seventeenth-century theologians taught that women were the weaker sex, spiritually as well as physically, and that the devil exploited their weakness in recruiting followers. Eve, the mother of the race, set the pattern by succumbing to the wiles of Satan and bringing upon mankind the curse of original sin. While the Puritans had more enlightened attitudes toward women than the views held by Catholics and many Protestants, the idea of innate female inferiority was a core belief.[32] The belief meshed perfectly with some of the lurid aspects of witchcraft. The devil was believed to recruit women not just because they were the weaker sex, but also because he lusted for their bodies.[33] When women confessed to sexual intercourse with the devil, they confessed only what the age took for granted about Satan and his female followers (see chapter 8). Had the devil been homosexual, more men might have been targeted for suspicion.

The devil not only preferred women, but apparently preferred them over the age of forty. Women belonging to this age group were likely to have confirmed reputations and enemies ready to accuse them.[34] Many of the suspects, particularly the older ones who were widowed or divorced, had reached the point in life when they no longer performed useful roles in society. Most were beyond their childbearing years, and some were no longer economically self-sufficient. According to one estimate, about 20 percent of the accused women were either impoverished or living at a subsistence level.[35] In effect, such women had become dispensable persons whose removal served public and private interests. This does not mean that a conscious effort was made to get rid of them, only that they made convenient scapegoats when witchcraft was suspected.

Her reputation and even appearance could target a woman for suspicion.[36] Just before the Salem trials, Cotton Mather noted with disapproval the tendency of people to mistake for a witch "every old woman whose temper with her visage is not eminently good."[37] Eunice Cole, a perennial suspect, had an unsavory reputation among her Massachusetts neighbors (see chapter 8). Mary Johnson's prior conviction for stealing probably made it easier for people to believe that she was also a witch.[38] The adultery charge included in the witchcraft indictment against Elizabeth Seager suggests that her reputation was not good.[39] That more than 50 percent of the witchcraft defendants had previous brushes with the law could not have been mere coincidence.[40] Witchcraft was a crime that fed on suspicion, and a bad reputation naturally attracted unfavorable notice.

Far less than an actual criminal conviction was needed to arouse suspicion. Any questionable behavior could start rumors leading people to suspect the worst. Even conflicts between family members could be dangerous. Jane Collins and Mary Parsons attracted unfavorable attention because of marital problems that had landed both in court. Family stability was the social norm, and signs of domestic discord would be carefully noted. Some family disputes resulted in witchcraft charges. Sarah Dribble's relations with her husband became so bad that he finally accused her of witchcraft. If the charges had stuck, his marital problems would have ended once and for all. Jane James, another suspected witch, had such bitter altercations with her son that the authorities had to intervene.[41] Though such incidents had nothing directly to do with witchcraft, they damaged reputations and sometimes turned family members into dangerous antagonists.

Disorderly women were more likely to arouse suspicion than disorderly men. Hierarchy and order were highly prized by the Puritans. Not to accept one's assigned place in God's scheme of things was a threat to society and an affront to God. Disorderly women posed a greater threat than disorderly men because male domination over females underpinned all other hierarchical relations. What better way for Satan to disrupt the natural order than to empower women and disrupt existing relations between the sexes? Women who broke the conventional mold of dutiful daughter, submissive wife, and devoted mother brought into question the prevailing social assumptions. They weakened the affective ties holding people together and put society in jeopardy. That such women might be in league with the devil seemed not only plausible but a real possibility.[42]

The conviction of a close relative could bring other family members under suspicion. John Carrington and Nathaniel Greensmith, the only men executed during the pre-Salem period, were both married to convicted witches. Witchcraft was thought sometimes to run in families, and almost always on the maternal side (see chapter 8). Jane Walford was twice accused by her Massachusetts neighbors, and the rumors followed her to the grave. They then focused on her daughter Hannah and four other daughters, and later Hannah's children were suspected.[43] A mother and daughter sometimes came under suspicion together. One complaint spanned three generations, accusing a woman, her daughter, and a granddaughter of witch-craft.[44] Satan apparently had no objection to nepotism among his followers.

Women who practiced folk medicine naturally aroused suspicion. Treatments involving herbs and potions must have seemed magical to superstitious people. Margaret Jones was a practitioner, and one of the charges against her was that her remedies produced "extraordinary, violent effects."[45] Elizabeth Morse's attempt to treat a sick child failed and almost sent her to the gallows when the child died.[46] Similarly, Rachel Fuller's treatment of a sick New Hampshire child brought her under suspicion when the child died.[47] There was not sufficient evidence to convict her, but her neighbors believed that she had killed the child by magic.[48] If the child had died under the care of a regular male physician, witchcraft would not have been suspected. The death then would have had no occult implications.

The law subjected women to stricter social controls than men. A married woman in Massachusetts could not entertain male guests during her husband's absence, though it was legal for a husband to entertain female friends while his wife was away.[49] Women who spoke out of turn were subject to penalties, while men were free to speak as they pleased.[50] Outspoken women were punished as scolds, an offense never alleged against men.[51] The usual penalty was a turn in the stocks or a soaking in the ducking pond, the sort of spectacle likely to remind other women to keep their tongues in check.[52] A Massachusetts court offered Goody Hunter the choice between a soaking and a gagging for speaking out of turn.[53] Only women were haled into court for speaking their minds.

Women who openly flouted moral standards were dealt with harshly by the courts. In 1662 Goody Wilson was sentenced to be whipped through the streets of Salem for the "barbarous and unhuman" offense of appearing in public stark naked. Her mother and sister were ordered to walk beside her and share her shame for their part in the affair. Since the law did not expressly forbid public nudity, the court was more than a little high-handed in ordering the punishment. Nor did Dorothy Hoyt break any law when she shocked Salem by wearing male clothing. Although the Bible forbade it, no statute covered the offense. So she was convicted of general misconduct and given the choice between a fine and a whipping.[54]

Some offenses correlated closely with social and economic status. Pilferage by servants, for example, obviously had something to do with their meager standard of living and access to the master's property.[55] The same can be said of running away, a generic offense among servants and slaves.[56]

The legal constraints on servants had implications for nonservants as well.[57] A female servant, for example, might not be courted or married by a nonservant without her master's consent.[58] To court her without first clearing things with the master could result in civil and criminal penalties.[59] Nor did ignorance of the law excuse an unwary suitor. In 1659 William Walker, a newcomer to Boston, spent a month in jail for becoming involved with a maidservant without her master's permission.[60] A Connecticut court fined Thomas Cooper for "inveigling the affections of a maid" without first getting consent.[61] The law expected men to behave prudently when they had designs on women.

The sexual harassment of female servants was another class-related offense. Women had to deal with unwanted advances not only of their masters but of male members of the household as well. Thomas Hawes, a Massachusetts resident, landed in court for forcing his brother's maidservant into an affair by threatening to make trouble for her if she refused. A Massachusetts court sentenced John Harris to a whipping for badgering his servant girl for sexual favors.[62] In 1677 the Suffolk County Court canceled Judith Platt's indenture on finding her master guilty of "wanton and lascivious carriages toward her."[63] The use of physical force by libidinous masters was severely punished. In 1681 William Cheney died on the Boston gallows for raping his maidservant.[64] The betrayal of trust seemed as reprehensible to the court as the rape itself. But despite the readiness of the system to punish the offender, most cases of sexual harassment probably went unreported and unpunished.

Crimes by servants were neither more serious nor common than offenses by nonservants. In Massachusetts, the court records of Middlesex County between 1650 and 1686 show that apprentices and servants were responsible for about 20 percent of the reported offenses. Masters were the principle targets of such crimes, and the offenses typically took the form of fraud, theft, and running away.[65] The only serious violence by a servant occurred in Massachusetts in 1674, when a Scottish servant killed his master.[66] But the killing was an isolated incident unrelated to class enmities. The offenses most frequently committed by servants were sexual in nature. They turned up repeatedly in court on fornication and lascivious misconduct charges.[67] The restrictions on courtship and marriage forced many to choose between celibacy and illicit sex. The court records suggest that the latter more often came out the winner.

The Middlesex records show that the majority of offenders were neither poverty-stricken nor drawn from the bottom of Puritan society. The poor comprise the smallest group in the case count, while the middle class is the largest. Offenders at the upper end of society actually outnumber those at the bottom. But class and economic standing did have a bearing on the type of offenses committed. The poor were more likely to commit property crimes than those who were better off economically. Similarly, the incidence of sexual misconduct was higher at the bottom, where marriage was not always a viable option.[68] In contrast to theft and sexual offenses, convictions for religious offenses rise on an ascending social scale. The correlation suggests that such offenses as Sabbath-breaking, Quakerism, Anabaptism, and other deviations from orthodoxy may have been a form of rebellion against the Puritan hegemony. As people rose in society, they apparently resented such dominance. Moreover, the wealthy were more likely to engage in intellectual pursuits that might undermine orthodox thinking. The same sort of class correlation exists for insults, sarcasm, and contempt directed against ministers and magistrates. Persons on the rise would likely resent a hierarchical system that set limits on their aspirations. The higher one rose, the more difficult it became to show deference to anyone.[69]

Slaves seldom appear in the criminal records. But this does not mean that they were models of propriety. There is a possibility that their crimes may have been underreported. The master's property interest in many cases would have caused him to think twice before reporting a serious offense to the authorities. A severe whipping might cost him the slave's services, and an execution would wipe out his investment completely. Since the law provided for no economic compensation to the master, only a keen sense of civic responsibility would move him to report a capital crime.[70] Self-interest sometimes prevailed even over the desire to avenge crimes committed against family members. In 1674 Robert Cox petitioned the Massachusetts Assistants Court to spare the life of his slave Basto. A jury had found Basto guilty of raping Cox's three-year-old daughter and voted the death penalty. The court commuted the punishment to thirty-nine lashes, thus preserving Cox's investment in the slave.[71] If his daughter had been raped by anyone else, Cox would likely have volunteered to assist at the hanging.

Indians committed far fewer crimes against whites than whites committed among themselves. Group fears in this regard generally bore no relation to how individuals in the group behaved (see chapter 7). In Massachusetts, only about twenty of the hundreds of cases tried by the Suffolk County Court in the 1670s involved Indian defendants. Crimes by whites outnumbered offenses by the natives by a ratio of thirty-seven to one.[72] The incidence of Indian crime was similarly low in other colonies.[73] In New Plymouth most crimes by Indians were committed against Indians.[74] This does not mean that close police control and regulation of the Indians served no purpose. Possibly, Indian crimes were infrequent precisely because the controls were in place.

Morals offenses involving whites with Indians were punished according to white standards. In 1631, before Massachusetts made adultery a capital crime, John Dawe was sentenced to a whipping for having an affair with a married Indian woman.[75] Such affairs had to be punished to hold the line against the laxer moral standards of the natives. A New Plymouth court sentenced William Makepeace to a whipping for making "lascivious attempts toward an Indian woman." Whites were sometimes punished more severely than their Indian partners. In 1639 Mary Mendame was whipped through the streets of Duxbury and ordered to wear a badge of shame for committing adultery with an Indian. The Indian's whipping was less severe, because the court found him less culpable than the woman.[76] Allowance was probably made for the fact that Indians did not regard such offenses as serious.

Some offenders had repeated brushes with the law. Compulsive drinkers were in and out of court with depressing regularity, and their long case histories suggest that the social costs of alcoholism must have been high. Thomas Lucas landed before the Plymouth courts at least a dozen times for drunkenness and alcohol-related offenses.[77] Because their habit was obviously uncontrollable, such persons were not treated as common criminals. Still, the offense could not be ignored without setting a bad example. The penalties imposed usually sought to break their habit rather than punish them for having it (see chapter 10).

Recidivism was also high among sex offenders. In 1639, just a year after being branded for rape, Aaron Stark was back in the Connecticut courts on bestiality charges.[78] In 1654 John Bradley, who had a prior record as a sex offender, was convicted of molesting a six-year-old New Haven girl.[79] John Knight was convicted of fornication before being sent to the New Haven gallows for sodomy in 1653.[80] The whipping and branding inflicted on Mary Batcheller for adultery in 1651 did not prevent her from returning to court on an adultery charge the following year.[81] John Bennett's fornication conviction was followed by charges of attempted seduction in another case.[82] Mary Parker made two court appearances during a two-year period on separate fornication charges.[83] Sex, like drinking, appears to have been addictive.

Apart from sex and alcohol, recidivism followed no particular pattern.

One offense might be followed by something so different that there would be no way to predict what the offender might do next. Joseph Gatchell appears in the Massachusetts records for such offenses as fornication, bastardy, and jail-breaking.[84] John Baker, a New Hampshire resident, was charged with assault, illegal trading with Indians, and Sabbath-breaking during just one court session.[85] Jonathan Lamson made his first court appearance as a youth and subsequently returned as an adult for several regulatory offenses.[86] In 1669 John Carr was arraigned before a Providence court on charges ranging from disturbing the peace to stealing and jail-breaking. Charges of theft and fornication were filed against Thomas Durfee during one three-year period.[87] Ralph Earle made several appearances before the Rhode Island courts over the years for such offenses as disorderly conduct and selling firearms to the Indians.[88] The only thing most repeat offenders had in common was a shared indifference to the rules of society.

Recidivism sometimes ran in families, apparently passed along from one member to another as a sort of social trait. Eli Faber's analysis of the court records of Middlesex County, Massachusetts, shows that wrongdoing occurred in particular families with striking regularity. About 42 percent of all reported offenses occurred in families with more than one offender. The phenomenon cut across class lines from the bottom to the top of society.[89] Indeed, family affiliation emerges as the most significant statistical correlation in the incidence of crime and antisocial conduct. Whether other family members simply followed the bad example of the first offender or whether some families had innate criminal tendencies cannot be determined. The only safe generalization is that recidivism bore almost no relation to class or social standing.

The court records of other colonies confirm the Middlesex findings. Recidivism correlated with particular families, passing from one member to another almost like a virus. The Thomas brothers, John and Daniel, appeared before the New Haven courts at least thirteen times on a wide range of charges.[90] In 1665 John Cole and his son stood trial together in New Plymouth, the father for keeping a disorderly house, and the son for assault and public disorders. The Winter family of New Plymouth had a case history spanning three generations. It began in 1639 when Christopher Winter was convicted of premarital sex with his first wife. He was back in court nine years later for committing the same offense with his second wife. In 1652 his daughter Katherine was prosecuted for fornication with her father-in-law. In 1669 Winter was accused of incest when his daughter Martha gave birth to an illegitimate child. The incest charges could not be proved, but Martha was convicted of fornication for conceiving the child out of wedlock. In 1678 another daughter, Anna, was charged with fornication, but the case was dropped when Anna jumped bail and fled the colony.[91]

Perhaps the most striking feature of crime in early New England is the low incidence of serious violence. Although fights and disorders became more common after 1650, serious harm seldom resulted. Petty thefts, illicit sex, and drinking violations predominated (see Appendix C). The records of the Suffolk County Court show that during the 1670s, Massachusetts citizens had little reason to fear criminal violence.[92] They were much safer than persons living in seventeenth-century England. But this fell far short of the goal of Puritan idealists who had hoped for something better than just a comparatively low crime rate. The Puritan dream of holy communities died within the lifetime of the founders, leaving some bewildered and dismayed.[93] "How came it to pass," William Bradford wondered, "that so many wicked persons and profane people should so quickly come over into this land?"[94] Perhaps, as the witchcraft superstition implied, it was because the world really belonged to the devil.

Thomas Carr . . . to be branded in the forehead with the
letter *B*, and to have one of his ears cut off, and to pay
treble damages to the persons from whom he
stole, and in case he make not payment that he be sold.
—Suffolk County Court (1675)

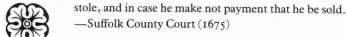

10   Deterrence and Retribution

Seventeenth-century penology was straightforward and uncomplicated by notions of societal responsibility for the wrongdoing of individuals. The prevailing theory was that offenders deserved to suffer for the harm they had done and to discourage others from following their example. The social or economic circumstances of the crime hardly counted; all that mattered was punishing the offender for his moral shortcomings. Public readings of the laws in the Puritan colonies made it unlikely that anyone would break the law inadvertently and without criminal intent.[1] The key assumption was that the offender was morally as well as legally culpable. This approach to wrongdoing gave the age a virtual blank check in meting out punishments.

Since the courts had considerable sentencing discretion, penalties were often tailored to fit the crime. Many petty offenders got off with warnings and admonitions, and some had to make public acknowledgment of the wrong they had done.[2] Sentences of humiliation sometimes required offenders to wear signs or badges stating the nature of their offense. Anyone convicted in Massachusetts of showing contempt for a minister had to stand "openly upon a block or stool, four-foot high, on a lecture day with a paper fixed on his breast, written in capital letters (AN OPEN AND OBSTINATE CONDEMNER OF GOD'S HOLY ORDINANCES) that others may fear and be ashamed of breaking into the like wickedness."[3] Connecticut made almost identical provisions for punishing the offense.[4] When New Plymouth removed adultery from its capital list, whipping and public humiliation were substituted for the death penalty. The adulterous couple had to wear "two capital letters, viz., *AD* cut in cloth and sewed on their upper garments on their arms or back." The punishment for appearing in public without the badge was a whipping for every omission.[5]

164

The courts imposed punishments of humiliation even in cases where such penalties were not specifically authorized by statute. In 1639, long before the lawmakers made it a statutory penalty, a New Plymouth court ordered Mary Mendame to wear a badge of shame for committing adultery.[6] A similar sentence was imposed on Thomas Braye and Goody Lindford in 1641, and the order reads like a verbatim draft of the statute later enacted. The order required them to wear "two letters, viz., an *AD* for adulterers, daily, upon the outside of their uppermost garment, in a most eminent place thereof."[7] Almost identical language was used seventeen years later in the statute making such badges mandatory in adultery cases.[8]

Adultery was not the only sexual offense punished with public humiliation.[9] John Davies had to wear a badge of shame following his whipping at Boston and Ipswich for "attempting lewdness with divers women." In 1642 Thomas Scott and his wife had to stand in the Boston marketplace with papers in their hats acknowledging that they had engaged in premarital sex.[10] In 1674 Hannah Gray was sentenced to stand in the Salem meetinghouse wearing the sign "I STAND HERE FOR MY LASCIVIOUS AND WANTON CARRIAGES." Standing in the meetinghouse guaranteed maximum exposure and humiliation. The previous year, Sarah Row had to stand in the same meetinghouse with a sign announcing "FOR MY BAUDISH CONDUCT."[11] Humiliating apparel sometimes took the place of signs and badges. In 1667 a Maine court ordered Elinor Bonighton, an unwed mother, to pay a five-pound fine or stand in front of the meetinghouse wearing a white sheet.[12]

The courts sometimes tried to shame drunkards into sobriety. New Plymouth published lists of excessive drinkers to put taverns on notice and to pressure those listed to mend their ways or suffer a loss of social standing.[13] In Massachusetts, the courts sometimes sentenced drunkards to wear identifying signs and symbols. In 1636 the Assistants Court ordered William Perkins to stand for an hour in public with "a white sheet of paper on his breast having a great *D* upon it." The Assistants issued a similar order requiring Robert Coles to wear a sign informing the public that he was a drunkard. When Coles returned to court a month later on another drinking charge, he was disfranchised and ordered to wear the letter *D* for a year.[14] This shocked him into a stretch of sobriety that led the court to suspend the sentence and restore his voting rights.[15]

Punishments of humiliation were ordered for a wide range of offenses. In 1639 Richard Wilson, a Massachusetts servant, was ordered to wear the letter *T* (thief) for stealing from his master.[16] For verbally abusing her husband, Sarah Morgan was ordered to pay a fifty-shilling fine or stand gagged in front of the Kittery meetinghouse with a sign identifying her offense.[17] Two sisters, Anstis and Margaret Manning, had to appear at a Salem town meeting with signs announcing that they had behaved lewdly with their brother. Susannah Boswell had to stand in front of the Salem meetinghouse with a sign identifying her as a burglar and liar.[18] In 1673 the Suffolk County Court ordered Sarah Scott to stand on a stool in the Boston marketplace with a sign acknowledging her "undutiful, abusive and reviling speeches and carriages to her natural mother."[19] Some punishments of humiliation lasted for years. In 1642 Daniel Fairfield was ordered to wear a rope about his neck as part of his punishment for debauching three young girls. He wore it for ten years until his wife successfully petitioned the General Court to remit the order.[20] Signs and badges could be used to warn the public as well as humiliate the offender. In 1670 the Essex County Court ordered two Indian rapists not to enter any Massachusetts settlement without signs identifying their offense.[21]

Punishments of humiliation for serious offenses were often carried out on the gallows. In 1641 the Massachusetts Assistants Court ordered Thomas Owens to stand on the Boston gallows for his "adulterous practices," a reminder that adultery itself was a capital crime. Philip Darland was ordered by the Assistants to stand on the gallows with a rope about his neck for his "vile, filthy and abominable" misconduct toward a married woman. Teagu Ocrimi, a servant, had to stand on the Boston gallows with a rope around his neck for his "foul and devilish attempt to bugger a cow."[22] If Ocrimi had succeeded in the attempt, the rope would have been drawn considerably tighter. Almost any serious offense could result in a gallows appearance. Abigail Betts had to stand on the ladder of the Hartford gallows for blasphemy, thus reminding onlookers that the offense was punishable by death.[23] Anna Negro, a servant, was sentenced to stand on the Boston gallows because she was strongly suspected of killing her illegitimate child. The two-witness rule made a murder conviction impossible, but the circumstantial evidence was convincing enough for a gallows appearance.[24] Alice Thomas, a Boston prostitute, had to stand on the gallows for her "shameful, notorious crimes and high misdemeanors," though none of her clients had to stand with her.[25]

Some forms of humiliation required no signs or symbols. Stripping the offender of voting rights and social standing could have the same effect. Josias Plastowe was demoted from the rank of gentleman for participating in the theft of some corn from the Indians.[26] John Godfrey, the perennial witchcraft suspect, was barred from testifying in the Massachusetts courts for abetting perjury in one of his many lawsuits.[27] New Plymouth barred Thomas Roberts from owning land after his conviction for lewdness, and John Combe was disfranchised by New Plymouth for his excessive drinking.[28] Massachusetts barred Robert Cannon from voting following his conviction for fraud, and Christopher Webb was disfranchised for sowing discord in the Bantry church congregation. Thomas Jay lost the right to vote in Massachusetts for slandering John Winslow.[29] Such penalties could be as humiliating as visible badges of shame in a society where rank and social standing really mattered.

Sentences of humiliation were far less frequent than fines and corporal punishments. Some of the latter involved humiliation by exposing offenders to shame and ridicule. One such device, the bilboes, which was used before the introduction of wooden stocks, consisted of an iron bar with sliding shackles to hold the prisoner's ankles in place. The bar could be hoisted off the ground, upending the offender and causing discomfort and humiliation.[30] The bilboes was used to restrain and punish all sorts of offenders in the early days.[31] Thomas Morton was kept in bilboes for punishment and restraint until he could be deported to England.[32] For asserting the right to appeal a judicial decision to England, Thomas Knower was clapped in bilboes by the Massachusetts Assistants Court. Almost any offense not serious enough for a whipping could land an offender in the bilboes.[33]

By the 1640s the bilboes gave way to wooden stocks. The latter were cheaper and easier to make and soon became common everywhere. In 1636 the New Plymouth General Court ordered every town to maintain at least one set for use against local offenders.[34] Similar laws and orders in the other colonies made the device ubiquitous. Towns failing to keep their stocks in good working order might be fined or censured.[35] Newport was rebuked in a grand jury presentment for neglecting to maintain a proper set of stocks.[36] The stocks marked the threshold of corporal punishment for numerous petty offenses.[37] The device filled the gray area between offenses calling for fines or admonitions and those serious enough for a whipping. Almost any offense qualified for a turn in the stocks. Edward Palmer, the carpenter who built the first set for Boston, was the first occupant of his own device. He was sentenced to be confined in it an hour for overcharging for his services.[38] If Palmer found the experience unpleasant, he had only himself to blame for not making it more comfortable.

Although stocks were not intended to cause physical harm, excessive time in the device could be painful and dangerous. Every colony set time limits to prevent overconfinement. New Plymouth, Massachusetts, and Connecticut set the upper limit at three hours, and New Haven allowed a maximum of four. Rhode Island permitted sentences of up to six hours, the most authorized by any New England colony.[39] These limits did not prevent offenders from being punished with additional time for other offenses, but they might not be confined beyond the limits for a continuous stretch.

The pillory resembled the stocks in design, though the prisoner was restrained in a standing position rather than sitting. The device was sometimes used for brutal punishments not associated with the stocks.[40] The ears of serious offenders might be nailed to the wooden crossbeam holding the head and arms in place.[41] In 1675 the Assistants Court sentenced Maurice Brett to have one of his ears nailed to the Boston pillory "and after an hour's standing there to be cut off." Brett made the mistake of swearing at the Assistants when a decision went against him. An apology saved his ear, but he still had to spend an hour in the pillory exposed to public scorn. Peter Lorphin was less fortunate. In 1679 both his ears were nailed to the Boston pillory and then cut off for lying and coin-clipping.[42]

The courts used their sentencing discretion to tailor punishments to the offense. Verbal offenses such as railing and scolding might be punished by orders for a public gagging. Goody Hunter was gagged at Springfield for scolding and railing, and Bridget Oliver got similar treatment at Salem for reviling her husband.[43] A cleft stick was sometimes used instead of a cloth gag. The stick would be tied around the prisoner's tongue, keeping the mouth open and stretching the tongue, something considerably more uncomfortable than a simple gagging. In 1636 the Massachusetts Assistants Court sentenced Elizabeth Applegate to the cleft-stick punishment for railing and swearing against her neighbors. The Assistants ordered the same punishment for Robert Shorthose and Robert Bartlett for cursing and swearing. Samuel Hawkes was sentenced to the Boston stocks with a stick tied to his tongue for stealing and some verbal offenses.[44] This was more uncomfortable than if the penalties had been administered separately. In 1646 the Essex County Court gave Mary Oliver the cleft-stick treatment for denouncing the Salem ministers as bloodthirsty men.[45] George Dill was sentenced to stand in front of the Salem meetinghouse with a cleft stick tied to his tongue, wearing a sign reading "FOR GROSS PREMEDITATED LYING."[46]

But such punishments were unusual and were applied only when the court decided to make an example of the offender. The most common corporal punishment was whipping, which was widely used in colonial times. It was used against children, servants, and apprentices as well as criminal offenders. There were few colonial people who at some time or another had not been whipped. One of its virtues was that it could be meted out according to the seriousness of the offense (see Appendix C). It was also the cheapest, simplest, and most immediate form of punishment available. An immediate whipping after conviction served to impress people with the effectiveness of the justice system. It brought home to onlookers the connection between wrongdoing and punishment, proving that the system worked and discouraging others from following the offender's example.[47]

Most whippings were administered at the town whipping post in full public view in order to maximize the deterrent effect. But in serious cases the whipping might be administered as the offender was drawn through the streets at the tail of a cart.[48] Carting was usually reserved for particularly shocking offenses. Goody Wilson was carted through the streets of Salem for appearing in public naked, and Sarah Ensigne was whipped through the streets of Plymouth for "common whoredom."[49] In 1672 the Suffolk County Court ordered Alice Thomas to be carted through Boston for setting up a brothel.[50] Her offense shocked the lawmakers into passing a statute with additional penalties.[51] The law was invoked six years later to banish Elinor May from the colony after she had been whipped through Boston for prostitution.[52]

Massachusetts ordered multiple whippings for Quakers who entered the colony illegally. The first whipping would be administered where the arrest was made, and additional whippings would follow from town to town until the prisoner was out of the colony. Since this could be fatal for a prisoner arrested far from the border, the law limited the whippings to three towns. The sentencing court would decide how many lashes would be inflicted and where the whippings would be carried out.[53] Quakers apprehended in Boston, the most common point of entry for Massachusetts, were usually whipped there first, then at Roxbury, and finally at Dedham, after which they would be driven into the wilderness.[54] With this sort of sendoff, only the most zealous or foolish were likely to return.

The courts sometimes ordered multiple whippings on their own authority without statutory sanction. In 1657 Robert Ferris was sentenced to be whipped at New Haven and again at Stamford for attempted bestiality. The court was convinced that Ferris had actually committed the offense, not just the attempted offense for which he was convicted. He escaped the gallows only because the two-witness rule prevented a capital conviction (see chapter 6). In 1643 the Massachusetts Assistants Court sentenced Robert Wyar and John Garland to separate whippings at Boston and Cambridge for debauching two young girls.[55] Another Massachusetts offender, Edward Sanders, got three separate whippings for sexually abusing a woman.[56] Thomas Braye and Anne Francis got double whippings for adultery, the first at Plymouth where they were tried and then at Yarmouth where the offense took place.[57] Adulterers got the same treatment in Rhode Island. In 1669 William Temerlake and Mary Stockes got fifteen lashes at Providence and another fifteen a week later at Newport.[58] Such sentences gave the punishment greater publicity than sentences inflicted in one place.

Recidivists were among the most likely candidates for multiple whippings. The Connecticut judges who sentenced Robert Beadle for theft in 1645 were furious when he returned a few months later on new criminal charges. So they ordered him to be whipped at every quarter session of the court until they were satisfied that he had mended his ways. In the same year the same court sentenced Susan Cole to a double whipping for fornication, possibly because of her previous conviction as a rebellious servant.[59] In 1667 Thomas Walwin was sentenced to a double whipping in Rhode Island after a second conviction for fornication. Fifteen lashes were administered at Newport and another fifteen in Providence. Ann Talman was sentenced the same year to be whipped twice at Newport after a second conviction for fornication.[60] In 1645 a Connecticut court sentenced Ruth Fishe to a double whipping for separate acts of fornication with two men. Her male partners got off with a single whipping each, probably because each had committed only one offense. Even a bad reputation might result in extra punishment. In 1646 Mary Johnson, a suspect later hanged for witchcraft, was whipped at Hartford and a second time at Wethersfield for stealing.[61]

While the courts had considerable leeway, they had no blank check in ordering whippings. No one could be whipped in Massachusetts unless at least two of the Assistants approved the order.[62] One Assistant could order a whipping in New Plymouth, but it might not exceed ten lashes.[63] Every colony set limits on the number of lashes that might be ordered at one time. Massachusetts and New Haven set the limit at forty, and the limit in Connecticut was thirty.[64] The fact that Massachusetts and Connecticut set their limits under code headings prohibiting torture suggests that anything more was considered cruel and excessive.[65] Rhode Island set no statutory limits but adopted instead the common-law rule that a whipping should stop when the offender's back had been bloodied.[66] As a practical matter, the Rhode Island courts seldom ordered more than fifteen lashes at a time, well within the limits of the Puritan colonies.[67]

The law in many cases gave offenders the option of paying a fine in lieu of corporal punishment. In Massachusetts, persons holding the rank of gentleman might not be whipped unless the offense was serious or the defendant's way of life "vicious and profligate."[68] When the Assistants Court degraded Josias Plastowe from the rank of gentleman for stealing some corn, it sentenced two of his accomplices to be whipped.[69] Plastowe would have gotten whipped as well if his rank had not protected him. In 1647 a New Haven court let John Heywood off for drunkenness on the ground that his expulsion from church membership was punishment enough.[70] If Heywood had not been a church member, a fine or some other penalty probably would have been ordered.

Sentences calling for fines or loss of status could later be modified or rescinded completely. But corporal punishments could not be taken back after they had been administered. When fines or orders of degradation were revoked, the beneficiaries were almost invariably upper-class offenders. Forty-four of the forty-seven sentences reduced or rescinded by the Massachusetts General Court in the 1630s involved offenders in the upper ranks of society.[71] Josias Plastowe was one of those whose rank was restored and the slate wiped clean. Plastowe's lower-class accomplices were less fortunate, because there was no way to rescind a whipping.

Offenses punishable by fine far outnumbered those calling for corporal punishments. Massachusetts authorized fines for offenses ranging from curfew violations to minor infractions of the moral code.[72] New Plymouth specified forty-two offenses as punishable by fine, and many more could be satisfied by fine at the discretion of the courts.[73] The Massachusetts Assistants Court imposed fines in about 47 percent of the cases dealt with in the 1630s, when the court tried both major and minor offenses. After county courts were established in the 1640s, fines continued to predominate among the penalties meted out. The pattern continued into the 1670s, even as more serious crimes increased. During the early 1670s, fines imposed by the Suffolk County Court outnumbered whippings by 144 to 88, and in 56 other cases the defendant was given a choice between a fine or whipping (see Appendix C). A sample of 190 cases tried in New Plymouth between 1633 and 1643 reveals that about 100 resulted in fines.[74] The fines collected must have generated considerable revenue, but whether this became a factor in sentencing cannot be ascertained. Making the justice system self-supporting would certainly have been a reasonable goal.

Corporal punishments for the most serious crimes went far beyond whipping. Massachusetts ordered branding for burglars and robbers, with additional penalties according to the circumstances of the offense. First-offenders were branded on the forehead with a *B* or *R* to identify the offense; second-offenders got another branding plus a whipping; and third-offenders got the death penalty.[75] Connecticut and New Haven ordered similar penalties, except in New Haven branding was on the hand instead of the forehead.[76] The provincial laws enacted by New Hampshire in 1679 also provided for branding on the hand for the first two offenses, but left it to the courts to decide whether the culprit should be put to death for a third offense.[77] Rhode Island ordered branding for all forms of grand larceny, which the law defined as stealing more than twelve pence.[78]

Some courts ordered brandings on their own authority even before statutes authorized the punishment. In 1639 a New Plymouth court warned Mary Mendame that she would be branded with the letters *AD* (adultery) if she appeared in public without the letters clearly visible on her sleeve. This was no empty threat, because only a year before the court had sentenced Edward Shaw, a servant, to be branded on the shoulder for stealing fifteen shillings. And two years later James Till was branded for stealing a shirt and some corn.[79] In 1651 a Maine court sentenced Mary Batcheller to be branded with the letter *A* for adultery.[80] At the time these brandings were ordered, there was no statutory sanction for such punishment. Not until the 1670s did the Plymouth lawmakers authorize branding as a statutory penalty.[81]

Quakers suffered the most brutal punishments of all in the Puritan colonies. Their missionaries who returned to Massachusetts a third time after banishment might have their tongues drilled through with a red-hot iron to prevent them from proselytizing. Tongue-drilling was later reduced to branding on the shoulder, but the death penalty was ordered for those who returned after the branding.[82] New Haven branded returnees on the hand the first two times they defied orders of banishment, and drilled them through the tongue for a third return. The New Haven courts sometimes went beyond the letter of the law in punishing religious subversives. Although not under an order of banishment and therefore not subject to branding, Humphrey Norton was nevertheless sentenced to be branded in 1658 for spreading heresy.[83]

Corporal punishment included a form of mutilation known as ear-cropping, which involved the amputation of one or both ears of the offender. Quakers faced the loss of an ear the first two times they returned to Massachusetts in defiance of orders of banishment.[84] Thus by the time their tongues were ready for drilling, they had already lost both ears. Burglaries and robberies on the Sabbath also called for loss of an ear besides the regular punishment of branding.[85] One such offender, Thomas Carr, was sentenced by the Suffolk County Court in 1675 "to be branded in the forehead with the letter *B*, and to have one of his ears cut off, and to pay treble damages to the person from whom he stole."[86] Connecticut ordered the same penalties for Sabbath burglaries and robberies.[87] Additional penalties were ordered by all the Puritan colonies, but only Massachusetts and Connecticut called for ear amputations. New Plymouth and New Hampshire ordered branding on the forehead instead of the hand, and New Haven settled for an extra whipping.[88] No special Sabbath penalties were needed in Rhode Island. All burglaries and robberies were capital crimes regardless of when they were committed.[89]

Multiple offenders usually drew separate sentences for each offense, and the sentences often involved different punishments. Webb Adey, for example, was sentenced to a turn in the Plymouth stocks for disorderly conduct and to a whipping for breaking out of jail. Thomas Lucas was fined for disorderly conduct and jailed for appearing in court drunk to answer the charge.[90] In 1667 a Rhode Island court imposed a fine on John Willis for jail-breaking, a whipping for fornication, and amputation of both his ears for perjury.[91] Only the death penalty canceled all other penalties for multiple offenses. After convicting John Knight of fornication and sodomy in 1655, a New Haven court sentenced him to death for sodomy but ordered no punishment for the other conviction.[92] To whip an offender bound for the gallows, though technically legal, would have been needlessly vindictive and cruel. A death sentence squared everything in every colony.

The death penalty, of course, was the ultimate form of corporal punishment. The seventeenth century regarded it as essential to the orderly administration of justice. It gave the justice system an awesome credibility that went beyond capital crimes. Persons contemplating less serious offenses were reminded that a life of crime might bring them to the gallows, a real possibility given the many crimes punishable by death. The number of hanging offenses grew over the years as new crimes were added to the capital lists. In New Plymouth, the crimes punishable by death grew from nine to sixteen over the years, and the Massachusetts list ballooned from twelve to twenty-seven capital offenses by the 1680s (see Appendix A).

But raw numbers can be misleading in dealing with capital crimes. Most of the capital laws were actually never enforced. The only crimes for which Massachusetts sent people to the gallows were adultery, rape, bestiality, arson, witchcraft, murder, piracy, and defiance of orders of banishment by

Quakers. Murder and bestiality were the only crimes for which people died in New Plymouth; and in Connecticut and New Haven, only sodomy, incest, bestiality, and witchcraft sent people to the gallows. The only death sentences handed down in Rhode Island were for capital forms of homicide.[93] The bulk of the offenses calling for the death penalty were punished as noncapital offenses. Many were scriptural crimes that Puritan lawmakers felt morally bound to include in the statutes, even though judges and juries were not likely to enforce the death penalty.

The divergence between theory and practice is best illustrated in adultery law. Although the Massachusetts Assistants Court had made it a capital crime, three adulterers got off with whippings and banishment in 1638 on the ground that the law had not been sufficiently published.[94] The General Court proceeded to confirm and publish the law, thus putting to rest any doubt as to its validity. But the only time the death penalty was ever applied was in 1644, when James Britton and Mary Latham were sent to the gallows for adultery. Both admitted the charges, and Mary even boasted of her infidelities. She implicated five other men, but they denied the charge and had to be released when no other evidence could be produced against them.[95] Although adultery remained on the capital list until the 1690s, no one was subsequently executed for the crime.

The other Puritan colonies likewise made adultery a capital offense, but none of them put adulterers to death. In 1658 New Plymouth removed adultery from the capital list, making it a whipping offense instead.[96] While it technically remained a capital offense in Connecticut and New Haven, neither colony sent adulterers to the gallows. Elizabeth Johnson and Thomas Newton were sentenced to death for adultery in Connecticut, but the sentences were not carried out. Newton broke jail and fled the colony, and Elizabeth was later apparently released.[97] An unnamed offender was executed for a sex crime in New Haven in 1650, but there is no reason to assume it was adultery. The court records describe the offense as "unnatural filthiness," making it more likely bestiality or sodomy than adultery.[98]

The Connecticut courts did not send adulterers to the gallows even when juries brought in guilty verdicts. The death penalty was not imposed on Elizabeth Seager when she was convicted in 1663, nor on Hannah Hackleton when she was found guilty two years later. Hackleton was whipped and made to stand on the gallows ladder for an hour with a rope about her neck.[99] Since the death penalty was not enforced, Connecticut removed adultery from the capital list in 1672, substituting harsh, noncapital penalties instead. The new law punished it with whipping, branding on the forehead with the letter *A*, and requiring adulterers to wear a rope about their necks when they appeared in public.[100] This left adultery a hanging offense only in Massachusetts, where it remained on the capital list until 1692. But in practice, Massachusetts punished adulterers less severely than Connecticut, which strictly enforced the brutal provisions of its 1672 adultery statute. Two adulterers, Abigail Betts and John Slade, were whipped and branded on the forehead the month the new law went into effect.[101]

No colony prescribed an official method of execution, probably because the common-law method of death by hanging was taken for granted. Except for two Indians beheaded at New Haven, one beheading in New Plymouth, and some executions by shooting in Massachusetts and New Plymouth during King Philip's War, hanging was virtually automatic in capital cases.[102] However, the 1681 execution of a black servant named Maria for arson has raised questions as to whether Massachusetts made an exception in her case. The Assistants Court ordered her to be burned, but the sentence does not make clear whether she was to be executed by burning or burned after execution by hanging. The latter seems more likely for several reasons. For one, the court ordered burning after hanging in another arson case tried at the same session.[103] For another, an execution by burning would have been an extraordinary event and almost certain to be noted in diaries and journals. The complete absence of contemporary comment suggests that such an execution never occurred. A live burning would not only have been unprecedented but probably contrary to the guarantee against cruel and barbarous punishments.[104]

While the justice system held everyone accountable, punishment varied with the social status of the offender. Massachusetts expressly excused upper-class defendants from whipping for minor offenses (see chapter 7). In New Haven, where crime patterns were similar, the courts made allowance for class without statutory prompting. Punishments of humiliation, for example, were reserved exclusively for persons of low social status. No one of even partially high status was sentenced to the stocks or required to wear locks or halters. But this happened to about 10 percent of all low-status offenders. Similarly, admonitions were occasionally given to lower-status defendants, but never to upper-status ones. The imposition of fines and corporal punishments also varied with status. Sentences of whipping were disproportionately ordered for those of low status, and fines were more frequently imposed on high-status offenders. An analysis of the court records by M. P. Baumgartner reveals that fines accounted for 60 percent of

175

the penalties imposed on high-status defendants, but only one-third of those imposed on low-status ones. The proportions reverse for corporal punishments. Only 20 percent of high-status defendants received corporal punishment, compared to 50 percent of the low-status defendants. The sentencing patterns make it clear that the chances of being whipped correlated inversely with class standing.[105]

But the correlation with class was not just a matter of differential severity. Whether punished corporally or by fine, the sentences imposed by New Haven courts on high-status offenders were likely to be more severe than those imposed on low-status defendants. The whippings ordered for persons higher on the social ladder were more likely to be designated "severe" and the fines imposed heavier than for low-status offenders.[106] So it would be wrong to conclude that there was across-the-board leniency for upper-class offenders. One reason the latter were less likely to receive corporal punishment is that they were less likely to be tried for crimes calling for the penalty. But when they did commit such crimes, they seem to have been punished with extra severity, perhaps because more was expected of them. This would also explain why fines became higher as rank increased. The greater ability of high-status defendants to pay required heavier fines to bring their punishment into line with the fines imposed on lower-class offenders. While the system took rank into account, it neither winked at upper-class offenses nor tolerated wrongdoing by offenders of any class.

One form of punishment almost never ordered in the seventeenth century was the long prison term. The long-term incarceration of offenders is a relatively recent development in Western penology.[107] Although long confinements occasionally occurred, they were the exception rather than the rule. Jails in the seventeenth century were primarily holding facilities for prisoners awaiting trial or punishment. They were not designed for long periods of detention. The Massachusetts Assistants Court tried over four hundred cases between 1630 and 1644, and only seven resulted in jail terms.[108] Most of the penalties imposed called for fines or corporal punishments. Sentencing offenders to jail would not have been a viable option, because colonial society could not afford long-term incarcerations. The Boston jail was the only regular jail in Massachusetts until 1652, when a second one was ordered for Ipswich. Jail construction was unpopular with taxpayers, and some towns had to be prodded into paying for such projects. In 1661 the General Court had to grant tax abatements to Springfield and Northampton to help cover the cost of building local jails.[109]

Massachusetts used Castle Island in Boston harbor for the detention of prisoners who could not be accommodated in the regular jails. In 1634 the island was fortified for the defense of the town, and it was almost continuously garrisoned with soldiers. Prisoners were confined there if they would not conform to jail rules or to isolate them from society. In 1636 Chausop, an Indian from Block Island, became the first prisoner sent to the island, and the following year Richard Osborn, apparently an idler, was threatened with confinement there if he did not mend his ways. Nicholas Upshall, who outraged the Puritan establishment by joining the Quakers, was warned that if he violated the terms of his parole he would be sent to the island for life.[110] Although not a regular prison, it was routinely used for the confinement of troublesome prisoners with problems the jails could not handle. In Upshall's case, confining him on the island would have isolated him from the sympathizers who embarrassed the government by visiting him in jail (see chapter 7). While not designed for such a purpose, the island was closer to a modern prison than any of the town jails.[111]

New Plymouth had no regular jail until 1638, when the General Court ordered one to be built for the town of Plymouth.[112] Prisoners had previously been held in other public buildings and sometimes on private premises. The Hartford jail served all of Connecticut until 1667, when the General Court ordered the towns to build their own jails.[113] The Rhode Island towns originally made their own arrangements for jail construction.[114] In 1656 the colony government authorized the use of cages for detaining prisoners, and the towns were required to maintain at least one cage under penalty of a fine.[115] Massachusetts and New Plymouth routinely used cages to relieve overcrowding in jails.[116] Keeping tax rates low took precedence over the comfort of prisoners.

Although resembling a jail, the house of correction was a separate and different sort of detaining facility. In theory, confinement there was not for punishment but rather to reform and rehabilitate the prisoner. Persons were detained not for actual crimes but to correct bad habits and antisocial tendencies. The idea of forced rehabilitation originated in England, where beggars, vagabonds, and prostitutes were rounded up and detained for training in useful labor.[117] In Massachusetts, the counties had responsibility for setting up houses of correction where idlers and misfits might be held until they could be turned into useful citizens.[118] This was one of the responsibilities of local government in New Plymouth as well. In 1658 the General Court ordered the town authorities to detain "all such vagrants as wander up and down without any calling, and also all idle persons or rebellious children or servants that are stubborn and will not earn their own bread."[119] Connecticut authorized the courts to send unruly children and servants to the house of correction until they learned correct behavior.[120]

Persons committed to the house of correction remained there until the court was satisfied they were ready to be returned to society. The conditions under which they lived were hard and sometimes brutal. Those committed to the Massachusetts house of correction were whipped upon admission to get their attention and point them in the right direction. The inmates were put to work processing flax and hemp and performing other tasks to make the facility self-supporting. Since any profits that accrued went to the master of the house, the arrangement invited exploitation of the inmates. Violations of the house rules were punished by whipping, and rations were kept at a subsistence level.[121] New Plymouth's house of correction operated in much the same way. The inmates were expected to be self-supporting, and they were limited to such rations as their own labor could provide.[122]

Time spent in jail was better in some respects than time spent in a house of correction. Inmates of the jails could at least supplement their meager rations with food provided by friends and relatives; the house of correction deliberately kept inmates hungry to motivate them to work and mend their ways. Moreover, jail inmates did not have to work for the benefit of their jailer. Still, by modern standards, their condition was deplorable. The daily maintenance allowance for prisoners in New Plymouth was set at two pence in 1646, and it remained unchanged for the next fourteen years despite sharp increases in the cost of living.[123] In 1663 Massachusetts set the jail allowance at thirty pence weekly.[124] While hardly generous, it at least set a colonywide minimum in some cases above the county level. Prisoners in the Essex County jail previously had to provide their own food or subsist on a diet of bread and water.[125] The records are silent on whether anyone actually starved, but hunger must have been a constant companion for many inmates.

Conditions were so deplorable that long-term imprisonment probably would have amounted to a death sentence. Most forms of corporal punishment seem humane when compared with living a half-starved existence in a filthy jail without proper light or sanitation. Thomas Gatchell, a frequent inmate, has left a graphic description of the Salem jail from the standpoint of persons confined there. He described it in 1679 as "a noisesome place not fit for a Christian man to breathe." In petitioning the court to release him, Gatchell cited the poor ventilation, pleading that he could not survive much longer "in so pestiferous a stink."[126] John Dunton, a visitor from London, observed similar conditions in the Boston jail. He described it as "a house of meager looks and ill smells . . . the suburbs of hell, and the persons much the same as there."[127] Even if Gatchell and Dunton exaggerated somewhat, a week or two in such a place would probably have made whipping seem preferable to jail time. Even severe whippings were soon over, leaving the offender free to return to society and resume normal living.

But the preferences of criminals hardly counted, for those who broke the rules got no sympathy. They deserved what they got for violating the social contract. The justice system dealt in fear, pain, and death, but it also stood for the moral ideals and social values that criminals had rejected. The protection of society by whatever means necessary took precedence over the suffering of wrongdoers. Apart from gratuitous cruelty, few New Englanders had qualms about punishing offenders, whether the punishment involved fines, whippings, or a trip to the gallows. Society owed offenders nothing except a fair trial and the opportunity to defend themselves. If convicted, they could expect to pay for the harm they had done both to individuals and society. Not to have exacted a full reckoning would have struck colonial people as dangerous and immoral.

We shall be as a city upon a hill, the eyes of all people are
upon us.—John Winthrop (1630)

11   The New England Way

The failure of the Puritans to keep New England Puritan and holy could
have been predicted from the outset. The idealism of the founders set a
standard beyond the reach of succeeding generations. Signs of this appeared early in the form of growing morals violations and the lamentations
of ministers about New England's fall from grace. There was constant
harping on the theme that the churches had had their best day and that
neither in faith nor behavior did the colonists equal their fathers.[1] If these
constantly reiterated fears did not mean New England's moral state was
getting steadily worse, they do suggest that the dreams of the founders had
not been realized. Their standards had been high indeed, even by the
measure of Scripture, which did not prohibit smoking, dictate the style of
clothing people might wear, or ban the drinking of toasts on social occasions. Such laws assumed a state of perfection to which few New Englanders could aspire. The piling of regulation upon regulation could not
make people better than they were. The very need for so much positive law
was itself a sign that the moral law had failed.

While failing to build a new Christian order, Puritan law remained a
powerful force in New England well into the eighteenth century. Crime
continued to be regarded as sinful; the criminal, as fundamentally a sinner;
and the criminal law, as the earthly instrument of God. The courts continued to function, as in the early seventeenth century, as the custodians of
public morality. Studies of the court records in Massachusetts indicate that
most of the developments that transformed Puritan law into the criminal
law of today occurred after 1760, when the law's basic function shifted from
the defense of morality to the protection of property.[2] The durability of
Puritan law can be attributed in part to its usefulness as a social regulator.
Even after the religious force behind it had been spent, all sorts of political,

180

social, and economic justifications could be cited for its continued enforcement. The moral law thus became a vehicle for promoting secular goals and interests.[3]

The idealism behind Puritan law had been lost long before its goals shifted. Like Jacob, the Puritans had attempted to wrestle with angels, fallen angels against whom corrupt human nature could never prevail. Wickedness and depravity followed the settlers to New England, and the moral rot set in almost from the beginning. Success in taming the wilderness and overcoming hardships and perils weakened the network of social interdependence that in the early years made people care about the good opinion of their neighbors. The moral consensus of New England faded within a generation, and the lights of the shining city gradually dimmed. By the 1690s all was gone—the dream, idealism, even political independence. The lights had gone out, and New England returned to the darker loop of secular history.

But not every light went out, for the New England Puritans were too dynamic and vital to fade away completely. Their great and lasting achievement was to put in place the foundations and building blocks of American constitutionalism. They brought to these shores and refined here the best legal traditions of the English nation. Discarding its anachronisms, they adjusted existing law to the needs of a dynamic new society. Their lawmakers set limits on governmental power that were much more explicit and binding than the then vague guarantees of the English common law. The list is familiar but still worth recounting: no unreasonable search or seizure, no double jeopardy, no compulsory self-incrimination, and no cruel or barbarous punishments. The right to bail, grand jury indictment, speedy trial, trial by jury, presumption of innocence, and the right to confront accusers in open court were all protected. Puritan law anticipated by nearly a century and a half the key guarantees of the United States Bill of Rights.

The Puritans accomplished all this by striking a reasonable balance between order and liberty. They never confused liberty with social license nor mistook arbitrary government for order. What kept their brand of order from becoming ruthlessly authoritarian was a criminal justice system geared to the protection of individual rights. People were held to a high standard of conduct by the state, but the state was held to equally high standards by the people. Both were subject to law and had to abide by the rules. This balancing of individual and public interests made the Puritan colonies far more successful than any others in preserving liberty while suppressing crime. Indeed, suppressing the latter was perceived as essential to preserving the former. There could be no real freedom for the individual in a society where fear of crime conditioned everyday social living. To the Puritan mind, liberty was a product of order, not its antithesis.

Although Puritan penal practices appear harsh today, they were not harsh by the standards of the seventeenth century. English law then allowed live evisceration and burning at the stake, and in Virginia capital offenders were broken on the wheel and burned alive.[4] Puritan law eschewed barbarous punishments and settled for hanging as the standard form of execution. Whatever we may think of hanging today, there were far worse ways to die in colonial times. Following a failed slave insurrection in 1712, New Yorkers were treated to a round of grisly spectacles as rebels were roasted over fires, racked and broken on the wheel, and gibbeted alive in chains.[5] Nothing comparable occurred in New England, not even for the most heinous crimes. Capital offenders were put to death without moral qualms, but they were dispatched swiftly without unnecessary suffering.

Nor were the punishments inflicted on noncapital offenders particularly brutal by the standards of the age. The harshest punishments were branding and ear-cropping, but both were reserved for the worst offenders. If the branding of burglars and robbers appears excessive today, it must be remembered that in seventeenth-century England both offenses were punishable by death. Nostril-slitting, a fairly common punishment in England, was inflicted only once, and for an offense many thought deserved the death penalty (see chapter 2). Whipping was by far the most common form of punishment, and the law set limits on the number of lashes that might be ordered. The upper limit was forty regardless of the nature or seriousness of the offense. However painful the experience, culprits emerged from even the most severe whippings with life and limb intact.

The Puritans were much more sparing with regard to the death penalty than a literal reading of their capital laws would suggest. For one thing, many of the capital prohibitions borrowed from Scripture were simply not enforced. No one ever went to the gallows for blasphemy, idolatry, or cursing a parent. For another, some of the offenses enacted under separate headings were already covered by other capital laws. The Massachusetts code of 1672, for example, made it a crime to kill intentionally, another to kill by guile or poison, and still another to kill in anger or cruelty (see Appendix A). If classified by modern definitions, the total number of capital crimes at any one time would not greatly exceed those calling for the death penalty until relatively recent times. Only five of the Puritan capital laws survived into the twentieth century: treason, murder, rape, arson,

and kidnapping. But these subsumed many other offenses separately proscribed in colonial times.[6] When discounted for Scripture and redundancy,
the Puritan capital lists do not appear particularly long.

Neither the death penalty nor corporal punishment raised any moral
issues in the seventeenth century. Both were taken for granted as part of
contemporary penology. They do cause moral qualms today, though not
because of moral progress or enlightenment over the past three centuries.
The virtual disappearance of corporal punishment from modern penology
can be more realistically attributed to changes in attitudes toward pain.
Colonial people experienced a great deal of pain. Lack of morphia and
effective anesthesia made it a constant companion for young and old alike.
Limbs were amputated from fully conscious people, and numerous agoniz-
ing ailments had to be endured through gritted teeth. In an age that
accepted pain as an ordinary part of life, the temporary suffering of criminals offended no one's moral sensibilities. That the deliberate infliction of
pain does offend moral sensibilities today can be attributed to modern
pharmacology, which has eliminated most of the old agonies. Deliberately
inflicting it is no longer morally acceptable because people no longer take
pain and suffering for granted.

Changing perceptions have similarly altered attitudes toward the death
penalty. Death was everywhere in the seventeenth century and seldom out
of sight. The sick and aged were not banished to hospitals and nursing
homes to die out of sight without reminding the living of their own mor-
tality. Death had a high level of visibility, and people took it for granted as a
part of everyday reality. Attitudes today are drastically different. Death
now shocks and affronts people whose social conditioning has not prepared
them to accept it as their forefathers accepted it. It is fear and repugnance of
death, not moral progress, that makes the death penalty so controversial
today. There was no controversy three centuries ago when death was a common experience. No one who had seen friends and family members die,
often in great agony, had any qualms over the speedy dispatch of criminals.

The guarantees of fairness built into Puritan law did not prevent witch
hunts or the persecution of Quakers. But this had less to do with law than
with the religious culture of early New England. The Puritans were preoc-
cupied with witchcraft to a greater extent than other English colonists of
the seventeenth century. Although not Puritan in origin, the superstition
meshed perfectly with their religious beliefs. It was the dark side of Puritanism, a horror spawned by idealism, like most of the horrors invented by
man. The intensity of Puritan spirituality made the struggle between good

and evil part of the consciousness of ordinary people. New England became part of the battleground where God contended with Satan for dominion over the world. If the Puritans had been less conscious of God, they would have been less fearful of the agents of Satan. These fears, not their legal institutions, bear responsibility for what happened.

The persecution of Quakers also needs perspective. The Quakers who entered New England in the 1650s were religious zealots bent on overthrowing church and state. They came not to worship peaceably but to destroy the existing order. Like the early Christian martyrs, they provoked persecution and gloried in the reprisals they suffered. Quakers defied civil authority, disrupted church services, and caused numerous disturbances. Without condoning what was done to them, it is difficult to imagine any society tolerating their provocations. The Puritans reacted as any dedicated group would have reacted to interlopers who threatened all they held holy. They had sacrificed too much to stand idly by while strangers destroyed what they had built. They would not have been Puritans had they not fought back with all the force at their command.[7]

Puritan penal theory differed from modern penology without being substantially different in practice. Penologists today make a mistake in distinguishing between the emphasis placed by the past on revenge and retribution and the modern aim of protecting society from the criminal. The latter is looked upon as enlightened and progressive, while the former is disparaged as characteristic of a more brutal era, though surviving to some extent in the criminal law of today. This sort of analysis is bad logic and worse history. Historically, penal brutality has varied over time in proportion to the threat posed by criminals to society. The sixteenth century was more brutal than the fifteenth from the standpoint of mass executions, because the threat had become greater in the sixteenth century. Every society has done whatever had to be done to suppress criminality, and notions of progress have had nothing to do with the measures taken. Moreover, the protection of society has always involved punishment—revenge of some sort upon the offender for violating social values. The Puritans were quite frank about the connection and willing to accept moral responsibility. They understood what modern penologists sometimes forget: that punishment cannot be turned into a gentle science without compromising its purpose.[8]

One key assumption underlying all Puritan penal practices was belief in the reality of evil. Puritans subscribed to the idea of innate human wickedness, a notion at odds with the sociological approach to crime. They saw no causal connection between crime and poverty. After all, the overwhelming majority of poor people were not criminals, while persons of wealth and social standing sometimes committed unspeakable crimes. Crime seemed to involve moral choices unrelated to the offender's place in society. These perceptions were reinforced by the fact that colonial people did not feel trapped by complex forces beyond their control. Hard work and good habits brought tangible rewards in a society where land was cheap and opportunities abounded. Those who chose crime over honest living could expect no sympathy when the time came for a reckoning. Sympathy went out to the victim, not to the perpetrator of the offense.

While the Puritans held offenders strictly accountable, they did not permanently exclude them from society. Once punishment had been inflicted, the books were considered closed on the offense. The offender could then start over with almost a clean slate. A policy of permanent exclusion would have been against the public interest, particularly during the early years when social cohesion was vitally important. Former offenders who mended their ways often managed to reintegrate themselves completely in the life of the community. Some even served as constables, selectmen, and tithingmen, and at least one became a justice of the peace. Social redemption usually brought with it restoration of church membership. Those who sincerely repented regained membership despite convictions for offenses ranging from fornication to homicide. Given the political and social importance of readmission, the churches played a useful role in turning wrongdoers into honest citizens.[9]

But forgiveness came only after offenders had suffered for the harm they had done. Their rehabilitation never took precedence over punishing the offense. To have neglected the latter would have caused moral confusion and undermined public confidence in the justice system. The first duty of the state was to punish offenses so severely that no one would be tempted to follow the culprit's example. Not to do so would breach the state's obligation to the victim, who had waived the right to private vengeance on the assumption that the offense would be punished. The just claims of the victim could not be ignored without bringing public justice into disrepute and weakening the social contract. So offenders had to be punished, not just for the sake of punishing them, but to hold society together. While the Puritans lived in a simpler time, their approach to crime and punishment speaks cogently across the centuries. The modern world has become a vastly different place, but they may yet have something important to say to the present.

Appendix A

Crimes Punishable by Death

New Plymouth[1]

LAWS OF 1636

1. Treason
2. Rebellion
3. Murder
4. Witchcraft
5. Arson
6. Sodomy (male)
7. Rape
8. Bestiality
9. Adultery (death penalty not mandatory)

LAWS OF 1658

1. Treason
2. Rebellion
3. Murder
4. Witchcraft
5. Arson
6. Sodomy (male)
7. Rape
8. Bestiality

LAWS OF 1671

1. Idolatry
2. Blasphemy
3. Treason
4. Rebellion
5. Murder
6. Manslaughter (involving anger or cruelty)
7. Killing through guile
8. Witchcraft
9. Bestiality
10. Sodomy (male)
11. Perjury (to take life)
12. Manstealing
13. Cursing a natural parent
14. Smiting a natural parent
15. Defiance by a rebellious son
16. Rape
17. Fornication with female under age ten
18. Arson
19. Burglary (3d offense)
20. Robbery (3d offense)
21. Profaning the Sabbath (provocatively)

187

Appendix A

LAWS OF 1684

1. Idolatry
2. Blasphemy
3. Treason
4. Rebellion
5. Murder
6. Manslaughter (involving anger or cruelty)
7. Killing through guile
8. Witchcraft
9. Bestiality
10. Sodomy (male)
11. Perjury (to take life)
12. Manstealing
13. Cursing a natural parent
14. Smiting a natural parent
15. Defiance by a rebellious son
16. Rape
17. Fornication with female under age ten
18. Arson
19. Burglary (3d offense)
20. Robbery (3d offense)
21. Profaning the Sabbath (provocatively)
22. Providing Indians with arms or ammunition
23. Military service with enemy state
24. Piracy

Massachusetts[2]

LAWS OF 1641

1. Idolatry
2. Witchcraft
3. Blasphemy
4. Murder
5. Manslaughter (involving anger or cruelty)
6. Killing through guile
7. Bestiality
8. Sodomy (male)
9. Adultery
10. Manstealing
11. Perjury (to take life)
12. Rebellion

LAWS OF 1648

1. Idolatry
2. Witchcraft
3. Blasphemy
4. Murder
5. Manslaughter (involving anger or cruelty)
6. Killing through guile
7. Bestiality
8. Sodomy (male)
9. Adultery
10. Manstealing
11. Perjury (to take life)
12. Rebellion
13. Cursing a natural parent
14. Smiting a natural parent
15. Defiance by a rebellious son
16. Rape
17. Burglary (3d offense)
18. Robbery (3d offense)
19. Return of Jesuit after banishment

LAWS OF 1660

1. Idolatry
2. Witchcraft
3. Blasphemy
4. Murder
5. Manslaughter (involving anger or cruelty)
6. Killing through guile
7. Bestiality
8. Sodomy (male)
9. Adultery
10. Manstealing
11. Perjury (to take life)
12. Rebellion
13. Cursing a natural parent
14. Smiting a natural parent
15. Defiance by a rebellious son
16. Rape
17. Burglary (3d offense)
18. Robbery (3d offense)
19. Arson

20. Return of Jesuit after banishment
21. Return of Quaker after banishment
22. Heresy

LAWS OF 1672

1. Idolatry
2. Witchcraft
3. Blasphemy
4. Murder
5. Manslaughter (involving anger or cruelty)
6. Killing through guile
7. Bestiality
8. Sodomy (male)
9. Adultery
10. Manstealing
11. Perjury (to take life)
12. Rebellion
13. Cursing a natural parent
14. Smiting a natural parent
15. Defiance by a rebellious son
16. Rape
17. Fornication with female under age ten
18. Burglary (3d offense)
19. Robbery (3d offense)
20. Arson
21. Return of Jesuit after banishment
22. Return of Quaker after banishment
23. Heresy

LAWS OF 1686

1. Idolatry
2. Witchcraft
3. Blasphemy
4. Murder
5. Manslaughter (involving anger or cruelty)
6. Killing through guile
7. Bestiality
8. Sodomy (male)
9. Adultery
10. Manstealing
11. Perjury (to take life)
12. Rebellion
13. Cursing a natural parent
14. Smiting a natural parent
15. Defiance by a rebellious son
16. Rape
17. Fornication with female under age ten
18. Burglary (3d offense)
19. Robbery (3d offense)
20. Arson
21. Return of Jesuit after banishment
22. Return of Quaker after banishment
23. Heresy
24. Piracy
25. Mutiny
26. Military service with enemy state
27. Treason

Connecticut[3]

LAWS OF 1642

1. Idolatry
2. Witchcraft
3. Blasphemy
4. Murder (killing with malice or cruelty)
5. Killing through guile
6. Bestiality
7. Sodomy (male)
8. Adultery
9. Rape
10. Manstealing
11. Perjury (to take life)
12. Rebellion

LAWS OF 1650

1. Idolatry
2. Witchcraft
3. Murder (killing with malice or cruelty)
4. Blasphemy
5. Killing through guile
6. Bestiality
7. Sodomy (male)
8. Adultery
9. Rape
10. Manstealing
11. Perjury (to take life)

Appendix A

12. Rebellion
13. Cursing a natural parent
14. Smiting a natural parent
15. Defiance by a rebellious son
16. Burglary (3d offense)
17. Robbery (3d offense)

LAWS OF 1673

1. Idolatry
2. Blasphemy
3. Witchcraft
4. Murder (killing with malice or cruelty)
5. Killing through guile
6. Bestiality
7. Sodomy (male)
8. Incest
9. Rape
10. Manstealing
11. Perjury (to take life)
12. Rebellion
13. Arson
14. Cursing a natural parent
15. Smiting a natural parent
16. Defiance by a rebellious son
17. Burglary (3d offense)
18. Robbery (3d offense)

New Haven Colony[4]

LAWS OF 1656

1. Idolatry
2. Witchcraft
3. Blasphemy
4. Murder
5. Manslaughter (involving anger or cruelty)
6. Killing through guile
7. Bestiality
8. Sodomy (male)
9. Sodomy (heterosexual)
10. Fornication with very young ("unripe") female
11. Masturbation (male)
12. Adultery
13. Manstealing
14. Perjury (to take life)
15. Rebellion
16. Cursing a natural parent
17. Smiting a natural parent
18. Defiance by a rebellious son
19. Rape (death penalty not mandatory)
20. Incest
21. Burglary (3d offense)
22. Robbery (3d offense)
23. Profaning the Sabbath (provocatively)

Rhode Island[5]

LAWS OF 1647

1. Treason
2. Murder
3. Manslaughter (intentional killing)
4. Witchcraft
5. Burglary
6. Robbery
7. Arson
8. Sodomy (male)
9. Bestiality
10. Rape
11. Fornication with female under age ten
12. Perjury (to take life)

LAWS OF 1684

1. Treason
2. Murder
3. Manslaughter (intentional killing)
4. Witchcraft
5. Burglary

190

6. Robbery
7. Arson
8. Sodomy (male)
9. Bestiality

10. Rape
11. Fornication with female under age ten

12. Military service with enemy state
13. Piracy

New Hampshire⁶

LAWS OF 1680

1. Idolatry
2. Blasphemy
3. Treason
4. Rebellion
5. Murder
6. Manslaughter (involving anger or cruelty)
7. Killing through guile
8. Witchcraft

9. Bestiality
10. Sodomy (male)
11. Perjury (to take life)
12. Manstealing
13. Cursing a natural parent
14. Smiting a natural parent

15. Defiance by a rebellious son
16. Rape
17. Fornication with female under age ten
18. Arson
19. Burglary (3d offense)
20. Robbery (3d offense)

Appendix B

Judicial Organization: Composition, Jurisdiction, and Evolution of the Courts

New Plymouth[1]

1620

GENERAL COURT

Composition	*Jurisdiction*
Governor, Deputy Governor, Assistants, Deputies	Unlimited

ASSISTANTS COURT

Governor, Deputy Governor, Assistants	Concurrent with General Court

---

1636

GENERAL COURT

Governor, Deputy Governor, Assistants, Deputies	Unlimited

ASSISTANTS COURT

Governor, Deputy Governor, Assistants	Concurrent with General Court

JUSTICES COURTS

Individual Assistants	Trial of minor offenses

1666

GENERAL COURT

Composition	*Jurisdiction*
Governor, Deputy Governor, Assistants, Deputies	Unlimited

ASSISTANTS COURT

Governor, Deputy Governor, Assistants	Concurrent with General Court; heard appeals from Justice Courts

JUSTICE COURTS

Individual Assistants	Trial of minor offenses

1671

ASSISTANTS COURT

Governor, Deputy Governor, Assistants	Unlimited (assumed all judicial functions of General Court)

JUSTICE COURTS

Individual Assistants	Trial of minor offenses

1686

ASSISTANTS COURT

Governor, Deputy Governor, Assistants	Crimes punishable by banishment, dismemberment, or death; heard appeals from County Courts

COUNTY COURTS

Assistants residing in county	Offenses not triable in Assistants Court; heard appeals from Town Courts

TOWN COURTS

Individual Assistants or Associates appointed by the General Court	Trial of minor offenses

Appendix B

Massachusetts[2]

1630

GENERAL COURT

Composition	Jurisdiction
Governor, Deputy Governor, Assistants, Deputies	Unlimited

ASSISTANTS COURT

Governor, Deputy Governor, Assistants	Concurrent with General Court

JUSTICE COURTS

Individual Assistants	Trial of minor offenses (two Assistants needed to order whippings)

1648

GENERAL COURT

Governor, Deputy Governor, Assistants, Deputies	Unlimited; heard appeals from Assistants Court

ASSISTANTS COURT

Governor, Deputy Governor, Assistants	Crimes punishable by banishment, dismemberment, or death; heard appeals from County Courts

COUNTY COURTS

Five Assistants (or substitutes appointed by General Court)	Offenses not triable in Assistants Court; heard appeals from Town Courts

STRANGERS COURT

Governor or Deputy Governor and two Assistants (three Assistants if Governor and Deputy Governor unavailable)	Concurrent with County Courts for trial of nonresidents; no right of appeal

194

TOWN COURTS

Composition	*Jurisdiction*
Resident Assistant (or three Commissioners appointed by General Court)	Trial of minor offenses

---

1660

GENERAL COURT

Governor, Deputy Governor, Assistants, Deputies	Unlimited; heard appeals from Assistants Court

ASSISTANTS COURT

Governor, Deputy Governor, Assistants	Crimes punishable by banishment, dismemberment, or death; heard appeals from County Courts and Commissioners Court of Boston

COUNTY COURTS

Five Assistants (or substitutes appointed by General Court)	Offenses not triable in Assistants Court; heard appeals from Town Courts

STRANGERS COURT

Governor or Deputy Governor and two Assistants (three Assistants if Governor and Deputy Governor unavailable)	Concurrent with County Courts for trial of nonresidents; no right of appeal

COMMISSIONERS COURT OF BOSTON

Seven Commissioners appointed by General Court (three if joined by an Assistant)	Trial of minor offenses

TOWN COURTS

Resident Assistant (or three Commissioners appointed by General Court)	Trial of minor offenses

Appendix B

Connecticut[3]

1639

GENERAL COURT

Composition	*Jurisdiction*
Governor, Deputy Governor, Magistrates, Deputies	Unlimited

PARTICULAR COURT

Governor, Deputy Governor, Magistrates	Unlimited (judicial subdivision of General Court)

1650

GENERAL COURT

Governor, Deputy Governor, Magistrates, Deputies	Unlimited

PARTICULAR COURT

Governor, Deputy Governor, Magistrates	Concurrent with General Court

TOWN COURTS

Individual Magistrates	Trial of minor offenses

1673

GENERAL COURT

Governor, Deputy Governor, Magistrates, Deputies	Unlimited; heard appeals from Assistants Court

ASSISTANTS COURT

Governor, Deputy Governor, Magistrates (Assistants)	Crimes punishable by banishment, dismemberment, or death; heard appeals from County Courts

COUNTY COURTS

Three Magistrates (or one Magistrate and two Commissioners appointed by General Court)	Offenses not triable in Assistants Court; heard appeals from Town Courts

TOWN COURTS

Composition	*Jurisdiction*
Individual Magistrates or Commissioners appointed by General Court	Trial of minor offenses

New Haven Colony[4]

Pre-1643

TOWN COURTS

Local governing body	Unlimited

1643

GENERAL COURT

Governor, Deputy Governor, Magistrates, Deputies	Unlimited

MAGISTRATES COURT

Governor, Deputy Governor, Magistrates	Serious offenses; heard appeals from Plantation Courts

PLANTATION COURTS

Local Magistrates or judges elected by freemen of the towns	Trial of minor offenses

1656

GENERAL COURT

Governor, Deputy Governor, Magistrates, Deputies	Unlimited; heard appeals from Magistrates Court

MAGISTRATES COURT

Governor, Deputy Governor, Magistrates	Serious offenses; heard appeals from Plantation Courts

PLANTATION COURTS

Local Magistrates or judges elected by freemen of the towns	Trial of minor offenses

Appendix B

STRANGERS COURTS

Composition	*Jurisdiction*
Three Magistrates	Trial of nonresidents for offenses not punishable by death (otherwise triable in Plantation Courts)

JUSTICE COURTS

Individual Magistrates or Deputies	Trial of minor offenses when Plantation Courts not in session

CONSTABLE'S COURT

Constable with one or two local freemen	Offenses involving profanity or cursing when no judicial officer was available

Rhode Island[5]

Pre-1640

TOWN COURTS

Local governing body	Unlimited

1640

(NEWPORT AND PORTSMOUTH)
PARTICULAR COURT

Governor, Deputy Governor, Assistants	Unlimited

JUSTICE COURTS

Governor, Deputy Governor, or individual Assistants sitting alone	Trial of minor offenses

---

1647

GENERAL COURT OF TRIALS

President, Assistants, and principal officers of host town	Crimes punishable by disfranchisement, banishment, dismemberment, or death

TOWN COURTS

Composition
Locally determined

Jurisdiction
Offenses not triable in General Court of Trials

JUSTICE COURTS

President or individual Assistants

Trial of minor offenses

1664

GENERAL COURT OF TRIALS

Governor, Deputy Governor, Assistants

Trial of serious offenses; heard appeals from Town Courts

ASSISTANTS COURTS (PROVIDENCE AND WARWICK)

Three Assistants

Concurrent with General Court of Trials

TOWN COURTS

Locally determined

Offenses not triable in General Court of Trials

JUSTICE COURTS

Governor, Deputy Governor, or individual Assistants

Trial of minor offenses

New Hampshire[6]

1680

GENERAL ASSEMBLY

President, Councillors, Deputies

Heard appeals from Inferior Court

INFERIOR COURT

President and Councillors

Unlimited; appeals allowed to England (automatic in capital cases)

JUSTICE COURTS

Individual Councillors

Trial of minor offenses punishable by fines up to 10 shillings or by whippings not exceeding 10 lashes

Appendix C

Typical Crimes and Penalties

Massachusetts Assistants Court, 1630–1644[1]

		PENALTIES								
CRIMES	CASES	Fine	Whipping	Stocks/Bilboes	Death	Restitution	Service	Admonition	Badge of Shame	Other[2]
1. Drunkenness	99	73	8	8				1	3	13
2. Fornication	22	8	12	2					2	4
3. Lewdness	14	1	10					1	1	3
4. Adultery	3		1		2					
5. Theft	50	4	27			15	8			9
6. Assault	9	2	4					1		2
7. Cursing/ swearing	24	9	5	3						7
8. Offensive speech	4							4		
9. Sabbath-breaking	4	1	2	1						
10. Murder	1				1					
11. Rape	1		1							
12. Attempted rape	3		3							2
13. Runaway servant	22		19				9			3
14. Stubbornness by servant	7		4							3
15. Overcharging for goods/ services	6	6								
16. Liquor offenses	17	15								2
17. Contempt of authority	17	12								5
18. Contempt of court	14	13								1
19. Attempted bestiality	1		1							1
20. Miscellaneous[3]	137	70	35	5	1	1		4	1	38
Totals	455	214	132	19	4	16	17	11	7	93

The case samples in Appendix C are illustrative and not quantifications of so-called crime rates for particular periods. Since the court sometimes imposed several penalties for the same offense, penalties often exceed the offenses tried.

Appendix C

Massachusetts Assistants Court, 1672–1684*

| | | PENALTIES | | | | | | | | | |
CRIMES	CASES	Fine	Whipping	Branding	Death	Restitution	Humiliation	Banishment	Pillory	Admonition	Other⁴
1. Adultery	5		4				4	1			
2. Adulterous behavior	8						8	1			
3. Abetting adultery	1		1			1					
4. Fornication	1		1								
5. Prostitution	1		1					1			
6. Bestiality	1				1						
7. Blasphemy	2		1								1
8. Arson	2				2						
9. Theft	6		4			4					2
10. Burglary	1		1	1		1					
11. Murder	6				6						
12. Manslaughter	1			1							1
13. Negligent homicide	6	5									6
14. Rape	5		1		4						1
15. Quaker meetings	11									11	
16. Coin clipping	1								1		1
17. Perjury	2								2		
18. Contempt of authority	2	1						1			
19. Piracy	5				5						
20. Concealing stolen property	3	3	2								
21. Miscellaneous⁵	26	12	3	1			1	2			4
Totals	96	21	19	3	18	5	14	6	3	11	16

*Reduced volume of cases reflects transfer of trial jurisdiction to County Courts.

Suffolk County Court, Massachusetts, 1671–1675[6]

PENALTIES

CRIMES	CASES	Fine	Whipping	Fine or whipping	Branding	Admonition	Restitution	Probation	Prison	Damages	Other[7]
1. Drunkenness	10	7	2					2			
2. Fornication	59	9	15	33							5
3. Lascivious behavior	13	1	7	2		1		1			1
4. Theft	50	5	28	4		1	37	2			2
5. Burglary	11		5		6		5				1
6. Cursing/ swearing	15	6	3	4		2		3			
7. Sabbath-breaking	17		5			9		5			
8. Lying	6	1	2			1			1		1
9. Liquor offenses	18	18				1		4			
10. Selling liquor to Indians	7	4	1			1		1			
11. Contempt of authority	5	2		1		2					
12. Curfew violations	12	6				3		3			
13. Assault	54	18	9	6		5		7		15	16
14. Absence from church	11	7				4					
15. Quaker meetings	12	8				4					
16. Bastardy	8		1			1		1			6
17. Idleness	6					2		2	2		
18. Jail-breaking	8	3	2	1				3			
19. Disorderly conduct	16	2	1	1		5		4	2		1
20. Miscellaneous[8]	81	47	7	4		10		5	1	2	5
Totals	419	144	88	56	6	52	42	43	6	17	38

Appendix C

Suffolk County Court, Massachusetts, 1676–1680

CRIMES	CASES	PENALTIES								
		Fine	Whipping	Fine or whipping	Branding	Admonition	Restitution	Probation	Damages	Other[9]
1. Drunkenness	11	7		2		2		1		
2. Fornication	47	5	17	26						
3. Lascivious behavior	14	5	4	4				1		
4. Theft	52	2	23	5			49			4
5. Burglary	1				1					
6. Cursing/ swearing	8	4		4		1				
7. Sabbath-breaking	6	3				3				
8. Liquor offenses	29	28				1				
9. Selling liquor to Indians	8	8								
10. Receiving stolen goods	3	1	1						2	
11. Curfew violations	10	8				1		1		
12. Assault	16	12	3					1	9	3
13. Fighting	10	10							1	
14. Absence from church	8	2		1		5				
15. Misconduct in church	6		4			2				
16. Bastardy	9									9
17. Disorderly conduct	10	4				3		3	1	
18. Idleness	4	1	2	1						1
19. Keeping a disorderly house	4	4				1				
20. Miscellaneous[10]	79	36	8	4		12	1	2	6	4
Totals	335	140	62	47	1	31	50	9	19	21

New Plymouth Judicial Records, 1633–1640[11]
(General Court and Assistants Court)

CRIMES	CASES	Fine	Whipping	Branding	Stocks	Admonition	Prison	Badge of shame	Other[12]
1. Drunkenness	13	7	2		2	2			1
2. Fornication	13	2	4		7				1
3. Lascivious behavior	6		6	1					1
4. Adultery	2		2					1	
5. Sabbath-breaking	5	2	2		1	1			
6. Assault	7	7							1
7. Fighting	4	4							1
8. Disorderly living	4								4
9. Lying	2								2
10. Speaking against government	4	3							1
11. Smoking in public	5	5							
12. Harboring strangers illegally	8						8		
13. Overcharging for goods/services	4	4							
14. Liquor offenses	5	5							
15. Miscellaneous[13]	26	11	4		4		2		6
Totals	108	50	20	1	14	3	10	1	18

PENALTIES

New Plymouth Judicial Records, 1652–1661 [14]
(General Court and Assistants Court)

PENALTIES

CRIMES	CASES	Fine	Whipping	Fine or whipping	Branding	Stocks	Admonition	Badge of shame	Other [15]
1. Drunkenness	14	14							
2. Fornication	21	13	3						6
3. Lascivious behavior	4	4							
4. Theft	12	4	2			5			
5. Assault	2	2							
6. Blasphemy	3			2				1	
7. Lying	3	3							
8. Selling firearms to Indians	5	5							
9. Manslaughter	1				1				1
10. Contempt of authority	15	13	1						1
11. Sabbath-breaking	4	2							2
12. Absence from church	4	1					3		
13. Attending Quaker meetings	26	26							
14. Holding Quaker meetings	4	4							
15. Harboring Quakers	2	2							
16. Miscellaneous [16]	52	22	7	2		7	5	1	9
Totals	172	115	12	5	1	12	8	2	19

Connecticut Judicial Records, 1636–1650 [17]
(General Court and Assistants Court)

PENALTIES

CRIMES	CASES	Fine	Whipping	Branding	Pillory	Stocks	Prison	Restitution	Admonition	Probation	Confession of fault	No disposition
1. Drunkenness	11	11							5	2		
2. Fornication	3		2									1
3. Lascivious behavior	3	1	2									
4. Theft	10	4	4	2				6				
5. Profanity	3	1	2		1		1					
6. Sabbath-breaking	3	1					2					
7. Adultery	1											1
8. Rape	1		1	1								
9. Bestiality	2											2
10. Masturbation (male)	4											4
11. Assault	2	1	1									
12. Abetting rape	2		2									
13. Liquor offenses	4	4										
14. Contempt of authority	3	3									1	
15. Selling firearms to Indians	5	5										
16. Miscellaneous [18]	21	17	5		1	2	1			2		
Totals	78	48	19	3	2	2	4	6	5	4	1	8

Connecticut Judicial Records, 1651–1663
(General Court and Particular Court)

CRIMES	CASES	Fine	Whipping	Pillory	Stocks	Fine or stocks	Restitution	Prison	Humiliation	Probation	Banishment
						PENALTIES					
1. Drunkenness	16	15			1						
2. Blasphemy	1							1	1		
3. Lascivious behavior	1	1						1		1	
4. Theft	1	1			1		1	1			
5. Profanity	1								1		
6. Sabbath-breaking	6	6			2						
7. Burglary	2		2					1			
8. Arson	1		1					1			
9. Assault	1	1									
10. Fighting	2		1		1			1			
11. Contempt of authority	4	1						1		2	1
12. Selling liquor to Indians	8	7							1		
13. Lying	3	1			2						
14. Card-playing	4	4									
15. Liquor violations	5	5									
16. Miscellaneous[19]	25	15	2	1		1		1		2	
Totals	81	57	6	1	7	1	1	8	1	7	1

New Haven Colony Judicial Records, 1639–1649 [20]
(General Court and Magistrates Court)

PENALTIES

CRIMES	CASES	Fine	Whipping	Stocks	Death	Restitution	Prison	Work in irons	Humiliation	Banishment	Unspecified	No disposition
1. Drunkenness	24	18	5	1							1	
2. Fornication	10	4	6				2	2				
3. Lascivious behavior	7	1	6						1			
4. Theft	10		9			5				1		
5. Burglary	1		1					1				
6. Sabbath-breaking	2		1	1								
7. Slander	1	1										
8. Bestiality	1				1							
9. Not reporting sexual solicitation	2		2									
10. Making false accusation	1			1								
11. Contempt of authority	1											1
12. Lying, stealing, counterfeiting	1		1					1				
13. Lying and running away by servant	1		1									
Totals	62	24	32	3	1	5	2	2	2	1	1	2

Rhode Island General Court of Trials, 1655–1670[21]

PENALTIES

CRIMES	CASES	Fine	Whipping	Fine or whipping	Restitution	Prison or bond	Confession of fault	Assist at whipping	Loss of ear	Death	Probation	No disposition
1. Fornication	19	8	2	6								4
2. Lascivious behavior	1	1										
3. Adultery	4	3	3	1								
4. Assault	5	2										3
5. Theft	7		5	1	7			1	1			
6. Murder	1									1		
7. Manslaughter	1									1		
8. Perjury	2	1										1
9. Disorderly conduct	6	4									3	
10. Jail-breaking	2											2
11. Absent from military training	2										2	
12. Drunk in court	1	1										
13. Sale of gunpowder to Indians	1	1										
14. Refusal to assist constable	1										1	
15. Contempt of authority	4					2	2				3	
Totals	57	21	10	8	7	2	2	1	1	2	9	10

Appendix D

Witchcraft Cases

Massachusetts

YEAR	DEFENDANT	OUTCOME
1648	Margaret Jones	Convicted and executed
1649 (?)	Alice Lake	Convicted and executed
1649 (?)	Goody Kendall	Convicted and executed
1651	Mary Parsons (of Springfield)	Not convicted of witchcraft,[1] but executed for murder
1651	Hugh Parsons	Guilty verdict overturned by court; released
1652	John Bradstreet	Not convicted of witchcraft; fined for lying
1656	Eunice Cole	Not convicted[2]
1656	Anne Hibbens	Convicted and executed
1656	Jane Walford	Not convicted
1659	John Godfrey	Not convicted
1659	Winifred Holman	Not convicted
1659	Mary Holman	Not convicted
1662	John Godfrey	Not convicted
1665	John Godfrey	Not convicted
1669	Susanna Martin	Not convicted
1669	Robert Williams	Not convicted of witchcraft; fined and whipped for lying
1670	Ann Burt	Not convicted

1673	Eunice Cole	Not convicted
1673	Anna Edmunds	Not convicted
1675	Mary Parsons (of Northampton)	Not convicted
1679	Caleb Powell	Not convicted
1679	Elizabeth Morse	Convicted; reprieved and released by court
1680	Bridget Oliver	Not convicted
1681	Mary Hale	Not convicted
1683	James Fuller	Not convicted
1683	Mary Webster	Not convicted
1688	Goody Glover	Confessed; executed

Connecticut

1647	Alice Young	Convicted and executed
1648	Mary Johnson	Confessed; executed
1651	Joan Carrington	Convicted and executed
1651	John Carrington	Convicted and executed
1651	Goody Bassett	Confessed; executed
1653	Goody Knapp	Convicted and executed
1654	Lydia Gilbert	Convicted; probably executed
1658	Elizabeth Garlick	Not convicted; bound to good behavior
1661	Margaret Jennings	Jury deadlocked; fled
1661	Nicholas Jennings	Jury deadlocked; fled
1662	Judith Varlet[3]	Case dropped; released
1662	Mary Sanford	Convicted and executed
1662	Andrew Sanford	Not convicted
1662	Goody Ayres	Fled before verdict
1663	Rebecca Greensmith	Confessed; executed
1663	Nathaniel Greensmith	Convicted and executed
1663	Mary Barnes	Convicted; probably executed
1663	Elizabeth Seager	Not convicted
1663	Elizabeth Seager	Not convicted
1665	John Browne[4]	Not convicted; admonished
1665	Elizabeth Seager	Convicted; verdict overturned by court

1669	Katherine Harrison	Convicted; verdict overturned by court; ordered to leave town
1692	Mercy Disborough	Convicted; reprieved and released by court
1692	Elizabeth Clawson	Not convicted

New Haven Colony

1655	Elizabeth Godman	Not convicted; bound to good behavior
1655	Goody Bailey	Not convicted; ordered to leave town
1655	Nicholas Bailey	Not convicted; ordered to leave town

New Plymouth

| 1676 | Mary Ingham | Not convicted |

New Hampshire

1680	Rachel Fuller	Not convicted
1680	Isabella Towle	Not convicted
1680	Eunice Cole	Not convicted of witchcraft, but jailed for misconduct

Abbreviations Used in the

Notes

AALHS	*Anglo-American Legal History Series*
AHR	*American Historical Review*
AJLH	*American Journal of Legal History*
ALR	*American Law Review*
CLR	*Columbia Law Review*
Conn. Col. Recs.	*The Public Records of the Colony of Connecticut, 1636–1776*, ed. J. Hammond Trumbull and Charles J. Hoadly, 15 vols. (Hartford: Lockwood & Brainard, 1850–90)
Conn. Laws (1673)	*The Laws of Connecticut: An Exact Reprint of the Edition of 1673*, ed. George Brinley (Hartford: Private printing, 1865)
"Conn. Part. Ct. Recs."	"Records of the Particular Court of Connecticut, 1639–1663," *Connecticut Historical Society Collections*, 22 (1928)
CSMP	*Colonial Society of Massachusetts Publications*
EIHC	*Essex Institute Historical Collections*
EHR	*English Historical Review*
Essex Ct. Recs.	*Records and Files of the Quarterly Courts of Essex County, Massachusetts*, ed. George F. Dow, 8 vols. (Salem, Mass.: Essex Institute, 1911–21)
Ind. L.J.	*Indiana Law Journal*
JHI	*Journal of the History of Ideas*
JIH	*Journal of Interdisciplinary History*
JSH	*Journal of Social History*

Abbreviations Used in the Notes

Mass. Assist. Ct. Recs.	*Records of the Court of Assistants of the Massachusetts Bay, 1630–1692*, ed. John B. Noble, 3 vols. (Boston: Pub. by Suffolk County, 1901–28)
Mass. Col. Laws (1648)	*The Laws and Liberties of Massachusetts, 1648*, ed. Max Farrand (Cambridge, Mass.: Harvard University Press, 1929)
Mass. Col. Laws (1660)	*The Colonial Laws of Massachusetts. Reprinted from the Edition of 1660, with the Supplements to 1672*, ed. William H. Whitmore (Boston: Rockwell & Churchill, 1889)
Mass. Col. Laws (1672)	*The Colonial Laws of Massachusetts. Reprinted from the Edition of 1672, with the Supplements through 1686*, ed. William H. Whitmore (Boston: Rockwell & Churchill, 1887)
Mass. Col. Recs.	*Records of the Governor and Company of the Massachusetts Bay in New England, 1628–1674*, ed. Nathaniel B. Shurtleff, 5 vols. (Boston: White, 1853–54)
Me. Ct. Recs.	*Province and Court Records of Maine*, 5 vols. (Portland: Maine Historical Society, 1928–64)
MHS Proc.	*Massachusetts Historical Society Proceedings*
Minn. L.R.	*Minnesota Law Review*
MLR	*Michigan Law Review*
NEQ	*New England Quarterly*
"New Hamp. Ct. Recs."	"New Hampshire Court Records, 1640–1692," *New Hampshire State Papers Series*, 40 (1943)
New Hamp. Laws	*Laws of New Hampshire, Including Public and Private Acts and Resolves and Royal Commissions and Instructions*, ed. Albert S. Batchellor et al., 10 vols. (Manchester, N.H.: Clarke, 1904–1922)
New Haven Col. Recs. 1	*Records of the Colony and Plantation of New Haven, 1638–1649*, ed. Charles J. Hoadly (Hartford: Case, Tiffany, 1857)
New Haven Col. Recs. 2	*Records of the Colony or Jurisdiction of New Haven, 1653 to the Union*, ed. Charles J. Hoadly (Hartford: Case, Lockwood, 1858)
New Haven Town Recs.	*New Haven Town Records, 1649–1769*, ed. Franklin B. Dexter and Zara J. Powers, 3 vols. (New Haven: New Haven Colony Historical Society, 1917–62)
PAH	*Perspectives in American History*

Ply. Col. Laws	*The Compact with the Charter and Laws of the Colony of New Plymouth,* ed. William Brigham (Boston: Dutton & Wentworth, 1836)
Ply. Col. Recs.	*Records of the Colony of New Plymouth in New England, 1620–1692,* ed. Nathaniel B. Shurtleff and David Pulsifer, 12 vols. (Boston: White, 1855–61)
Ply. Town Recs.	*Records of the Town of Plymouth,* 3 vols. (Plymouth, Mass.: Avery & Doten, 1889–1903)
Provid. Ct. Recs.	*Records of the Court of Trials of the Colony of Providence Plantations, 1647–1670,* 2 vols. (Providence: Rhode Island Historical Society, 1920–22)
Provid. Town Recs.	*The Early Records of the Town of Providence,* 21 vols. (Providence: Snow & Fornbrow, 1892–1915)
Pyn. Ct. Rec.	*Colonial Justice in Western Massachusetts (1639–1702): The Pynchon Court Record,* ed. Joseph H. Smith (Cambridge, Mass.: Harvard University Press, 1961)
R.I. Col. Laws	*Laws and Acts of Her Majesty's Colony of Rhode Island and Providence Plantations, Made from the First Settlement in 1636 to 1705* (Providence: Rider, 1896)
R.I. Col. Recs.	*Records of the Colony of Rhode Island and Providence Plantations in New England, 1636–1792,* ed. John R. Bartlett, 10 vols. (Providence: Greene, 1856–65)
R.I. Gen. Assem. (1647)	*The Proceedings of the First General Assembly of "The Incorporation of Providence Plantations," and the Code of Laws Adopted by That Assembly, in 1647,* ed. William R. Staples (Providence: Burnett, 1847)
RLS	*Research in Law and Sociology*
"Suffolk Ct. Recs."	"Records of the Suffolk County Court, 1671–1680," ed. Samuel E. Morison, 2 vols. *Colonial Society of Massachusetts Publications* 29–30 (1933)
Va. L.R.	*Virginia Law Review*
VULR	*Valparaiso University Law Review*
WMQ	*William and Mary Quarterly*
YLJ	*Yale Law Journal*

Notes

Chapter 1: Laws for Living Saints

Relevant dates not in the text or citation, follow the page reference. When two dates follow a code citation, the first indicates the year of the code and the second, following the pagination, indicates the year in which the law was passed.

1. See *The Works of Mr. Richard Hooker in Eight Books of the Laws of Ecclesiastical Polity*, 3 vols. (London: Clarke, 1821), 1:184–95.

2. Richard B. Morris, *Studies in the History of American Law*, 2d ed. (1930; reprint Philadelphia: Mitchell, 1959), 21–23.

3. See Carol F. Lee, "Discretionary Justice in Early Massachusetts," *EIHC* 112 (1976): 120ff.

4. George L. Haskins, *Law and Authority in Early Massachusetts* (New York: Macmillan, 1960), 174.

5. David T. Konig, *Law and Society in Puritan Massachusetts: Essex County, 1629–1692* (Chapel Hill: University of North Carolina Press, 1979), 5–6, 9.

6. Bradley Chapin, *Criminal Justice in Colonial America, 1606–1660* (Athens: University of Georgia Press, 1983), 20.

7. Lee, "Discretionary Justice in Early Massachusetts," 122–25.

8. William Bradford, *Of Plymouth Plantation*, ed. Samuel E. Morison (New York: Knopf, 1952), 234.

9. *Mass. Assist. Ct. Recs.* 2:19.

10. Chapin, *Criminal Justice in Colonial America*, 19–20.

11. John Winthrop, *History of New England* (or *Journal*), ed. James K. Hosmer, 2 vols. (New York: Scribner's, 1908), 1:151, 2:49–52.

12. *The Winthrop Papers*, 5 vols. (Boston: Massachusetts Historical Society, 1929–47), 4:473. See Edwin Powers, *Crime and Punishment in Early Massachusetts, 1620–1692* (Boston: Beacon Press, 1966), 273, 449.

13. Winthrop, *Journal* 1:323–24.

14. Thomas G. Barnes, "Law and Liberty (and Order) in Early Massachusetts," in *The English Legal System: Carryover to the Colonies* (Los Angeles: University of California, 1975), 72–73.

15. *Mass. Col. Recs.* 2:12–13.

16. Star Chamber punishments were fine, imprisonment, and mutilation without reference to statutory limits. See George M. Trevelyan, *England under the Stuarts* (New York: Barnes & Noble, 1965), 157.

17. *Mass. Col. Recs.* 2:199.

18. Winthrop, *Journal* 1:323.

19. Haskins, *Law and Authority in Early Massachusetts*, 123.

20. *Mass. Col. Recs.* 1:147, 174–75.

21. *Ply. Col. Laws*, 19–20, 35–43.

22. George D. Langdon, Jr., *Pilgrim Colony* (New Haven: Yale University Press, 1966), 92–96.

23. Charles M. Andrews, *The Colonial Period of American History*, 4 vols. (New Haven: Yale University Press, 1934–38), 1:430–31; Julius Goebel, Jr., "King's Law and Local Custom in Seventeenth Century New England," *CLR* 31 (1931): 429n.

24. George L. Haskins, "Codification of the Law in Colonial Massachusetts: A Study in Comparative Law," *Ind. L.J.* 30 (1954): 6.

25. Winthrop, *Journal* 1:196.

26. Morris, *Studies in the History of American Law*, 28–29.

27. Isabel M. Calder, "John Cotton's 'Moses His Judicials,'" *CSMP* 28 (1931): 86–94; Worthington C. Ford, "Cotton's 'Moses His Judicials,'" *MHS Proc.* 16 (1902): 274–84.

28. Samuel E. Morison, *Builders of the Bay Colony* (Boston: Houghton Mifflin, 1930), 228–29.

29. Calder, "John Cotton's 'Moses His Judicials,'" 88–89.

30. Morison, *Builders of the Bay Colony*, 228–29; Haskins, *Law and Authority in Early Massachusetts*, 126–27.

31. Winthrop, *Journal* 1:323–24, 2:48–49.

32. Andrews, *Colonial Period of American History*, 1:455–56; Haskins, *Law and Authority in Early Massachusetts*, 106, 127–29.

33. *Mass. Col. Laws* (1660), 33–53.

34. Ibid., 33.

35. Haskins, "Codification of the Law in Colonial Massachusetts," 8; Morris, *Studies in the History of American Law*, 29–30.

36. Winthrop, *Journal* 2:48–49.

37. Ibid., 271, 289, 297–99.

38. Morison, *Builders of the Bay Colony*, 261–63.

39. *Mass. Col. Recs.* 2:168–69.

40. *Mass. Col. Laws* (1648), A2.

41. Haskins, "Codification of the Law in Colonial Massachusetts," 3–4.

42. Morison, *Builders of the Bay Colony*, 264.

43. *Mass. Col. Recs.* 1:147.

44. *Mass. Col. Laws* (1648), 1.

45. Julius Goebel, Jr., *Felony and Misdemeanor* (New York: The Commonwealth Fund, 1937), 237–38.

46. Theodore F. T. Plucknett, *A Concise History of the Common Law* (Boston: Little, Brown, 1956), 442–43.

47. George W. Dalzell, *Benefit of Clergy in America* (Winston-Salem, N.C.: John F. Blair, 1955), 9–26.

48. See N. E. H. Hull, *Female Felons* (Urbana: University of Illinois Press, 1987), 21–23.

49. Goebel, *Felony and Misdemeanor*, xxviii–xxix.

50. Plucknett, *Concise History of the Common Law*, 455–59.

51. Michael Dalton, *The Country Justice* (London: Society of Stationers, 1618).

52. William Lambarde, *Eirenarcha, or Of the Office of the Justices of the Peace* (London: n.p., 1581).

53. Barnes, "Law and Liberty (and Order) in Early Massachusetts," 85. See also Haskins, *Law and Authority in Early Massachusetts*, 135.

54. *Mass. Col. Recs.* 2:212.

55. Sir Edward Coke, *The First of the Institutes of the Laws of England; or a Commentary upon Littleton*, 2 vols. (Philadelphia: Small, 1853), 1:11b.

56. Mark DeWolfe Howe, "The Sources and Nature of Law in Colonial Massachusetts," in *Law and Authority in Colonial America*, ed. George A. Billias (Barre, Mass.: Barre Publishers, 1965), 11–12.

57. Haskins, *Law and Authority in Early Massachusetts*, 163–75.

58. F. Douglas Price, "The Abuses of Excommunication and the Decline of Ecclesiastical Discipline under Queen Elizabeth," *EHR* 57 (1942): 114.

59. Ronald A. Marchant, *The Puritans and the Church Courts in the Diocese of York, 1560–1642* (London: Longmans, Green, 1960), 1–2.

60. Carson I. A. Ritchie, *The Ecclesiastical Courts of York* (Arbroath: The Herald Press, 1956), 7–8.

61. Price, "The Abuses of Excommunication," 108.

62. Marchant, *The Puritans and the Church Courts in the Diocese of York*, 204.

63. Trevelyan, *England under the Stuarts*, 167.

64. Haskins, *Law and Authority in Early Massachusetts*, 13, 183–84.

65. Emil Oberholzer, Jr., *Delinquent Saints: Disciplinary Action in the Early Congregational Churches of Massachusetts* (New York: Columbia University Press, 1958), passim.

66. George L. Haskins, "Ecclesiastical Antecedents of Criminal Punishment in Early Massachusetts," *MHS Proc.* 72 (1960): 24–27.

67. *Mass. Col. Recs.* 1:242 (1638).

68. David H. Flaherty, "Law and the Enforcement of Morals in Early America," *PAH* 5 (1971): 219–22.

69. Trevelyan, *England under the Stuarts*, 157.

70. Plucknett, *Concise History of the Common Law*, 459.

71. Barnes, "Law and Liberty (and Order) in Early Massachusetts," 78–79.

72. Goebel, "King's Law and Local Custom in Seventeenth Century New England," 433 n.

73. *Ply. Col. Laws*, 36.

74. *Mass. Col. Laws* (1660), 33.

75. *Mass. Col. Laws* (1648), A2.

76. Haskins, *Law and Authority in Early Massachusetts*, 120, 136.

77. Introduction to *Mass. Col. Laws* (1648), viii.

78. Stefan A. Riesenfeld, "Law-Making and Legislative Precedent in American Legal History," *Minn. L.R.* 33 (1949): 106.

79. Barnes, "Law and Liberty (and Order) in Early Massachusetts," 65–72.

80. *Mass. Col. Laws* (1648), A3.

81. Riesenfeld, "Law-Making and Legislative Precedent in American Legal History," 132.

82. William H. Fry, *New Hampshire as a Royal Province* (New York: Columbia University Press, 1908), 37–39; John G. Reid, *Maine, Charles II and Massachusetts* (Portland, Me.: Maine Historical Society, 1977), 14–22.

83. Henry S. Burrage, *The Beginnings of Colonial Maine* (Portland, Me.: Marks Printing House, 1914), 370–82; Jeremy Belknap, *The History of New Hampshire*, 2 vols. (New York: Johnson Reprint, 1970), 1:53–65, 85–90; Fry, *New Hampshire as a Royal Province*, 52–65.

84. Herbert L. Osgood, *The American Colonies in the Seventeenth Century*, 3 vols. (New York: Columbia University Press, 1904–1907), 3:338–39.

85. *Provincial Papers: Documents and Papers Relating to the Province of New Hampshire, from the Earliest Period of Settlement, 1623–1770*, ed. Nathaniel Bouton, 7 vols. (Concord and Nashua: Jenks, 1867–73), 1:474.

86. Fry, *New Hampshire as a Royal Province*, 431–32.

87. Langdon, *Pilgrim Colony*, 208–10.

88. *Ply. Col. Laws*, 105–21; Riesenfeld, "Law-Making and Legislative Precedent in American Legal History," 132.

89. *Conn. Col. Recs.* 1:20–25.

90. *New Haven Col. Recs.* 1:14–15, 112; Andrews, *Colonial Period of American History* 2:157–58; Isabel M. Calder, "John Cotton and the New Haven Colony," *NEQ* 3 (1930): 89–94.

91. Osgood, *American Colonies in the Seventeenth Century* 1:309–11; Morison, *Builders of the Bay Colony*, 229.

92. *Conn. Col. Recs.* 1:509–63; Riesenfeld, "Law-Making and Legislative Precedent in American Legal History," 132.

93. *New Haven Col. Recs.* 2:569.

94. Morison, *Builders of the Bay Colony*, 229.

95. Calder, "John Cotton and the New Haven Colony," 87–89. See also Gail Sussman Marcus, " 'Due Execution of the Generall Rules of Righteousnesse': Criminal Procedure in New Haven Town and Colony, 1638–1658," in *Saints and Revolutionaries: Essays on Early American History*, ed. David D. Hall, John M. Murrin, and Thad W. Tate (New York: Norton, 1984), 99–137.

96. Morison, *Builders of the Bay Colony*, 229.

97. *New Haven Col. Recs.* 2:571 ff.

98. Osgood, *American Colonies in the Seventeenth Century*, 1:322–59; Andrews, *Colonial Period of American History* 2:1–27.

99. John E. Pomfret, *Founding the American Colonies, 1583–1660* (New York: Harper & Row, 1970), 213–16, 221.

100. Andrews, *Colonial Period of American History* 2:23.

101. *R.I. Col. Recs.* 1:27–31, 111–15, 143–208.

102. Pomfret, *Founding the American Colonies*, 219–20.

103. *R.I. Col. Recs.* 1:147–49.

104. Ibid., 156 ff.

105. Dalton, *Country Justice*, passim.

106. *R.I. Col. Recs.* 2:504–5; Riesenfeld, "Law-Making and Legislative Precedent in American Legal History," 132–33 n.

107. *R.I. Col. Recs.* 1:157.

108. *Mass. Col. Laws* (1648), 1; *Mass. Col. Laws* (1660), 33; *Ply. Col. Laws*, 241; *Conn. Col. Recs.* 1:509; *New Haven Col. Recs.* 2:571–72.

109. *R.I. Col. Recs.* 1:157.

110. Ibid., 180–81.

111. Peter J. Coleman, *Debtors and Creditors in America* (Madison: State Historical Society of Wisconsin, 1974), 40, 74.

112. *Mass. Col. Laws* (1648), 2–3.

113. Coleman, *Debtors and Creditors in America*, 40.

114. *Ply. Col. Laws*, 154 (1665).

115. See Samuel H. Brockunier, *The Irrepressible Democrat—Roger Williams* (New York: Ronald Press, 1940), 175–77.

116. *Mass. Col. Laws* (1660), 33.

117. *Conn. Col. Recs.* 1:509 (1650).

118. *R.I. Col. Recs.* 1:157.

119. Joseph H. Smith, "The English Criminal Law in Early America," in *The English Legal System: Carryover to the Colonies* (Los Angeles: University of California, 1975), 22–29.

120. Konig, *Law and Society in Puritan Massachusetts*, 158–62.

121. Viola F. Barnes, *The Dominion of New England* (New Haven: Yale University Press, 1923), 71–72, 77–79.

122. *Acts and Resolves, Public and Private, of the Province of the Massachusetts Bay*, 5 vols. (Boston: Wright & Potter, 1869–1922), 1:1 ff.

Chapter 2: Crime and Scripture

1. Quoted in George L. Haskins, *Law and Authority in Early Massachusetts* (New York: Macmillan, 1960), 143–44.

2. Ibid., 143, 145.

3. *Ply. Col. Laws*, 42–43.

4. *Mass. Col. Laws* (1660), 55.

5. *Mass. Col. Laws* (1648), 5–6.

6. *Conn. Col. Recs.* 1:77 (1642), 515 (1650).

7. *New Haven Col. Recs.* 2:575–78, 593.

8. F. Douglas Price, "The Abuses of Excommunication and the Decline of Ecclesiastical Discipline under Queen Elizabeth," *EHR* 57 (1942): 111–12.

9. David H. Flaherty, "Law and the Enforcement of Morals in Early America," *PAH* 5 (1971): 221.

10. C. H. Firth and R. S. Rait, eds., *Acts and Ordinances of the Interregnum, 1642–1660*, 3 vols. (London: H.M.S.O., 1911), 2:387–88.

11. *Mass. Assist. Ct. Recs.* 2:19; *Mass. Col. Recs.* 1:91–92.
12. *Mass. Col. Recs.* 1:225.
13. *Mass. Col. Laws* (1660), 55.
14. *Mass. Col. Laws* (1648), 6; *Conn. Col. Recs.* 1:77; *New Haven Col. Recs.* 2:577; *Ply. Col. Laws*, 245–46. Cf. Leviticus 18:20, 20:19; Deuteronomy 22:23, 27.
15. Haskins, *Law and Authority in Early Massachusetts*, 271 n.58.
16. Firth and Rait, *Acts and Ordinances of the Interregnum* 2:387–88.
17. Deuteronomy 22:23–24.
18. Leviticus 18:20; Deuteronomy 22:22.
19. *Mass. Col. Laws* (1648), 6.
20. Caroline Bingham, "Seventeenth-Century Attitudes toward Deviant Sex," *JIH* 1 (1971): 448–64.
21. Haskins, *Law and Authority in Early Massachusetts*, 147, 271 n.41.
22. See Bingham, "Seventeenth-Century Attitudes toward Deviant Sex," 447.
23. *New Haven Col. Recs.* 2:577. Cf. Leviticus 20:13.
24. *Ply. Col. Laws*, 106.
25. Bradley Chapin, *Criminal Justice in Colonial America, 1606–1660* (Athens: University of Georgia Press, 1983), 6.
26. *Ply. Col. Laws*, 243–44.
27. See Leviticus 20:11–12, 14, 17, 19–21.
28. *New Haven Col. Recs.* 2:593 (1656).
29. *Conn. Laws* (1673), 9.
30. *Mass. Assist. Ct. Recs.* 1:342, 361 (1691).
31. *Mass. Col. Laws* (1648), 6; *Ply. Col. Laws*, 245 (1672); *Conn. Col. Recs.* 1:515 (1650); *New Haven Col. Recs.* 2:578 (1656).
32. See Deuteronomy 21:18–21.
33. *Mass. Col. Laws* (1648), 5; *New Haven Col. Recs.* 2:576. Cf. Leviticus 24:15–16.
34. David H. Wrinn, "Manslaughter and Mosaicism in Early Connecticut," *VULR* 21 (1986–87): 277.
35. *Mass. Col. Laws* (1660), 55.
36. *Conn. Col. Recs.* 1:77.
37. Wrinn, "Manslaughter and Mosaicism in Early Connecticut," 280–81; Isabel M. Calder, "John Cotton and New Haven Colony," *NEQ* 3 (1930): 86–94.
38. *Mass. Col. Laws* (1648), 37.
39. *Conn. Col. Recs.* 1:539.
40. Wrinn, "Manslaughter and Mosaicism in Early Connecticut," 283.
41. *Conn. Laws* (1673), 9, 42.
42. Wrinn, "Manslaughter and Mosaicism in Early Connecticut," 283.
43. *Ply. Col. Laws*, 42, 244.
44. *New Haven Col. Recs.* 2:577, 599.
45. For scriptural law on homicide, see Exodus 21:12–13, 14; Leviticus 24:17; Numbers 35:20–21, 31.
46. *Mass. Col. Laws* (1648), 6; *Ply. Col. Laws*, 244 (1671); *Conn. Col. Recs.* 1:77 (1642), 515 (1650); *New Haven Col. Recs.* 2:577 (1656). Cf. Deuteronomy 19:16–19.

47. *Mass. Col. Laws* (1648), 6; *Ply. Col. Laws*, 245 (1671); *Conn. Col. Recs.* 1:515 (1650); *New Haven Col. Recs.* 2:578 (1656). Cf. Exodus 21:15, 17.

48. *Mass. Col. Laws* (1648), 6; *Ply. Col. Laws*, 245 (1671); *Conn. Col. Recs.* 1:515 (1650); *New Haven Col. Recs.* 2:578 (1656). Cf. Deuteronomy 21:18–21.

49. *Mass. Col. Laws* (1648), 6; *Ply. Col. Laws*, 244 (1671); *Conn. Col. Recs.* 1:77 (1642), 515 (1650); *New Haven Col. Recs.* 2:577 (1656). Cf. Exodus 21:16.

50. Quoted in Wrinn, "Manslaughter and Mosaicism in Early Connecticut," 286 n.50.

51. *R.I. Gen. Assem.* (1647), 32 n.

52. *R.I. Col. Recs.* 1:163–65.

53. Chapin, *Criminal Justice in Colonial America*, 5, 182.

54. *Mass. Col. Laws* (1648), 4–5; *Ply. Col. Laws*, 246 (1671); *Conn. Col. Recs.* 1:513–14 (1650); *New Haven Col. Recs.* 2:575 (1656). Cf. Numbers 15:30–31.

55. *Mass. Col. Recs.* 2:22.

56. *Mass. Col. Laws* (1660), 127; *Conn. Col. Recs.* 1:84, 110, 115, 143–44, 203, 513–14.

57. *New Haven Col. Recs.* 1:26, 46, 51, 77, 89–90, 153; 2:575.

58. *Ply. Col. Laws*, 246.

59. *R.I. Col. Recs.* 1:166–67 (1647).

60. *Mass. Col. Laws* (1660), 127 (1647).

61. *Conn. Col. Recs.* 1:513–14 (1650); *New Haven Col. Recs.* 2:575 (1656).

62. *Ply. Col. Laws*, 246 (1671).

63. *R.I. Gen. Assem.* (1647), 32.

64. Deuteronomy 22:28.

65. *Mass. Col. Recs.* 2:12–13.

66. Ibid., 12–13, 21 (1641).

67. John Winthrop, *History of New England* (or *Journal*), ed. James K. Hosmer, 2 vols. (New York: Scribner's, 1908), 2:38.

68. *Mass. Col. Laws* (1648), 5–6.

69. *Mass. Assist. Ct. Recs.* 3:199–200.

70. *Mass. Col. Recs.* 4 (pt. 2): 437–38 (1669); *Mass. Col. Laws* (1672), 15–16 (1669).

71. *Ply. Col. Laws*, 43, 245.

72. *Conn. Col. Recs.* 1:28 (1639), 77 (1642).

73. *Conn. Laws* (1673), 9.

74. *New Haven Col. Recs.* 2:577–78 (1656).

75. *R.I. Col. Recs.* 1:173 (1647).

76. *Ply. Col. Laws*, 43.

77. *Mass. Col. Laws* (1660), 152.

78. *New Haven Col. Recs.* 2:175–76; *Conn. Laws* (1673), 9.

79. *R.I. Col. Recs.* 1:167 (1647).

80. 1 Jac. I, c. 12–14 (1603).

81. *Mass. Col. Laws* (1660), 55 (1641); *Conn. Col. Recs.* 1:77 (1642); *Ply. Col. Laws*, 43 (1636). The Plymouth law of 1671 followed the Massachusetts statute almost verbatim. *Ply. Col. Laws*, 244.

82. *New Haven Col. Recs.* 2:576 (1656).

83. *R.I. Col. Recs.* 1:166 (1647).

84. See Exodus 22:1–4.

85. *Essex Ct. Recs.* 1:24, 38; 4:121; 5:138.

86. *Mass. Assist. Ct. Recs.* 2:86 (1639); *Essex Ct. Recs.* 1:57 (1643); *Conn. Col. Recs.* 1:110, 115.

87. *Ply. Col. Laws*, 81 (1645), 246–47 (1671).

88. *New Haven Col. Recs.* 2:575–76 (1656).

89. *Mass. Col. Laws* (1660), 127–28 (1646, 1653); *Conn. Col. Recs.* 1:514 (1650).

90. *R.I. Col. Recs.* 1:174 (1647).

91. *Ply. Col. Laws*, 82 (1645), 248 (1671); *Mass. Col. Laws* (1660), 153 (1646).

92. *Conn. Col. Recs.* 1:526 (1650); *New Haven Col. Recs.* 2:589–90 (1656).

93. *R.I. Gen. Assem.* (1647), 41–42.

94. *Ply. Col. Laws*, 249 (1671); *Mass. Col. Laws* (1660), 261 (1668).

95. *Conn. Col. Recs.* 1:78 (1642).

96. *New Haven Col. Recs.* 2:601 (1656).

97. *R.I. Col. Recs.* 1:171 (1647).

98. *Mass. Assist. Ct. Recs.* 1:54, 60, 114, 272; 3:255–56.

99. *Mass. Col. Laws* (1672), 349 (1678).

100. Thomas A. Green, *Verdict According to Conscience: Perspectives on the English Criminal Trial Jury, 1200–1800* (Chicago: University of Chicago Press, 1985), 106–7, 236–49.

101. "Conn. Part. Ct. Recs.," 106.

102. *Ply. Col. Laws*, 42–43 (1636), 243–44 (1671).

103. *Conn. Col. Recs.* 1:77, 513–15; *Conn. Laws* (1673), 7–10.

104. *Mass. Col. Laws* (1672), 12–16, 52, 58–60, 62–63, 67, 211, 315–16; *Mass. Col. Recs.* 5:194.

105. *New Haven Col. Recs.* 2:575–78, 593 (1656).

106. *R.I. Col. Recs.* 1:157 ff. (1647); *R.I. Col. Laws*, 1–7 (1663).

107. Numbers 35:30.

108. *Mass. Col. Laws* (1660), 43 (1641); *Ply. Col. Laws*, 101 (1656); *New Haven Col. Recs.* 2:572 (1656); *Conn. Laws* (1673), 69.

109. *R.I. Col. Recs.* 1:160 (1647).

110. *Mass. Col. Laws* (1660), 33 (1641).

111. *Conn. Col. Recs.* 1:509 (1650); *New Haven Col. Recs.* 2:571–72 (1656).

112. *Ply. Col. Laws*, 241 (1671).

113. William Bradford, *Of Plymouth Plantation*, ed. Samuel E. Morison (New York: Knopf, 1952), 234.

114. *Conn. Col. Recs.* 2:184.

115. *Conn. Laws* (1673), 9.

116. *Mass. Col. Laws* (1672), 13, 19, 27, 51, 54, 58, 81, 91, 145; *Ply. Col. Laws*, 43, 65–66, 81, 88, 99, 101, 113; *Conn. Col. Recs.* 1:514, 527–28, 547; *Conn. Laws* (1673), 14, 40, 56; *New Haven Col. Recs.* 2:585–86, 597–601, 605, 608, 611.

117. *Ply. Col. Laws*, 243–44.

118. *Mass. Col. Laws* (1672), 15; *Conn. Laws* (1673), 9; *New Haven Col. Recs.* 2:578 (1656).

119. *R.I. Col. Recs.* 1:160–68, 171–72, 174, 182 (1647).
120. See chapter 6.

Chapter 3: The Reach of the Law

1. John Calvin, *Institutes of the Christian Religion,* ed. John T. McNeill (Philadelphia: Westminster Press, 1960), 835.
2. See David T. Konig, *Law and Society in Puritan Massachusetts: Essex County, 1629–1692* (Chapel Hill: University of North Carolina Press, 1979), 128 ff., and Carl Stephenson and Frederick G. Marcham, eds., *Sources of English Constitutional History* (New York: Harper, 1937), 18–19.
3. *Mass. Col. Laws* (1648), 51.
4. *Mass. Col. Laws* (1672), 149.
5. *Ply. Col. Laws,* 156 (1669).
6. *Conn. Col. Recs.* 1:8 (1636); *New Haven Col. Recs.* 1:70 (1641).
7. *New Haven Col. Recs.* 2:608–9.
8. *Mass. Col. Laws* (1660), 172.
9. *Conn. Col. Recs.* 1:350 (1660).
10. *New Haven Col. Recs.* 2:600 (1656).
11. *Ply. Col. Laws,* 44, 61 (1638).
12. *Mass. Col. Laws* (1660), 171–72.
13. *Conn. Col. Recs.* 1:47–48, 92.
14. *New Haven Col. Recs.* 2:600.
15. *Mass. Col. Laws* (1648), 6; *Ply. Col. Laws,* 245 (1671); *Conn. Col. Recs.* 1:515 (1650); *New Haven Col. Recs.* 2:578 (1656).
16. *Mass. Col. Recs.* 4 (pt. 2): 216–17.
17. *Mass. Col. Laws* (1660), 136–37.
18. *Conn. Col. Recs.* 1:515 (1650).
19. *Ply. Col. Laws,* 270 (1671); *Mass. Col. Laws* (1660), 136 (1642); *Conn. Col. Recs.* 1:521 (1650).
20. *Mass. Col. Laws* (1660), 136 (1642); *Mass. Col. Laws* (1648), 61; *Ply. Col. Laws,* 245, 270–71 (1671); *Conn. Col. Recs.* 1:515, 520–21 (1650); *New Haven Col. Recs.* 2:578, 583–84 (1656).
21. *Mass. Col. Laws* (1660), 189–90.
22. See Gustavus Myers, *Ye Olden Blue Laws* (New York: Century Company, 1921), 28 ff.
23. *Mass. Col. Recs.* 1:126.
24. Ibid., 183.
25. Ibid., 274–75.
26. *Mass. Col. Laws* (1660), 123.
27. Ibid.
28. Ibid.
29. Ibid., 220–21.
30. *Mass. Col. Laws* (1672), 232–33.

31. *Conn. Col. Recs.* 1:64. The "particular court" was a judicial court of trial jurisdiction. See chapter 5.

32. *Conn. Col. Recs.* 2:283.

33. Myers, *Ye Olden Blue Laws*, 91.

34. Babette May Levy, *Preaching in the First Half Century of New England History* (Hartford: The American Society of Church History, 1945), 170–71.

35. *Mass. Col. Recs.* 1:140.

36. *Mass. Col. Laws* (1660), 148.

37. Levy, *Preaching in the First Half Century of New England History*, 170.

38. *Mass. Col. Laws* (1660), 148.

39. Levy, *Preaching in the First Half Century of New England History*, 172.

40. *Mass. Col. Recs.* 2:358.

41. *Mass. Col. Laws* (1672), 234.

42. Ibid., 249–50.

43. *Mass. Col. Recs.* 5:155 (1677).

44. *Mass. Col. Laws* (1660), 189.

45. *Mass. Col. Laws* (1672), 269.

46. *Ply. Col. Laws*, 92 (1650), 96 (1652), 113 (1658), 137–38 (1662), 158 (1669), 247 (1671).

47. *Conn. Col. Recs.* 1:524.

48. *New Haven Col. Recs.* 2:605 (1656).

49. *Conn. Laws* (1673), 58.

50. *Conn. Col. Recs.* 2:280.

51. *R.I. Col. Recs.* 2:503–4; 3:30–31.

52. John M. O'Brien and Sheldon C. Seller, "Attributes of Alcohol in the Old Testament," *The Drinking and Drug Practices Surveyor*, no. 18 (Aug. 1982), 18–20.

53. William Bradford, *Of Plymouth Plantation*, ed. Samuel E. Morison (New York: Knopf, 1952), 328–29.

54. Edwin Powers, *Crime and Punishment in Early Massachusetts, 1620–1692* (Boston: Beacon Press, 1966), 371.

55. John Winthrop, *History of New England* (or *Journal*), ed. James K. Hosmer, 2 vols. (New York: Scribner's, 1908), 1:325 (1639); *Mass. Col. Recs.* 2:121 (1645).

56. *Ply. Col. Laws*, 86, 125, 136, 140, 155; *Mass. Col. Laws* (1660), 126, 163–64, 166, 173, 228; *Mass. Col. Laws* (1672), 80; *New Haven Col. Recs.* 2:595–96; *Conn. Col. Recs.* 1:533–35; *Conn. Laws* (1673), 20; *R.I. Col. Recs.* 1:185–86.

57. *Mass. Col. Laws* (1648), 30.

58. *Ply. Col. Laws*, 84 (1646).

59. *Mass. Col. Laws* (1660), 164–65.

60. *Conn. Col. Recs.* 1:533–34 (1650).

61. *New Haven Col. Recs.* 2:596–97 (1656).

62. *Ply. Col. Laws*, 62 (1638).

63. *Mass. Col. Laws* (1660), 153 (1646); *Ply. Col. Laws*, 155 (1669); *Conn. Col. Recs.* 1:527 (1650); *New Haven Col. Recs.* 2:590 (1656); *R.I. Col. Recs.* 1:185 (1647).

64. *Ply. Col. Laws*, 251 (1671).

65. *New Haven Col. Recs.* 2:313 (1659).

66. *Conn. Col. Recs.* 2:282 (1676).

67. *Mass. Col. Laws* (1672), 80.

68. *Ply. Col. Laws*, 287 (1671); *New Haven Col. Recs.* 2:596 (1656).

69. Powers, *Crime and Punishment in Early Massachusetts*, 385.

70. *Conn. Col. Recs.* 1:41; *New Haven Col. Recs.* 1:170–71, 306–7, 449; 2:311–13; *Mass. Assist. Ct. Recs.* 2:120.

71. *Mass. Col. Recs.* 1:107, 118; *Mass. Assist. Ct. Recs.* 2:34–35, 41, 62.

72. *Mass. Col. Laws* (1660), 164–65; *Ply. Col. Laws*, 47, 83–84, 251; *Conn. Col. Recs.* 1:533–34; *New Haven Col. Recs.* 2:596–97; *R.I. Col. Recs.* 1:86; *Me. Ct. Recs.* 3:19.

73. Dean Albertson, "Puritan Liquor in the Planting of New England," *NEQ* 23 (1950): 482–83.

74. *Mass. Col. Laws* (1660), 161; *Ply. Col. Laws*, 89, 151, 290; *Conn. Col. Recs.* 1:254–55, 263; *Conn. Laws* (1673), 41; *New Haven Col. Recs.* 2:597; *R.I. Col. Recs.* 1:279.

75. *Mass. Col. Laws* (1660), 161–62 (1657).

76. *Conn. Laws* (1673), 41; *R.I. Col. Recs.* 1:279 (1654).

77. *Mass. Col. Laws* (1660), 236 (1666).

78. *Ply. Col. Laws*, 290 (1671); *Conn. Laws* (1673), 41; *Mass. Col. Laws* (1660), 236 (1666).

79. George L. Haskins, *Law and Authority in Early Massachusetts* (New York: Macmillan, 1960), 177–78.

80. Powers, *Crime and Punishment in Early Massachusetts*, 414–15.

81. *Mass. Col. Laws* (1660), 195 (1638, 1647).

82. *Ply. Col. Laws*, 59 (1630).

83. *New Haven Col. Recs.* 1:241 (1646).

84. *Conn. Col. Recs.* 1:558.

85. *Conn. Laws* (1673), passim.

86. *Mass. Col. Laws* (1660), 158, 195 (1633, 1638, 1647).

87. *Ply. Col. Laws*, 59 (1630), 68 (1640), 158 (1669).

88. *Mass. Col. Laws* (1648), 24 (1646).

89. *Mass. Col. Laws* (1660), 153.

90. *Mass. Col. Laws* (1672), 58.

91. *Ply. Col. Laws*, 101 (1656), 250 (1671).

92. *Ply. Col. Recs.* 4:47.

93. *Conn. Col. Recs.* 1:289–90 (1656).

94. *New Haven Col. Recs.* 2:590 (1656); *R.I. Col. Recs.* 1:185–86 (1647).

95. *New Haven Col. Recs.* 2:366–67 (1660).

96. Edmund S. Morgan, "The Puritans and Sex," *NEQ* 15 (1942): 591–92. See also David H. Flaherty, "Law and the Enforcement of Morals in Early America," *PAH* 5 (1971): 215–16.

97. *Mass. Col. Laws* (1660), 153; *Ply. Col. Laws*, 79–80; *Conn. Col. Recs.* 1:527; *New Haven Col. Recs.* 2:590. Cf. Exodus 22:16.

98. *Ply. Col. Laws*, 79–80 (1645).

99. *New Hamp. Laws* 1:60 (1682).

100. *Ply. Col. Recs.* 4:47, 83, 106; 5:51, 86, 112, 130, 162, 168, 173, 221; 6:115,

172, 201; *Me. Ct. Recs.* 2:406, 424; 3:63; "Suffolk Ct. Recs." 1:22, 80; 2:629, 870; *Essex Ct. Recs.* 3:61; 5:120; 6:169–70, 180, 213, 342; 7:79, 265; 8:47, 87, 146, 367, 422, 424; "New Hamp. Ct. Recs.," 160.
  101. *Essex Ct. Recs.* 6:213.
  102. "New Hamp. Ct. Recs.," 294.
  103. *Mass. Assist. Ct. Recs.* 1:29, 51, 114, 125, 127–28.
  104. See Peter C. Hoffer and N. E. H. Hull, *Murdering Mothers: Infanticide in England and New England, 1558–1803* (New York: New York University Press, 1981), passim.
  105. 21 Jac. I, c. 27 (1624).
  106. See chapter 9. The English statute was not adopted until 1696. *Acts and Resolves, Public and Private, of the Province of the Massachusetts Bay,* 5 vols. (Boston: Wright & Potter, 1869–1922), 1:255.
  107. *Mass. Assist. Ct. Recs.* 1:114, 125, 227–28.
  108. *Essex Ct. Recs.* 5:143.
  109. *New Haven Col. Recs.* 2:289–91, 363–68 (1659).
  110. *Essex Ct. Recs.* 5:143, 147.
  111. *Ply. Col. Recs.* 6:195 (1686).
  112. *Me. Ct. Recs.* 1:146; 2:42–43, 49, 93, 252, 468.
  113. *Mass. Assist. Ct. Recs.* 2:81 (1639), 109 (1642).
  114. *New Haven Col. Recs.* 1:81 (1642); 2:135–36 (1655).
  115. *Mass. Assist. Ct. Recs.* 2:93.
  116. *Mass. Col. Laws* (1660), 55, 128; *Ply. Col. Laws,* 43, 244; *Conn. Col. Recs.* 1:77; *New Haven Col. Recs.* 2:576–77; *R.I. Col. Recs.* 1:172–73.
  117. *New Haven Col. Recs.* 2:576–77 (1656).
  118. *Mass. Col. Laws* (1672), 208.
  119. Keith W. Thomas, "The Double Standard," *JHI* 20 (1959): 198.
  120. *Ply. Col. Recs.* 4:106; 5:260.
  121. Flaherty, "Law and the Enforcement of Morals in Early America," 215–16.
  122. *R.I. Col. Recs.* 1:157 (1647).

Chapter 4: Enforcing the Laws

  1. William Bradford, *Of Plymouth Plantation,* ed. Samuel E. Morison (New York: Knopf, 1952), 75.
  2. *Mass. Col. Laws* (1648), A2; David H. Flaherty, "Law and the Enforcement of Morals in Early America," *PAH* 5 (1971): 217–18.
  3. *Ply. Col. Laws,* 37, 40, 264 (1636, 1671).
  4. *Mass. Col. Recs.* 1:76, 79 (1630); *Mass. Col. Laws* (1660), 195–96.
  5. Royal R. Hinman, *The Blue Laws of New Haven Colony* (Hartford: Case, Tiffany, 1838), 69.
  6. *Conn. Col. Recs.* 1:522 (1650).
  7. *New Haven Col. Recs.* 2:2, 95–96, 172, 304, 369.
  8. *R.I. Col. Recs.* 1:65 (1638).
  9. *Ply. Col. Laws,* 40 (1636), 266 (1671).

10. *Mass. Col. Recs.* 1:252 (1639).

11. *Mass. Col. Laws* (1648), 13 (1646).

12. *Conn. Col. Recs.* 1:522 (1650).

13. *Mass. Col. Recs.* 2:38 (1643).

14. Edwin Powers, *Crime and Punishment in Early Massachusetts, 1620–1692* (Boston: Beacon Press, 1966), 432, 622 n.

15. *R.I. Col. Recs.* 1:191–92, 196, 197–98, 202 (1647).

16. See *Ply. Col. Laws*, 40 (1636).

17. *Mass. Col. Laws* (1648), 13 (1646); *Conn. Col. Recs.* 1:522 (1650); *Ply. Col. Laws*, 266 (1671); *R.I. Col. Recs.* 1:198 (1647).

18. John Winthrop, *History of New England* (or *Journal*), ed. James K. Hosmer, 2 vols. (New York: Scribner's, 1908), 2:191–93.

19. *R.I. Col. Recs.* 1:157, 168–69 (1647).

20. *Ply. Col. Laws*, 241 (1671).

21. *Mass. Col. Laws* (1648), 1 (1641); *Conn. Col. Recs.* 1:509 (1650).

22. *New Haven Col. Recs.* 2:411–12, 570.

23. William Cuddihy and B. Carmon Hardy, "A Man's House Was Not His Castle: Origins of the Fourth Amendment to the United States Constitution," *WMQ*, 3d ser., 37 (1980): 388–92.

24. *Mass. Col. Laws* (1660), 129, 132, 135, 139, 145, 148, 159, 174, 192–94.

25. *Salem Town Records, 1659–91*, 3 vols. (Salem, Mass.: Essex Institute, 1913–34), 1:26 (1662); *The Records of the Town of Cambridge (formerly Newtowne) Massachusetts, 1630–1703* (Cambridge, Mass.: Pub. by the City Council, 1901), 23 (1636), 351 (1646).

26. *Conn. Col. Recs.* 1:449–50, 556–57, 561 (1650); *Conn. Laws* (1673), 23, 58, 71.

27. *Ply. Col. Laws*, 41, 68, 102, 152, 156, 267–69; *Ply. Town Recs.* 1:7, 34, 43.

28. *New Haven Col. Recs.* 2:598–99 (1656).

29. *The Early Records of the Town of Warwick* (Providence: Johnson, 1926), 77 (1653), 155 (1665); *Provid. Town Recs.* 2:83 (1655); 4:35 (1675).

30. *Mass. Col. Laws* (1660), 196.

31. *Mass. Col. Laws* (1672), 148.

32. *Ply. Col. Laws*, 37 (1636), 109 (1658), 258 (1671).

33. *Conn. Col. Recs.* 1:21 (1639).

34. *Conn. Laws* (1673), 23, 26.

35. *New Haven Col. Recs.* 2:567 (1656).

36. *R.I. Col. Recs.* 1:150 (1647).

37. *Mass. Col. Laws* (1660), 139, 158, 164; *Mass. Col. Laws* (1672), 101–2; *Ply. Col. Laws*, 250–52; *Conn. Laws* (1673), 15, 52; *New Haven Col. Recs.* 2:590, 596–97; *New Haven Col. Recs.* 1:241.

38. *Mass. Col. Laws* (1660), 139 (1646); *Ply. Col. Laws*, 265 (1671); *Conn. Col. Recs.* 1:525 (1650); *Conn. Laws* (1673), 24.

39. *Mass. Col. Laws* (1660), 173; *Ply. Col. Laws*, 267 (1671); *Conn. Col. Recs.* 1:540–41 (1650); *New Haven Col. Recs.* 2:600 (1656); *R.I. Col. Recs.* 1:207 (1647).

40. *Mass. Col. Laws* (1660), 153; *Conn. Laws* (1673), 66; *Ply. Col. Laws*, 99 (1654).

41. *Ply. Col. Laws,* 127–28 (1660); *Mass. Col. Laws* (1660), 196 (1658); *Mass. Col. Laws* (1672), 247 (1676).

42. *Ply. Col. Laws,* 264 (1671).

43. *Conn. Laws* (1673), 15, 60.

44. *Ply. Col. Laws,* 265, 267–68 (1671).

45. *Mass. Col. Laws* (1660), 140 (1646); *Ply. Col. Laws,* 267 (1671); *Conn. Col. Recs.* 1:522 (1650).

46. *Mass. Col. Laws* (1660), 198–99 (1636, 1646, 1652, 1657).

47. Ibid., 173.

48. *Conn. Laws* (1673), 39–40.

49. *New Haven Col. Recs.* 2:601 (1656); *Conn. Laws* (1673), 47.

50. *Mass. Col. Laws* (1660), 154, 171 (1645, 1651); *Ply. Col. Laws,* 130 (1661).

51. Sumner C. Powell, *Puritan Village* (Garden City, N.Y.: Doubleday, 1965), 124.

52. *Ply. Col. Laws,* 41 (1636), 462–63 (1671).

53. *Conn. Col. Recs.* 1:91 (1643), 536 (1650); 2:280–83 (1676); 3:148 (1684).

54. *Mass. Col. Laws* (1660), 167 (1657).

55. See *Ply. Col. Laws,* 64 (1639).

56. *Ply. Col. Recs.* 1:68, 75, 86, 98; 2:4, 12, 36–37, 42, 96, 140, 156, 162, 165, 173–74; 3:5–6, 36, 41, 82, 96.

57. Richard D. Younger, *The People's Panel: The Grand Jury in the United States, 1634–1941* (Providence: Brown University Press, 1963), 6–7.

58. *Conn. Col. Recs.* 2:61 (1667), 98–99 (1668).

59. *R.I. Col. Recs.* 1:198–99 (1647).

60. Younger, *The People's Panel,* 5–6.

61. Theodore F. T. Plucknett, *A Concise History of the Common Law* (Boston: Little, Brown, 1956), 97.

62. *Mass. Col. Laws* (1672), 249–50.

63. *Watertown Records from 1634,* 8 vols. (Watertown, Mass.: Historical Society of Watertown, 1894–1939), 1:144. See John Dickinson, "Economic Regulations and Restrictions on Personal Liberty in Early Massachusetts," *Pocumtuck Valley Memorial Association Proceedings* 7 (1927): 497.

64. Flaherty, "Law and the Enforcement of Morals in Early America," 241.

65. Ibid.

66. *Mass. Col. Laws* (1660), 140; *Ply. Col. Laws,* 266 (1671); *Conn. Col. Recs.* 1:522 (1650).

67. Plucknett, *Concise History of the Common Law,* 430.

68. Statute of Westminster, 13 Edw. I (1285).

69. *R.I. Col. Recs.* 1:167, 194 (1647).

70. See *Mass. Col. Laws* (1660), 139–40 (1646); *Ply. Col. Laws,* 266–67 (1671); *Conn. Col. Recs.* 1:522 (1650); *Conn. Laws* (1673), 14–15.

71. Harry M. Ward, *The United Colonies of New England, 1643–90* (New York: Vantage Press, 1961), 388.

72. Winthrop, *Journal* 2:161–63.

73. Bradford, *Of Plymouth Plantation,* 299–301.

74. See *Ply. Col. Laws,* 266 (1671); *Mass. Col. Laws* (1660), 139 (1646); *Conn. Col. Recs.* 1:521 (1650).

75. *Mass. Col. Laws* (1660), 198–99.

76. *Mass. Col. Laws* (1672), 154–55 (1652, 1657).

77. *Conn. Col. Recs.* 1:2 (1636), 74 (1642), 560–61 (1650).

78. *Conn. Laws* (1673), 68.

79. *New Haven Col. Recs.* 1:33–35, 74–75, 204, 274, 381; 2:603–4 (1656).

80. *Ply. Col. Laws,* 33 (1633), 57 (1636).

81. *Ply. Town Recs.* 1:15; *Ply. Col. Laws,* 76.

82. *Ply. Col. Recs.* 5:186–87 (1676).

83. *Provid. Town Recs.* 2:82 (1655), 94 (1656); 4:53 (1675); Clarence S. Brigham, ed., *The Early Records of Portsmouth, R.I.* (Providence: Freeman, 1901), 64 (1664).

84. Carl Stephenson and Frederick G. Marcham, eds., *Sources of English Constitutional History* (New York: Harper, 1937), 18–19.

85. *Mass. Col. Laws* (1672), 154–55 (1657, 1661).

86. *Conn. Col. Recs.* 1:15 (1638), 48 (1640), 62 (1640), 74 (1642), 99 (1644), 234 (1652), 298 (1657).

87. *New Haven Col. Recs.* 2:604 (1656).

88. *Mass. Col. Laws* (1660), 199 (1657).

89. *Ply. Col. Laws* 76 (1644); *Conn. Col. Recs.* 1:561 (1650).

90. *Mass. Col. Laws* (1660), 198 (1657).

91. George L. Haskins, *Law and Authority in Early Massachusetts* (New York: Macmillan, 1960), 91.

92. David H. Flaherty, *Privacy in Colonial New England* (Charlottesville: University of Virginia Press, 1972), 151, 166.

93. Ibid., 21.

94. *Mass. Col. Laws* (1660), 129, 137, 153, 161–62, 182, 195, 293; *Ply. Col. Laws,* 45, 95, 148; *Conn. Laws* (1673), 27, 41; *New Haven Col. Recs.* 2:590, 592, 594.

95. Flaherty, *Privacy in Colonial New England,* 207.

96. *R.I. Col. Recs.* 1:155 (1647).

97. *Essex Ct. Recs.* 5:231. See Powers, *Crime and Punishment in Early Massachusetts,* 173.

98. *Essex Ct. Recs.* 8:285–87 (1682).

99. Winthrop, *Journal* 1:126.

100. *Essex Ct. Recs.* 3:51–53, 65–66. See Flaherty, *Privacy in Colonial New England,* 203.

101. Flaherty, *Privacy in Colonial New England,* 205–6.

102. *Mass. Col. Laws* (1672), 58.

103. *Conn. Laws* (1673), 26–27.

104. Flaherty, *Privacy in Colonial New England,* 207.

105. Ibid., 206–8.

106. Thomas Hooker, *A Survey of the Sum of Church Discipline* (London: n.p., 1648), pt. 3, 23; William Ames, *Conscience with the Power and Cases Thereof . . . Translated out of Latin into English* (London: n.p., 1643), bk. 5, 280–81. Cited in Flaherty, *Privacy in Colonial New England,* 208–9.

107. *Mass. Col. Laws* (1648), 47, 58.

108. *Conn. Laws* (1673), 59–60.

109. *Mass. Col. Recs.* 5:59–60.

110. Emil Oberholzer, Jr., *Delinquent Saints: Disciplinary Action in the Early Churches of Massachusetts* (New York: Columbia University Press, 1955), 127–29.

111. Flaherty, "Law and the Enforcement of Morals in Early America," 226, 229, 233, 241–44.

112. Flaherty, *Privacy in Colonial New England*, 16–17.

113. See Keith Wrightson, "Two Concepts of Order: Justices, Constables and Jurymen in Seventeenth-Century England," in *An Ungovernable People: The English and Their Law in the Seventeenth and Eighteenth Centuries*, ed. John Brewer and John Styles (London: Hutchinson, 1980), 25–26.

Chapter 5: The Judicial System

1. Lawrence M. Friedman, *A History of American Law* (New York: Simon & Schuster, 1973), 32–34.

2. Francis N. Thorpe, ed., *The Federal and State Constitutions, Colonial Charters, and Other Organic Laws*, 7 vols. (Washington, D.C.: G.P.O., 1909), 3:1852–54.

3. John Winthrop, *History of New England* (or *Journal*), ed. James K. Hosmer, 2 vols. (New York: Scribner's, 1908), 2:64–66, 116–21, 164.

4. B. Katherine Brown, "A Note on the Puritan Concept of Aristocracy," *Mississippi Valley Historical Review* 41 (1954): 105–12.

5. Thomas L. Philips, "The Courts of Justice in the Province of Massachusetts Bay under the First Charter, 1630–1684," *ALR* 34 (1900): 567–69.

6. *Mass. Col. Recs.* 1:74, 82.

7. *Mass. Col. Laws* (1672), 3, 152.

8. See Richard B. Morris, *Fair Trial* (New York: Knopf, 1952), 3 ff.

9. Zechariah Chafee, Jr., introduction to "Suffolk Ct. Recs.," xx–xxiii.

10. *Mass. Col. Recs.* 1:169; 2:38; *Mass. Col. Laws* (1660), 143.

11. *Mass. Col. Recs.* 1:169. See Edwin Powers, *Crime and Punishment in Early Massachusetts, 1620–1692* (Boston: Beacon Press, 1966), 60–61.

12. Herbert L. Osgood, *The American Colonies in the Seventeenth Century*, 3 vols. (New York: Columbia University Press, 1904–1907), 1:190.

13. Chafee, "Suffolk Ct. Recs.," xvii–xix.

14. *Mass. Col. Laws* (1672), 36–37.

15. *Me. Ct. Recs.* 2:ix–x.

16. Philips, "Courts of Justice in Massachusetts," 569.

17. *Mass. Col. Recs.* 1:239 (1638).

18. *Mass. Col. Laws* (1660), 132 (1647).

19. *Mass. Col. Recs.* 5:139 (1677).

20. *Mass. Col. Laws* (1660), 122.

21. *Mass. Col. Recs.* 1:264.

22. *Mass. Col. Laws* (1648), 15.

23. *Mass. Col. Recs.* 4 (pt. 1): 20 (1650).

24. *Mass. Col. Laws* (1672), 207.

25. *Mass. Col. Recs.* 1:276.

26. Charles J. Hilkey, *Legal Development in Colonial Massachusetts, 1630–1686* (New York: Columbia University Press, 1910), 37–38.

27. *Mass. Col. Recs.* 4 (pt. 1): 59–63; *Mass. Col. Laws* (1660), 133.

28. *Mass. Col. Laws* (1660), 133; *Mass. Col. Laws* (1672), 21–22.

29. *Mass. Col. Laws* (1672), 217.

30. *Mass. Col. Laws* (1648), 50–51 (1636); *Mass. Col. Laws* (1660), 143; *Mass. Col. Recs.* 2:4, 8–9; Hilkey, *Legal Development in Colonial Massachusetts*, 45.

31. *Mass. Col. Laws* (1660), 41 (1641).

32. The *Laws and Liberties* provided that "all general laws not here inserted nor mentioned to be still of force are to be accounted repealed." *Mass. Col. Laws* (1648), A2.

33. *Mass. Col. Laws* (1660), 122, 143.

34. While the statutes guaranteed just one appeal as a matter of right, some historians have mistakenly assumed that a right to multiple appeals existed. See Powers, *Crime and Punishment in Early Massachusetts*, 92–93; Philips, "Courts of Justice in Massachusetts," 569; Mark De Wolfe Howe and Louis F. Eaton, Jr., "The Supreme Judicial Power in the Colony of Massachusetts Bay," *NEQ* 20 (1947), 298. Cf. *Mass. Col. Laws* (1660), 122, 143.

35. Joseph H. Smith, *Appeals to the Privy Council from the American Colonies* (New York: Columbia University Press, 1950), 41–42.

36. *Mass. Col. Recs.* 1:94.

37. Smith, *Appeals to the Privy Council from the American Colonies*, 45–46.

38. Ibid., 48–49.

39. Ibid., 54.

40. Ibid., 55–56.

41. Powers, *Crime and Punishment in Early Massachusetts*, 285–86.

42. Smith, *Appeals to the Privy Council from the American Colonies*, 56–58; Hilkey, *Legal Development in Colonial Massachusetts*, 50.

43. Winthrop, *Journal* 2:64–66, 116–20; Howe and Eaton, "The Supreme Judicial Power in the Colony of Massachusetts Bay," 294.

44. Howe and Eaton, "The Supreme Judicial Power in the Colony of Massachusetts Bay," 293.

45. *The Winthrop Papers*, 5 vols. (Boston: Massachusetts Historical Society, 1929–47), 4:282–83, 388, 390.

46. *Mass. Col. Recs.* 2:285; 4 (pt. 1): 82.

47. Howe and Eaton, "The Supreme Judicial Power in the Colony of Massachusetts Bay," 302–3, 311–12, 315.

48. Charles M. Andrews, *The Colonial Period of American History*, 4 vols. (New Haven: Yale University Press, 1934–38), 1:293–94.

49. *Ply. Col. Laws*, 28.

50. Ibid., 39 (1636), 98 (1653), 139 (1662).

51. Ibid., 70, 74, 128.

52. Ibid., 149–50, 151 (1666).

53. Ibid., 259–60.

54. Ibid., 294–97; George D. Langdon, Jr., *Pilgrim Colony* (New Haven: Yale University Press, 1966), 206.

55. *Ply. Col. Laws*, 294–98; Langdon, *Pilgrim Colony*, 206.
56. *Mass. Col. Recs.* 1:170 (1636).
57. Osgood, *American Colonies in the Seventeenth Century* 1:305–6; Andrews, *Colonial Period of American History* 2:92; *Conn. Col. Recs.* 1:21, 24.
58. "Conn. Part. Ct. Recs.," vii–viii.
59. *Conn. Col. Recs.* 1:81 (1643), 118–19 (1645), 150 (1647).
60. Ibid., 522, 528, 534–35, 537–38, 547, 558, 561 (1650); Andrews, *Colonial Period of American History* 2:113–15.
61. *Conn. Col. Recs.* 1:53, 528, 537–38, 547, 558, 561.
62. *New Haven Col. Recs.* 1:113–16.
63. Ibid., 191–92.
64. Ibid., 115–16.
65. *New Haven Col. Recs.* 2:570–71, 585.
66. Ibid., 576, 606.
67. Ibid., 515.
68. *Conn. Col. Recs.* 2:28–29, 34–35, 38, 118, 132, 531.
69. *Conn. Laws*, 3, 4, 17–18, 28, 31, 40, 58.
70. *R.I. Col. Recs.* 1:27.
71. Amasa M. Eaton, "The Development of the Judicial System in Rhode Island," *YLJ* 14 (1905): 149.
72. *R.I. Col. Recs.* 1:52, 63 (1638), 70–71, 87 (1639); Eaton, "The Development of the Judicial System in Rhode Island," 149.
73. *R.I. Col. Recs.* 1:101–3.
74. Eaton, "The Development of the Judicial System in Rhode Island," 149.
75. *R.I. Col. Recs.* 1:191–92, 202. See Howard M. Chapin's preface in *Records of the Court of Trials of Warwick, 1659–1674* (Providence: Shepley Press, 1922).
76. *R.I. Col. Recs.* 1:202, 218.
77. Andrews, *Colonial Period of American History*, 2:28–29.
78. *R.I. Col. Recs.* 1:191–92, 202 (1647), 237; Stephen O. Edwards, "The Supreme Court of Rhode Island," *The Green Bag* 2 (1890): 525.
79. *Provid. Ct. Recs.* 1:9, 45–46, 50–53, 57, 76; 2:25–28, 35–36, 40, 43, 45–46, 48, 56–58, 65–67, 71, 82, 84–85, 87–88, 91–92.
80. Thorpe, *Federal and State Constitutions* 6:3214–15.
81. *R.I. Col. Recs.* 2:26.
82. *R.I. Col. Laws*, 14.
83. *R.I. Col. Recs.* 2:26–27, 30–31 (1664).
84. Edwards, "The Supreme Court of Rhode Island," 526.
85. Andrews, *Colonial Period of American History* 2:48.
86. Nathaniel Bouton, ed., *Provincial Papers: Documents and Papers Relating to the Province of New Hampshire, from the Earliest Period of Its Settlement, 1623–1776*, 7 vols. (Concord and Nashua: Jenks, 1867–73), 1:373–82, 387, 395–96, 474.

Chapter 6: Legal Due Process

1. Richard D. Younger, *The People's Panel: The Grand Jury in the United States, 1634–1941* (Providence: Brown University Press, 1963), 1–2.

2. Bradley Chapin, *Criminal Justice in Colonial America, 1606–1660* (Athens: University of Georgia Press, 1983), 33.

3. John M. Taylor, *The Witchcraft Delusion in Colonial Connecticut, 1647–1697* (1908; reprint New York: Franklin, 1971), 152–53.

4. Chapin, *Criminal Justice in Colonial America*, 33.

5. Theodore F. T. Plucknett, *A Concise History of the Common Law* (Boston: Little, Brown, 1956), 430.

6. Ibid., 438.

7. Chapin, *Criminal Justice in Colonial America*, 28–30.

8. *Mass. Col. Laws* (1648), 46, 49.

9. Chapin, *Criminal Justice in Colonial America*, 35–40.

10. *Mass. Col. Laws* (1660), 129, 168.

11. Chapin, *Criminal Justice in Colonial America*, 27.

12. George L. Haskins, *Law and Authority in Early Massachusetts* (New York: Macmillan, 1960), 199–200.

13. *Mass. Col. Laws* (1660), 201–2; *Conn. Laws* (1673), 69.

14. *New Haven Col. Recs.* 2:614 (1656).

15. William S. Holdsworth, *A History of English Law*, 13 vols. (Boston: Little, Brown, 1922–52), 9:225–30.

16. Haskins, *Law and Authority in Early Massachusetts*, 200; *R.I. Col. Recs.* 1:194 (1647).

17. See Edmund S. Morgan, "The Case against Anne Hutchinson," *NEQ* 10 (1937): 644–48; John Winthrop, *History of New England* (or *Journal*), ed. James K. Hosmer, 2 vols. (New York: Scribner's, 1908), 1:236 (1637); *Essex Ct. Recs.* 1:70 (1644).

18. 3 Coke's *Institutes* 137, cited in Felix Rackow, "The Right to Counsel: English and American Precedents," *WMQ*, 3d ser., 11 (1954): 6.

19. Rackow, "The Right to Counsel," 5–6.

20. Frederick Pollack and Frederic Maitland, *The History of English Law before the Time of Edward I* (Cambridge: Cambridge University Press, 1968), 213.

21. Plucknett, *Concise History of the Common Law*, 438, 455–59.

22. Rackow, "The Right to Counsel," 4–5.

23. Plucknett, *Concise History of the Common Law*, 434–35, 438.

24. *Conn. Col. Recs.* 2:59 (1667).

25. Nathan Matthews, "The Results of the Prejudice against Lawyers in Massachusetts in the 17th Century," *Massachusetts Law Quarterly* 13 (1928): 73; Dwight Loomis and J. Gilbert Calhoun, *The Judicial and Civil History of Connecticut* (Boston: Boston Book Company, 1895), 182. See Edwin Powers, *Crime and Punishment in Early Massachusetts, 1620–1692* (Boston: Beacon Press, 1966), 433–34.

26. Anton-Hermann Chroust, *The Rise of the Legal Profession in America*, 2 vols. (Norman: University of Oklahoma Press, 1965), 1:75.

27. *Mass. Col. Laws* (1660), 39.

28. Chroust, *Rise of the Legal Profession in America* 1:73–75.

29. *Mass. Col. Recs.* 3:168 (1649).

30. J. Hammond Trumbull, "A Sketch of the Life of Thomas Lechford," *American Antiquarian Society Transactions* 7 (1885): xv–xxi.

31. Chroust, *Rise of the Legal Profession in America* 1:73–75.

32. Ibid., 76–80, 117–18.
33. *Mass. Col. Laws* (1660), 9.
34. *Mass. Col. Recs.* 4 (pt. 2): 87.
35. Chroust, *Rise of the Legal Profession in America* 1:116–17.
36. *R.I. Col. Recs.* 1:200–201.
37. Rackow, "The Right to Counsel," 4.
38. *R.I. Col. Recs.* 1:200–201.
39. Chroust, *Rise of the Legal Profession in America* 1:137–38.
40. *R.I. Col. Recs.* 2:238–39.
41. Plucknett, *Concise History of the Common Law,* 434–35.
42. *Salem Town Records, 1659–91,* 3 vols. (Salem, Mass.: Essex Institute, 1913–34), 1:167 (1673); 2:46 (1681).
43. *R.I. Col. Recs.* 1:225–26.
44. *R.I. Col. Laws,* 27. See Oliver W. Hammonds, "The Attorney General in the American Colonies," *AALHS* 1, no. 2 (1939): 15–16.
45. *Conn. Col. Recs.* 1:388, 426.
46. *MHS Proc.,* 3d ser., 56 (1922): 172–73.
47. Hammonds, "The Attorney General in the American Colonies," 15–16; *MHS Proc.,* 3d ser., 56:172–73. For Checkley's later appointment as attorney general for the Salem witch trials, see *MHS Proc.,* 1st ser., 19 (1881): 142; George L. Burr, ed., *Narratives of the Witchcraft Cases, 1648–1706* (New York: Scribner's, 1914), 31 n., 412.
48. James F. Stephen, *A History of the Criminal Law of England,* 3 vols. (London: Macmillan, 1883), 1:233–39.
49. *Mass. Col. Laws* (1660), 37 (1641); *Mass. Col. Laws* (1672), 59–60 (1646, 1651).
50. *Conn. Laws* (1673), 32; *Ply. Col. Laws,* 255–56 (1671).
51. *New Haven Col. Recs.* 1:449 (1649). See also *New Haven Col. Recs.* 2:151–52 (1655).
52. *R.I. Col. Recs.* 1:198, 207–8 (1647).
53. *Mass. Col. Laws* (1660), 43, 187; *Mass. Col. Laws* (1648), 46; *Mass. Col. Laws* (1672), 129.
54. *Conn. Laws* (1673), 58.
55. *Mass. Col. Laws* (1660), 163 (1652).
56. *Ply. Col. Laws,* 262 (1671); *Conn. Laws* (1673), 34.
57. S. F. C. Milsom, *Historical Foundations of the Common Law* (London: Butterworths, 1969), 359.
58. A. L. Goodhart, *English Law and the Moral Law* (London: Stevens & Sons, 1953), 134–35.
59. *Ply. Col. Laws,* 28, 42, 87, 242, 247. See Julius Goebel, Jr., "King's Law and Local Custom in Seventeenth Century New England," *CLR* 31 (1931): 441–42.
60. *Mass. Col. Recs.* 1:118.
61. *Mass. Col. Laws* (1660), 153, 158, 164, 171, 194, 197.
62. Charles J. Hilkey, *Legal Development in Colonial Massachusetts, 1630–1686* (New York: Columbia University Press, 1910), 89–90.

63. *R.I. Col. Recs.* 1:71, 103. See John T. Farrell, *The Early History of Rhode Island's Court System* (Reprint from *Rhode Island History* 9, no. 3), 5–6.

64. *R.I. Col. Recs.* 1:198–99.

65. *Conn. Col. Recs.* 1:535–36 (1650).

66. *Conn. Laws* (1673), 37.

67. "Conn. Part. Ct. Recs." 22 (1928): 145, 188, 251; *Conn. Col. Recs.* 2:118, 132.

68. *New Haven Col. Recs.* 1:62–69, 137–39; 2:175–76.

69. Milsom, *Historical Foundations of the Common Law,* 360.

70. *Mass. Col. Laws* (1648), 51.

71. *R.I. Col. Recs.* 1:199.

72. *Ply. Col. Laws,* 242 (1671), 293 (1685).

73. Robert C. Palmer, "Conscience and the Law: The English Criminal Jury," *MLR* 84 (Feb.–Apr. 1986): 788.

74. See P. G. Lawson, "Lawless Juries? The Composition and Behavior of Hertfordshire Juries, 1573–1624," in *The Criminal Trial Jury in England, 1200–1800,* ed. J. S. Cockburn and Thomas A. Green (Princeton, N.J.: Princeton University Press, 1988), 117.

75. Palmer, "Conscience and the Law," 794.

76. Thomas A. Green, *Verdict According to Conscience: Perspectives on the English Criminal Trial Jury, 1200–1800* (Chicago: University of Chicago Press, 1985), 106–7.

77. Palmer, "Conscience and the Law," 788–89.

78. Green, *Verdict According to Conscience,* 236–49.

79. Palmer, "Conscience and the Law," 789–90.

80. *Mass. Col. Laws* (1648), 32 (1641); *Ply. Col. Laws,* 263 (1671).

81. *Mass. Col. Laws* (1648), 32 (1641).

82. Ibid.

83. Haskins, *Law and Authority in Early Massachusetts,* 213–14.

84. *R.I. Col. Recs.* 1:199, 204 (1647).

85. David J. Bodenhamer, *Fair Trial: Rights of the Accused in American History* (New York: Oxford University Press, 1992), 22–23. See also John M. Murrin, "Magistrates, Sinners, and a Precarious Liberty: Trial by Jury in Seventeenth-Century New England," in *Saints and Revolutionaries: Essays on Early American History,* ed. David D. Hall, John M. Murrin, and Thad W. Tate (New York: Norton, 1984), 163.

86. Murrin, "Magistrates, Sinners, and a Precarious Liberty," 152–206.

87. *Conn. Laws* (1673), 9; *Mass. Col. Laws* (1660), 152.

88. *Ply. Col. Laws,* 244 (1671); *New Haven Col. Recs.* 2:577 (1656); *Mass. Col. Laws* (1648), 5–6; *Conn. Laws* (1673), 9.

89. *R.I. Col. Recs.* 1:166 (1647).

90. Powers, *Crime and Punishment in Early Massachusetts,* 439–40.

91. *Mass. Col. Laws* (1660), 45 (1641).

92. *Conn. Col. Recs.* 1:515 (1650); *New Haven Col. Recs.* 2:578 (1656).

93. *R.I. Col. Recs.* 1:167 (1647).

94. "Suffolk Ct. Recs." 1:436.

95. Sanford J. Fox, *Science and Justice: The Massachusetts Witchcraft Trials* (Baltimore: Johns Hopkins University Press, 1968), 100.

96. Winthrop, *Journal* 1:282–83 (1638); *Mass. Col. Recs.* 3:229 (1651).

97. Winthrop, *Journal* 1:282–83.

98. *Ply. Col. Recs.* 6:98.

99. Fox, *Science and Justice*, 91–98.

100. Winthrop, *Journal* 1:282–83.

101. David H. Wrinn, "Manslaughter and Mosaicism in Early Connecticut," *VULR* 21 (1986–87): 313–14.

102. E. M. Morgan, "The Privilege against Self-Incrimination," *Minn. L.R.* 34 (1949): 18.

103. Plucknett, *Concise History of the Common Law*, 437.

104. *Mass. Col. Laws* (1660), 236 (1666); *Ply. Col. Laws*, 290 (1671); *Conn. Laws* (1673), 41.

105. Leonard W. Levy, *Origins of the Fifth Amendment* (New York: Oxford University Press, 1968), 43–82, 203–4, 301–32. See also R. Carter Pittman, "The Colonial and Constitutional History of the Privilege against Self-Incrimination in America," *Va. L.R.* 21 (1935): 769–73.

106. John Winthrop, *A Short History of the Rise, Reign, and Ruin of the Antinomians, Familists, and Libertines That Infected the Churches of New England* (London: Smith, 1644), reprinted in Charles F. Adams, ed., *Antinomianism in the Colony of Massachusetts Bay, 1636–1638* (Boston: Prince Society, 1894), 194–95; Haskins, *Law and Authority in Early Massachusetts*, 200–201; Levy, *Origins of the Fifth Amendment*, 341–42.

107. Morgan, "The Privilege against Self-Incrimination," 19.

108. *Mass. Col. Laws* (1660), 33 (1641).

109. *Conn. Laws* (1673), 55.

110. Pittman, "The Colonial and Constitutional History of the Privilege against Self-Incrimination," 773–74.

111. Levy, *Origins of the Fifth Amendment*, 33–35, 263.

112. John H. Langbein, *Torture and the Law of Proof* (Chicago: University of Chicago Press, 1977), 73–74.

113. Morgan, "The Privilege against Self-Incrimination," 14–15.

114. Langbein, *Torture and the Law of Proof*, 134–36.

115. Ibid., 6–8, 11–12, 75.

116. 3 Coke's *Institutes* 35, quoted in Langbein, *Torture and the Law of Proof*, 73.

117. *Mass. Col. Laws* (1660), 43 (1641).

118. *Conn. Laws* (1673), 65.

119. Powers, *Crime and Punishment in Early Massachusetts*, 88, 490–92.

120. Statute of Westminster 1, c. 12 (1275).

121. Levy, *Origins of the Fifth Amendment*, 17–18; Plucknett, *Concise History of the Common Law*, 126; Langbein, *Torture and the Law of Proof*, 75.

122. James F. Stephen, *A History of the Criminal Law of England*, 3 vols. (London: Macmillan, 1883), 1:297–301; Plucknett, *Concise History of the Common Law*, 125–26.

123. Plucknett, *Concise History of the Common Law*, 126 n.2.

124. Winthrop, *Journal* 1:282–83.

125. Morgan, "The Privilege against Self-Incrimination," 20.

126. Robert Calef, *More Wonders of the Invisible World* (London: Nath. Hillar, 1700), 106.

127. *Mass. Col. Laws* (1660), 43 (1641); *Conn. Laws* (1673), 69; *New Haven Col. Recs.* 2:572 (1656); *Ply. Col. Laws*, 101 (1656).

128. Winthrop, *Journal* 1:235.

129. Massachusetts retained the two-witness rule until 1692, when the new provincial laws restricted it to treason cases, thus bringing application of the rule into conformity with English law. *Acts and Resolves, Public and Private, of the Province of the Massachusetts Bay*, 5 vols. (Boston: Wright & Potter, 1869–1922), 1:55, 255.

130. *Mass. Assist. Ct. Recs.* 3:191–93 (1667). See Powers, *Crime and Punishment in Early Massachusetts*, 280–81.

131. *Mass. Assist. Ct. Recs.* 2:121.

132. *New Haven Col. Recs.* 2:223–24.

133. "New Hamp. Ct. Recs.," 16, 126, 182–83.

134. *Mass. Col. Laws* (1660), 55 (1641).

135. *New Haven Col. Recs.* 1:29, 62–69. See Robert F. Oaks, " 'Things Fearful to Name': Sodomy and Buggery in Seventeenth-Century New England," *JSH* 12 (1978): 275.

136. *New Haven Col. Recs.* 1:62–73 (1642).

137. Ibid., 295–96 (1647), 378 (1648).

138. John M. Zane, "The Five Ages of the Bench and Bar of England," in *Select Essays in Anglo-American Legal History*, 3 vols. (Boston: Little, Brown, 1907–1909), 1:688–90.

139. J. H. Baker, "Criminal Courts and Procedure at Common Law, 1550–1800," in *Crime in England, 1550–1800*, ed. J. S. Cockburn (Princeton, N.J.: Princeton University Press, 1977), 41–42.

140. George W. Dalzell, *Benefit of Clergy in America* (Winston-Salem: John F. Blair, 1955), 1–42. See also Edward J. White, "Benefit of Clergy," *ALR* 46 (1912): 78–94; Stephen, *History of the Criminal Law of England* 1:459.

141. Dalzell, *Benefit of Clergy in America*, 24–42; Chapin, *Criminal Justice in Colonial America*, 48–49.

142. Baker, "Criminal Courts and Procedure at Common Law," 41–42.

143. Dalzell, *Benefit of Clergy in America*, 181.

144. Chapin, *Criminal Justice in Colonial America*, 49–50.

145. Haskins, *Law and Authority in Early Massachusetts*, 199–200.

146. Stephen, *History of the Criminal Law of England* 1:233–39; Haskins, *Law and Authority in Early Massachusetts*, 198–99.

147. Haskins, *Law and Authority in Early Massachusetts*, 199.

148. *Mass. Col. Laws* (1660), 43; *Conn. Laws* (1673), 58.

149. Plucknett, *Concise History of the Common Law*, 133–34; Stephen, *History of the Criminal Law of England* 1:306–7; Levy, *Origins of the Fifth Amendment*, 37–38, 315.

150. *Mass. Col. Laws* (1660), 41 (1641).
151. *Ply. Col. Laws*, 68 (1640).

Chapter 7: Unequal Protection of the Law

1. *Mass. Col. Laws* (1648), 2.
2. *Mass. Col. Laws* (1660), 155–56, 219–20, 222, 224.
3. Edwin Powers, *Crime and Punishment in Early Massachusetts, 1620–1692* (Boston: Beacon Press, 1966), 324.
4. *Ply. Col. Laws*, 102–3, 114, 122, 126–27, 130; *New Haven Col. Recs.* 2:238–41; *Conn. Col. Recs.* 1:283–84, 303, 308, 324; *Conn. Laws* (1673), 28.
5. *Ply. Col. Recs.* 3:123–24, 139–40, 154.
6. *New Haven Col. Recs.* 2:238–40 (1658).
7. *Mass. Col. Laws* (1660), 160.
8. Bradley Chapin, *Criminal Justice in Colonial America, 1606–1660* (Athens: University of Georgia Press, 1983), 54–55.
9. Powers, *Crime and Punishment in Early Massachusetts*, 321.
10. See *Mass. Col. Laws* (1660), 33 (1641).
11. *Mass. Col. Recs.* 4 (pt. 1): 385 (1659).
12. Ibid., 279–80; (pt. 2): 21, 27, 50.
13. Powers, *Crime and Punishment in Early Massachusetts*, 221–22.
14. *Mass. Col. Recs.* 4 (pt. 1): 238–44, 384–86 (1659). See Powers, *Crime and Punishment in Early Massachusetts*, 333–34, 337.
15. *Mass. Col. Laws* (1660), 171 (1645); *Ply. Col. Laws*, 98 (1653); *Conn. Col. Recs.* 1:537–38 (1650); *New Haven Col. Recs.* 2:598–99 (1656).
16. *Ply. Col. Laws*, 244 (1671); *Conn. Laws* (1673), 9; *Mass. Col. Laws* (1648), 5–6; *R.I. Col. Recs.* 1:158–59 (1647).
17. Alice M. Earle, *Child Life in Colonial Days* (New York: Macmillan, 1937), 1–33.
18. John P. Demos, *A Little Commonwealth: Family Life in Plymouth Colony* (New York: Oxford University Press, 1970), 145–50.
19. *Mass. Col. Laws* (1660), 55 (1641); *Conn. Col. Recs.* 1:77–78 (1642).
20. *Conn. Laws* (1673), 9; *Mass. Col. Laws* (1648), 5–6; *Mass. Col. Laws* (1660), 128–29; *Mass. Col. Laws* (1672), 14–15.
21. Keith W. Thomas, "The Double Standard," *JHI* 20 (1959): 198.
22. See chapter 2; *Mass. Col. Laws* (1660), 55 (1641); *Ply. Col. Laws*, 245 (1671); *Conn. Col. Recs.* 1:77 (1642); *New Haven Col. Recs.* 2:577 (1656); *R.I. Col. Recs.* 1:173 (1647).
23. *Mass. Col. Laws* (1648), 17; *Ply. Col. Recs.* 3:221 (1661). See Demos, *A Little Commonwealth*, 96–97.
24. "Suffolk Ct. Recs." 1:222, 233, 249, 254–55, 312, 442, 480–81; 2:809; *Essex Ct. Recs.* 5:103, 154, 155. See also *Me. Ct. Recs.* 3:136.
25. *Essex Ct. Recs.* 3:242 (1665), 309 (1666); 5:103 (1672); 6:73 (1675), 169 (1676), 256 (1677).
26. 21 Jac. I, c. 27 (1624).

27. Roger Thompson, *Women in Stuart England and America: A Comparative Study* (London: Routledge & Paul, 1974), 9.

28. Thomas, "The Double Standard," 212, 216.

29. See *Mass. Col. Laws* (1660), 35, 51 (1641); *Ply. Col. Laws*, 86 (1646), 281 (1671); *Ply. Col. Recs.* 4:46 (1663); *New Haven Town Recs.* 2:214 (1668).

30. Richard B. Morris, *Studies in the History of American Law*, 2d ed. (1930; reprint Philadelphia: Mitchell, 1959), 134–35.

31. John Winthrop, *History of New England* (or *Journal*), ed. James K. Hosmer, 2 vols. (New York: Scribner's, 1908), 2:225.

32. Quoted in Thompson, *Women in Stuart England*, 10.

33. *Mass. Col. Laws* (1660), 43 (1641), 164, 171, 189–90, 194; *Ply. Col. Laws*, 65–66, 82, 92, 247; *Conn. Col. Recs.* 1:533, 538, 547; *New Haven Col. Recs.* 2:595, 606; *R.I. Col. Recs.* 1:186.

34. *Mass. Col. Laws* (1660), 136–37.

35. *Conn. Col. Recs.* 1:124 (1645).

36. "Conn. Part. Ct. Recs.," 74.

37. *New Haven Col. Recs.* 1:46–47.

38. *Essex Ct. Recs.* 8:303.

39. See Donald Black, *The Behavior of Law* (New York: Academic Press, 1976), 116–17.

40. M. P. Baumgartner, "Law and Social Status in Colonial New Haven, 1639–1665," *RLS* 1 (1978): 155–60.

41. Ibid., 166–68.

42. Ibid., 168–69.

43. Ibid., 170.

44. *Ply. Col. Recs.* 6:108 (1683), 190 (1686); *New Haven Col. Recs.* 2:384–87 (1660), 504–9 (1673); "Suffolk Ct. Recs." 1:189 (1680), 2:869 (1677), 912 (1678); *Mass. Assist. Ct. Recs.* 1:283–84 (1685); 2:32 (1632), 79 (1637), 86 (1638), 99 (1640), 122 (1643).

45. See A. Roger Ekirch, *Bound for America: The Transportation of British Convicts to the Colonies, 1718–1775* (New York: Oxford University Press, 1987), 1–8.

46. James D. Butler, "British Convicts Shipped to American Colonies," *AHR* 2 (1896): 13.

47. Abbot E. Smith, *Colonists in Bondage* (Gloucester, Mass.: Peter Smith, 1965), 165–67.

48. Butler, "British Convicts Shipped to American Colonies," 20.

49. Ibid.

50. Wilcomb E. Washburn, *Red Man's Land/White Man's Law: A Study of the Past and Present Status of the American Indian* (New York: Scribner's, 1971), 22–23, 41.

51. Alden T. Vaughan, *New England Frontier: Puritans and Indians, 1620–1675* (Boston: Little, Brown, 1965), passim.

52. G. E. Thomas, "Puritans, Indians, and the Concept of Race," *NEQ* 48 (1975): 3–27.

53. Francis Jennings, *The Invasion of America: Indians, Colonialism, and the Cant of Conquest* (Chapel Hill: University of North Carolina Press, 1975), passim.

54. Yasuhide Kawashima, *Puritan Justice and the Indian: White Man's Law in Massachusetts* (Middletown, Conn.: Wesleyan University Press, 1986), passim.

55. Vaughan, *New England Frontier*, 188–90.

56. Washburn, *Red Man's Land/White Man's Law,* 41–42.

57. Yasuhide Kawashima, "Jurisdiction of the Colonial Courts over the Indians in Massachusetts, 1689–1763," *NEQ* 42 (1969): 538.

58. *New Haven Col. Recs.* 1:23–24, 134, 135, 146 n.; *Ply. Col. Recs.* 5:204–6.

59. Kawashima, *Puritan Justice and the Indian*, 150–51, 176–79.

60. *Mass. Col. Laws* (1660), 162.

61. *Ply. Col. Laws*, 194 (1682).

62. *Mass. Col. Laws* (1660), 163 (1633).

63. *Ply. Col. Laws*, 96 (1652), 298 (1685); *Conn. Laws* (1673), 34.

64. *Mass. Col. Laws* (1672), 77.

65. *Mass. Col. Laws* (1660), 161; *Ply. Col. Laws*, 74 (1643); *Conn. Col. Recs.* 1:402; *New Haven Col. Recs.* 2:593; *R.I. Col. Recs.* 1:403–4 (1658).

66. Jennings, *Invasion of America*, 135.

67. *Mass. Col. Laws* (1672), 289 (1681).

68. Lorenzo J. Greene, *The Negro in Colonial New England* (New York: Atheneum, 1968), 100–23, 290–315.

69. *Mass. Col. Laws* (1672), 251–52 (1677).

70. *Mass. Col. Laws* (1660), 163 (1658); *Mass. Col. Laws* (1672), 77.

71. *Mass. Col. Laws* (1672), 3.

72. *Conn. Col. Recs.* 2:575–76 (1675).

73. *Conn. Laws* (1673), 17.

74. Kawashima, "Jurisdiction of the Colonial Courts over Indians," 541–46.

75. Vaughan, *New England Frontier*, 191–92.

76. *Ply. Col. Laws*, 171 (1674).

77. *R.I. Col. Recs.* 2:509 (1673).

78. Ibid.

79. *Mass. Assist. Ct. Recs.* 1:21–22.

80. *Mass. Col. Recs.* 5:25.

81. *Ply. Col. Recs.* 5:159, 167–68.

82. *Mass. Assist. Ct. Recs.* 3:216–17 (1672); *Ply. Col. Recs.* 6:98 (1682).

83. *Mass. Assist. Ct. Recs.* 1:50, 74, 199, 295–96.

84. *Essex Ct. Recs.* 4:174.

85. *Conn. Col. Recs.* 1:576 (1660).

86. *Mass. Col. Laws* (1660), 236 (1666); *Conn. Laws* (1673), 41; *Ply. Col. Laws*, 290 (1671).

87. *R.I. Col. Recs.* 2:509 (1673); *Ply. Col. Laws*, 171 (1674).

88. *Watertown Records from 1634,* 8 vols. (Watertown, Mass.: Historical Society of Watertown, 1894–1939), 1:106.

89. *Salem Town Records, 1659–91,* 3 vols. (Salem, Mass.: Essex Institute, 1913–34), 1:304 (1679).

90. Samuel A. Green, ed., *Early Records of Groton, 1662–1707* (Groton, Mass.: Wilson, 1880), 69 (1681).

91. *Ply. Col. Laws*, 193–94.

92. *Mass. Col. Laws* (1660), 164–65, 236; *Ply. Col. Laws*, 41, 83–84, 141–42, 194, 251; *Conn. Col. Recs.* 1:533–34; 2:257; 3:94; *R.I. Col. Recs.* 1:186.

93. *R.I. Col. Recs.* 1:308 (1655).

94. *Ply. Col. Laws*, 41 (1636), 195 (1682).

95. *Conn. Col. Recs.* 1:105 (1644); 2:308–9 (1676).

96. Ibid. 6:163.

97. *Ply. Col. Laws*, 172 (1674).

98. *Ply. Col. Recs.* 5:270 (1678); 6:163 (1685).

99. *R.I. Col. Recs.* 1:413 (1659).

100. Jennings, *Invasion of America*, 146–49.

101. Greene, *Negro in Colonial New England*, 179–86.

102. William D. Piersen, *Black Yankees* (Amherst: University of Massachusetts Press, 1988), passim.

103. Evarts B. Greene and Virginia D. Harrington, *American Population before the Federal Census of 1790* (New York: Columbia University Press, 1932), 10. See Greene, *Negro in Colonial New England*, 73.

104. Vaughan, *New England Frontier*, 196–97.

105. *Mass. Assist. Ct. Recs.* 1:25, 74, 197, 304; *Essex Ct. Recs.* 3:101; 5:179–80; 7:329, 373, 410; 8:341. See Greene, *Negro in Colonial New England*, 179–81, 182–86.

106. Edgar J. McManus, *Black Bondage in the North* (Syracuse, N.Y.: Syracuse University Press, 1973), 83–85.

107. *Pyn. Ct. Rec.*, 105.

108. *Mass. Assist. Ct. Recs.* 1:50, 74, 199; "Suffolk Ct. Recs." 2:1067.

109. *Ply. Col. Recs.* 6:141–42; *Mass. Assist. Ct. Recs.* 1:304–5, 321.

110. Racial restrictions against blacks were a later development. See *Conn. Col. Recs.* 4:40 (1690); *R.I. Col. Recs.* 3:492 (1703); *The Acts and Resolves, Public and Private, of the Province of the Massachusetts Bay*, 5 vols. (Boston: Wright & Potter, 1869–86), 1:578 (1705), 606–7 (1707).

Chapter 8: The Devil and the Law

1. Thomas Hobbes, *Leviathan*, ed. C. B. Macpherson (London: Penguin Books, 1981), 92.

2. Chadwick Hansen, *Witchcraft at Salem* (New York: Braziller, 1969), 6–8.

3. *Ply. Col. Laws*, 43 (1636). The revised code adopted in 1671 followed the Massachusetts statute almost verbatim. Ibid., 244.

4. *Mass. Col. Laws* (1660), 55 (1641); *Mass. Col. Laws* (1672), 14; *Conn. Col. Recs.* 1:77 (1642), 515 (1650); *Conn. Laws* (1673), 9.

5. *New Haven Col. Recs.* 2:576 (1656); *R.I. Col. Recs.* 1:166 (1647); *R.I. Col. Laws*, 3 (1665).

6. "Conn. Part. Ct. Recs.," 56. See Samuel G. Drake, *Annals of Witchcraft in New England, and Elsewhere in the United States, from Their First Settlement* (1869; reprint New York: Blom, 1972), 62–63; John P. Demos, *Entertaining Satan* (New

York: Oxford University Press, 1982), 345–46; George L. Burr, ed., *Narratives of the Witchcraft Cases, 1648–1706* (New York: Scribner's, 1914), 135–36.

7. John Winthrop, *History of New England* (or *Journal*), ed. James K. Hosmer, 2 vols. (New York: Scribner's, 1908), 2:344–45 (1648).

8. See A. D. J. Macfarlane, "Witchcraft in Tudor and Stuart Essex," in *Crime in England, 1550–1800*, ed. J. S. Cockburn (Princeton, N.J.: Princeton University Press, 1977), 73, 82.

9. Michael Dalton, *The Country Justice* (London: Society of Stationers, 1618), 243.

10. Hansen, *Witchcraft at Salem*, 48.

11. John M. Taylor, *The Witchcraft Delusion in Colonial Connecticut, 1647–1697* (1908; reprint New York: Franklin, 1971), 40–44.

12. Drake, *Annals of Witchcraft*, 135.

13. Winthrop, *Journal* 2:344.

14. Taylor, *Witchcraft Delusion in Connecticut*, 43–44.

15. Ibid., 40–42.

16. Winthrop, *Journal* 2:344.

17. Burr, *Narratives of the Witchcraft Cases*, 31 n., 412.

18. Wallace Notestein, *A History of Witchcraft in England from 1558 to 1718* (New York: Russell & Russell, 1965), 164 ff.

19. Burr, *Narratives of the Witchcraft Cases*, 363 n.

20. Winthrop, *Journal* 2:344–45.

21. Burr, *Narratives of the Witchcraft Cases*, 20–21.

22. Hansen, *Witchcraft at Salem*, 49.

23. Winthrop, *Journal* 2:344–45.

24. Drake, *Annals of Witchcraft*, 144–49 (1679); Burr, *Narratives of the Witchcraft Cases*, 412.

25. Richard Weisman, *Witchcraft, Magic, and Religion in 17th-Century Massachusetts* (Amherst: University of Massachusetts Press, 1984), 103–4, 150–52.

26. Demos, *Entertaining Satan*, 44, 83, 140–41, 188, 190, 213–17, 355, 360–61.

27. Drake, *Annals of Witchcraft*, 62–64, 78–79, 120–22; Taylor, *Witchcraft Delusion in Connecticut*, 148–49; Demos, *Entertaining Satan*, 402–9.

28. Burr, *Narratives of the Witchcraft Cases*, 18–21, 135–36.

29. Taylor, *Witchcraft Delusion in Connecticut*, 152–53.

30. Drake, *Annals of Witchcraft*, 145–46.

31. Ibid.

32. Taylor, *Witchcraft Delusion in Connecticut*, 57; Burr, *Narratives of the Witchcraft Cases*, 411.

33. Drake, *Annals of Witchcraft*, 219–22, 225–27.

34. Taylor, *Witchcraft Delusion in Connecticut*, 99–100.

35. Demos, *Entertaining Satan*, 319–39, 404, 406–7. See Drake, *Annals of Witchcraft*, 99–103; Montague Summers, *The Geography of Witchcraft* (New Hyde Park, N.Y.: University Books, 1965), 263.

36. *Mass. Assist. Ct. Recs.* 3:151–52. See Demos, *Entertaining Satan*, 36–56, 404–5.

37. Drake, *Annals of Witchcraft*, 128–29, 196–97.

38. *New Haven Town Recs.* 1:245–46.

39. Royal R. Hinman, *The Blue Laws of New Haven Colony* (Hartford: Case, Tiffany, 1838), 296–97. See Taylor, *Witchcraft Delusion in Connecticut*, 152–53.

40. See Demos, *Entertaining Satan*, 44–45.

41. *Essex Ct. Recs.* 7:355 (1680). See Drake, *Annals of Witchcraft*, 142–43; Demos, *Entertaining Satan*, 132–36.

42. *Conn. Col. Recs.* 1:572–73 (1658).

43. *Mass. Assist. Ct. Recs.* 1:11 (1673). See also *Ply. Col. Recs.* 3:211 (1660); Drake, *Annals of Witchcraft*, 134–35.

44. *Mass. Col. Laws* (1660), 202 (1647); *Mass. Col. Laws* (1672), 86, 126; *Conn. Laws* (1673), 65; *New Haven Col. Recs.* 2:614–15 (1656).

45. Demos, *Entertaining Satan*, 44–45, 132–36; *Essex Ct. Recs.* 7:355 (1680). See Drake, *Annals of Witchcraft*, 142–43.

46. *Conn. Col. Recs.* 2:132 (1670).

47. *New Haven Col. Recs.* 2:151–52 (1655); *New Haven Town Recs.* 2:174, 179.

48. Carl Stephenson and Frederick G. Marcham, eds., *Sources of English Constitutional History* (New York: Harper, 1937), 78–80.

49. Burr, *Narratives of the Witchcraft Cases*, 31 n., 412.

50. Drake, *Annals of Witchcraft*, 64–70.

51. Demos, *Entertaining Satan*, 286 (1665).

52. *Conn. Col. Recs.* 2:132 (1669). See Taylor, *Witchcraft Delusion in Connecticut*, 47–61, 76–78; Demos, *Entertaining Satan*, 355–63.

53. Drake, *Annals of Witchcraft*, 146–47.

54. *Provincial Papers: Documents and Records Relating to the Province of New Hampshire, from the Earliest Period of Its Settlement, 1623–1776*, ed. Nathaniel Bouton, 7 vols. (Concord and Nashua: Jenks, 1867–73), 1:219 (1656), 415 (1680).

55. Burr, *Narratives of the Witchcraft Cases*, 20–21; Drake, *Annals of Witchcraft*, 169–71, 179.

56. Demos, Entertaining Satan, 40–41, 45–46, 141, 356.

57. Drake, *Annals of Witchcraft*, 141–43 (1679); Summers, *Geography of Witchcraft*, 263–71.

58. Demos, *Entertaining Satan*, 132–36.

59. *Essex Ct. Recs.* 2:160 (1659).

60. John P. Demos, "John Godfrey and His Neighbors: Witchcraft and the Social Web in Colonial Massachusetts," *WMQ*, 3d ser., 33 (1976): 247–49.

61. Demos, *Entertaining Satan*, 44–46.

62. Drake, *Annals of Witchcraft*, 74–75.

63. *New Haven Town Recs.* 2:129–32.

64. *New Haven Col. Recs.* 2:29 (1652).

65. Demos, *Entertaining Satan*, 76–79.

66. Demos, "John Godfrey and His Neighbors," 161.

67. Drake, *Annals of Witchcraft*, 171.

68. Demos, *Entertaining Satan*, 88–89.

69. Drake, *Annals of Witchcraft*, 65–72.

70. Demos, *Entertaining Satan*, 75, 87–88 (1656).

71. Hansen, *Witchcraft at Salem*, 12–13; Edwin Powers, *Crime and Punishment in Early Massachusetts, 1620–1692* (Boston: Beacon Press, 1966), 460–61.

72. Demos, "John Godfrey and His Neighbors," 258–60.

73. Demos, *Entertaining Satan*, 75, 87–88, 286.

74. Burr, *Narratives of the Witchcraft Cases*, 18–21.

75. Hansen, *Witchcraft at Salem*, 13–15.

76. Demos, *Entertaining Satan*, 99–105; Summers, *Geography of Witchcraft*, 261–62; Hansen, *Witchcraft at Salem*, 17.

77. Demos, *Entertaining Satan*, 99–131.

78. Drake, *Annals of Witchcraft*, 19, 112.

79. Hansen, *Witchcraft at Salem*, 18.

80. Burr, *Narratives of the Witchcraft Cases*, 19.

81. See Sanford J. Fox, *Science and Justice: The Massachusetts Witchcraft Trials* (Baltimore: Johns Hopkins University Press, 1968), 91–98.

82. Demos, *Entertaining Satan*, 99–131, 345–46; Burr, *Narratives of the Witchcraft Cases*, 18–21, 135–36; Hansen, *Witchcraft at Salem*, 13–15.

83. Taylor, *Witchcraft Delusion in Connecticut*, 99–100.

84. Hansen, *Witchcraft at Salem*, 12–13.

85. *New Haven Town Recs.* 1:318–19 (1657).

86. John P. Demos, *A Little Commonwealth: Family Life in Plymouth Colony* (New York: Oxford University Press, 1971), 83n; Drake, *Annals of Witchcraft*, 77–79; Taylor, *Witchcraft Delusion in Connecticut*, 125 ff.

87. Hansen, *Witchcraft at Salem*, 1–11; Summers, *Geography of Witchcraft*, 346–48. See Weisman, *Witchcraft, Magic, and Religion*, 23–38.

88. Taylor, *Witchcraft Delusion in Connecticut*, 42.

89. George L. Kittredge, *Witchcraft in Old and New England* (Cambridge, Mass.: Harvard University Press, 1929), 331, 367–68.

90. Cotton Mather, *The Wonders of the Invisible World* (Boston: Benjamin Harris, 1693); Robert Calef, *More Wonders of the Invisible World* (London: Nath. Hillar, 1700); Paul Boyer and Stephen Nissenbaum, *Salem Possessed* (Cambridge, Mass.: Harvard University Press, 1974); Linnda R. Caporael, "Ergotism: The Satan Loosed in Salem?" *Science* 194 (Dec. 24, 1976): 1390–94; Marion L. Starkey, *The Devil in Massachusetts* (New York: Knopf, 1949); Hansen, *Witchcraft at Salem*.

91. N. E. H. Hull, *Female Felons* (Urbana: University of Illinois Press, 1987), 50; David T. Konig, *Law and Society in Puritan Massachusetts: Essex County, 1629–1692* (Chapel Hill: University of North Carolina Press, 1979), 175.

92. Samuel Sewall, *The Diary of Samuel Sewall, 1674–1729*, ed. M. Halsey Thomas, 2 vols. (New York: Farrar, Straus & Giroux, 1973), 1:xxvi, 366–67.

Chapter 9: Patterns of Criminality

1. Kai T. Erikson, *Wayward Puritans: A Study in the Sociology of Deviance* (New York: Wiley, 1966), 168–69.

2. Thomas J. Wertenbaker, *The Puritan Oligarchy* (New York: Scribner's, 1947), 159–60, 165.

3. *Mass. Assist. Ct. Recs.*

4. *Ply. Col. Recs.* 1; *Conn. Col. Recs.* 1; "Conn. Part. Ct. Recs."; *New Haven Col. Recs.* 1; *Provid. Ct. Recs.*

5. David T. Konig, *Law and Society in Puritan Massachusetts: Essex County, 1629–1692* (Chapel Hill: University of North Carolina Press, 1979), 129–30.

6. Roger Thompson, *Sex in Middlesex: Popular Mores in a Massachusetts County, 1649–1699* (Amherst: University of Massachusetts Press, 1986), 35.

7. Ibid., 193–94.

8. Edwin Powers, *Crime and Punishment in Early Massachusetts, 1620–1692* (Boston: Beacon Press, 1966), 404–5.

9. Thompson, *Sex in Middlesex*, 51.

10. *Me. Ct. Recs.* 1:146, 160, 236–38, 240, 263; 2:12, 84, 87, 91, 106, 119, 151, 153, 184, 196, 202, 222–23, 239, 247, 284, 286–87, 306, 319, 433, 436.

11. See *Essex Ct. Recs.* 1–2.

12. See *Ply. Col. Recs.* 3–6.

13. Statistical data from John P. Demos, *Entertaining Satan* (New York: Oxford University Press, 1982), 402–7.

14. Ibid., 368–70, 382.

15. *Ply. Col. Laws*, 203–4, 249–50; *New Haven Col. Recs.* 2; *Mass. Col. Laws* (1672), 359–95; *Conn. Laws* (1673); *R.I. Col. Laws*, 33–34.

16. "Suffolk Ct. Recs."

17. N. E. H. Hull, *Female Felons* (Urbana: University of Illinois Press, 1987), 37, 44, 46–48, 61–64.

18. *Mass. Assist. Ct. Recs.* 1:30, 32, 71–73, 242–43, 357; 2:78; John Winthrop, *History of New England* (or *Journal*), ed. James K. Hosmer, 2 vols. (New York: Scribner's, 1908), 1:282–83. See Powers, *Crime and Punishment in Early Massachusetts*, 406.

19. *Mass. Assist. Ct. Recs.*, 1–3.

20. *Essex Ct. Recs.* 4:24, 43, 55, 74, 86–87, 119, 142, 165, 178, 181, 187, 214, 239, 243–44, 266–67, 270–71, 274–75, 289, 304, 316, 325, 394, 410–11, 415, 441, 448; "Suffolk Ct. Recs." 1:22, 26, 89–90, 92, 114, 146, 148, 183, 189, 223–24, 231–33, 253, 255–57, 264, 267, 302, 305–7, 336–38, 398, 403, 410, 412, 433, 481, 488, 490, 548, 561; 2:599–601, 603–5, 630, 645; "Conn. Part. Ct. Recs.," 5, 12, 14, 29, 31–34, 36, 38–39, 48, 50, 54, 74, 78, 81, 86, 96–98, 105, 112, 126–27, 129, 138, 144, 152, 166, 169, 174, 187, 191, 196, 205, 213, 236–37, 241, 253, 269; *New Haven Col. Recs.* 1:26, 28–29, 46, 56, 77, 89, 120, 133, 153, 170–71, 229–30, 306–7; *Provid. Ct. Recs.* 1:6, 9, 20, 26, 36–38, 43, 52–53, 57, 63, 70–71, 76, 79; 2:26, 38, 43–44, 51–52, 56–57, 68–70, 97–98; *Pyn. Ct. Rec.*, 107, 109–11, 121, 231, 243, 247, 249, 252–53, 268, 275, 280, 283–84, 287, 290, 293–94, 310, 323, 326; *R.I. Col. Recs.* 1:60, 72.

21. *Mass. Assist. Ct. Recs.* 2:65, 81, 86–87, 90, 92–93, 109; *Essex Ct. Recs.* 3:226, 254, 264; 4:180; "Suffolk Ct. Recs." 1:22, 442–43; 2:677, 697, 807, 1061; *Ply. Col. Recs.* 1:65; 2:35, 54, 96, 112, 137, 165, 172, 174; 3:36, 41, 75, 97; 4:8, 22; 5:143, 253; *New Haven Col. Recs.* 1:81; 2:135–36, 466–67; "Conn. Part. Ct. Recs.," 170.

22. *Mass. Assist. Ct. Recs.* 1:10–11, 251; 2:121; 3:66–67; *Ply. Col. Recs.* 1:64; 2:35–36, 44; 6:74–75; *Conn. Col. Recs.* 1:344; "Conn. Part. Ct. Recs.," 13; *New Haven Col. Recs.* 1:70–73, 295–96; 2:223–24, 440–43, 527n.

23. *Ply. Col. Recs.* 2:148 (1649), 163 (1650).

24. See *Essex Ct. Recs.* 3:16, 270, 289, 344; 4:266, 271; 7:67, 245–46; *Ply. Col. Recs.* 4:115, 137, 183; 5:9, 10, 169; *Conn. Col. Recs.* 1:130; "Conn. Part. Ct. Recs.," 5, 324–25.

25. *Mass. Assist. Ct. Recs.* 1:357.

26. Ibid., 227–28.

27. Ibid., 29–30, 115, 125–26.

28. Peter C. Hoffer and N. E. H. Hull, *Murdering Mothers: Infanticide in England and New England, 1558–1803* (New York: New York University Press, 1981), 59–60.

29. *Acts and Resolves, Public and Private, of the Province of the Massachusetts Bay,* 5 vols. (Boston: Wright & Potter, 1869–1922), 1:255. Concealment of the death of a bastard was first made a capital crime in 1692, but the entire capital list was disallowed by the Privy Council because the provisions relating to witchcraft, blasphemy, incest, homicide by poisoning, and treason were contrary to the laws of England. Ibid., 55–56.

30. Connecticut Archives: Crimes and Misdemeanors 1:219–23. Ms. Coll., Connecticut State Library, Hartford.

31. *Conn. Col. Recs.* 4:285.

32. Carol F. Karlsen, *The Devil in the Shape of a Woman* (New York: Norton, 1987), 160–73.

33. Montague Summers, *The Geography of Witchcraft* (New Hyde Park, N.Y.: University Books, 1965), 259, 263.

34. Demos, *Entertaining Satan,* 64–68.

35. Karlsen, *Devil in the Shape of a Woman,* 64–76, 78.

36. Samuel G. Drake, *Annals of Witchcraft in New England, and Elsewhere in the United States, from Their First Settlement* (1869; reprint New York: Blom, 1972), 99–102; Summers, *Geography of Witchcraft,* 263; Demos, *Entertaining Satan,* 320–21.

37. Karlsen, *Devil in the Shape of a Woman,* 69.

38. *Conn. Col. Recs.* 1:143, 171, 209–22, 226–32; "Conn. Part. Ct. Recs.," 43. See John M. Taylor, *The Witchcraft Delusion in Colonial Connecticut, 1647–1697* (1908; reprint New York: Franklin, 1971), 144–45.

39. Taylor, *Witchcraft Delusion in Connecticut,* 152–53.

40. Demos, *Entertaining Satan,* 76–79.

41. Ibid., 19–35, 74–75.

42. See Karlsen, *Devil in the Shape of a Woman,* 181.

43. Demos, *Entertaining Satan,* 70; Karlsen, *Devil in the Shape of a Woman,* 62.

44. Demos, *Entertaining Satan,* 70.

45. Winthrop, *Journal* 2:344–45.

46. George L. Burr, ed., *Narratives of the Witchcraft Cases, 1648–1706* (New York: Scribner's, 1914), 412. See Drake, *Annals of Witchcraft,* 140–49.

47. *Provincial Papers: Documents and Records Relating to the Province of New Hampshire, from the Earliest Period of Its Settlement, 1623–1776,* ed. Nathaniel Bouton, 7 vols. (Concord and Nashua: Jenks, 1867–73), 1:415–19 (1680).

48. Demos, *Entertaining Satan,* 82.

49. *Mass. Col. Laws* (1672), 216 (1674). See "Suffolk Ct. Recs." 2:943 (1678), 1161 (1680).
50. *Mass. Col. Laws* (1672), 206; *R.I. Col. Recs.* 1:185 (1647).
51. *Essex Ct. Recs.* 6:54 (1675).
52. *Me. Ct. Recs.* 1:136 (1649).
53. *Pyn. Ct. Rec.*, 114, 278 (1673).
54. *Essex Ct. Recs.* 3:17 (1662); 6:341 (1677).
55. *Mass. Assist. Ct. Recs.* 1:200; 2:59, 62, 86, 118, 126; *Essex Ct. Recs.* 1:6, 20; 2:307; 3:143, 254, 351; 4:234; 5:230; "Suffolk Ct. Recs." 1:24, 184, 249–50; 2:751, 753, 847, 884, 958–59, 992, 1158; *Ply. Col. Recs.* 1:7, 15; 2:30, 36, 59; 3:204; 4:234; 5:23, 230; 6:20; *New Haven Col. Recs.* 1:26, 28, 38–39; 2:187–88; "Conn. Part. Ct. Recs.," 74; *Provid. Ct. Recs.* 2:38.
56. *Mass. Assist. Ct. Recs.* 1:200; 2:16–17, 40, 57, 59, 86, 95, 97, 112, 118, 122–23, 126, 132; *Pyn. Ct. Rec.*, 275, 299; *Essex Ct. Recs.* 1:3, 5, 6, 20, 286; 3:143, 182, 254, 263, 351, 435; 4:10, 234, 425; 7:74; 8:301, 365; "Suffolk Ct. Recs." 1:184, 250; 2:605, 847, 884, 894, 958; *Ply. Col. Recs.* 1:7, 15; 2:30, 36, 59; 3:204; 4:234; 5:23, 230; 6:20; *New Haven Col. Recs.* 1:38–39, 162.
57. *Essex Ct. Recs.* 2:151, 247; 4:38; 5:155, 411, 428; 6:205, 256; 7:94, 141; "Suffolk Ct. Recs." 1:185, 232–33, 480; 2:809, 841, 991, 1025; *Ply. Col. Recs.* 1:15, 65; 3:82, 91; "Conn. Part. Ct. Recs.," 4; *New Haven Col. Recs.* 1:81, 88–89, 105; *Provid. Ct. Recs.* 2:24–25.
58. Edmund S. Morgan, "The Puritans and Sex," *NEQ* 15 (1942): 597–602.
59. *Ply. Col. Laws*, 61 (1638); *Conn. Col. Recs.* 1:540 (1650); *New Haven Col. Recs.* 2:599–600 (1656); *Mass. Col. Laws* (1660), 172 (1647).
60. *Mass. Col. Recs.* 4 (pt. 2), 66.
61. *Conn. Col. Recs.* 1:142 (1646).
62. Morgan, "Puritans and Sex," 599–600.
63. "Suffolk Ct. Recs." 2:807.
64. *Mass. Assist. Ct. Recs.* 1:199 (1681).
65. Eli Faber, "Puritan Criminals: The Economic, Social, and Intellectual Background to Crime in Seventeenth-Century Massachusetts," *PAH* 11 (1978): 99–102.
66. *Mass. Assist. Ct. Recs.* 1:30.
67. Faber, "Puritan Criminals," 99–102.
68. Ibid., 103–7. Cf. Thompson, *Sex in Middlesex*, 199.
69. Faber, "Puritan Criminals," 117–22.
70. Edgar J. McManus, *Black Bondage in the North* (Syracuse, N.Y.: Syracuse University Press, 1973), 86–87.
71. *Mass. Assist. Ct. Recs.* 1:74 (1674); *Mass. Col. Recs.* 5:117–18 (1676).
72. "Suffolk Ct. Recs." 1–2.
73. *Essex Ct. Recs.* 1–8; *Pyn. Ct. Rec.*, 123, 246, 262, 274, 281–82, 341.
74. *Ply. Col. Recs.* 6:108, 113, 153–54.
75. *Mass. Assist. Ct. Recs.* 2:19 (1631).
76. *Ply. Col. Recs.* 1:132; 5:107.
77. Powers, *Crime and Punishment in Early Massachusetts*, 389–91.
78. "Conn. Part. Ct. Recs.," 3, 13; *Conn. Col. Recs.* 1:55.
79. *New Haven Town Recs.* 1:179–220.

80. *New Haven Col. Recs.* 2:137–39 (1653).

81. *Me. Ct. Recs.* 1:164, 176 (1651).

82. "Conn. Part. Ct. Recs.," 4, 53.

83. *Essex Ct. Recs.* 5:102, 298.

84. Ibid. 7:146, 224; 8:342, 378.

85. "New Hamp. Ct. Recs.," 16–17 (1654).

86. *New Haven Town Recs.* 2:30, 198, 300, 312.

87. *Provid. Ct. Recs.* 2:39 (1664), 65 (1667), 87 (1669).

88. Howard M. Chapin, ed., *Documentary History of Rhode Island*, 2 vols. (Providence: Preston & Rounds, 1916–19), 2:150, 158.

89. Faber, "Puritan Criminals," 133–34.

90. *New Haven Town Recs.* 2:24–31, 43, 51–55, 110–12, 116–17, 126–27, 134, 164–65, 179, 187–88, 198, 228–29.

91. *Ply. Col. Recs.* 4:88, 107; 5:13–14, 21; 1:132; 2:135; 3:5; 5:13–14, 260.

92. "Suffolk Ct. Recs." 1–2.

93. See James T. Adams, *The Founding of New England* (1921; reprint Boston: Little, Brown, 1949), 121–22.

94. William Bradford, *Of Plymouth Plantation*, ed. Samuel E. Morison (New York: Knopf, 1952), 321.

Chapter 10: Deterrence and Retribution

1. *Mass. Col. Laws* (1660), 93–94 (1650); *Ply. Col. Laws,* 121 (1658); *Conn. Col. Recs.* 1:590 (1650); *New Haven Col. Recs.* 2:571–72 (1656).

2. George L. Haskins, *Law and Authority in Early Massachusetts* (New York: Macmillan, 1960), 206–11; Edwin Powers, *Crime and Punishment in Early Massachusetts, 1620–1692* (Boston: Beacon Press, 1966), 206–8.

3. *Mass. Col. Laws* (1660), 148.

4. *Conn. Col. Recs.* 1:524 (1650).

5. *Ply. Col. Laws,* 42–43, 113 (1658).

6. *Ply. Col. Recs.* 1:132 (1639).

7. Ibid. 2:28.

8. *Ply. Col. Laws,* 113 (1658).

9. See Andrew M. Davis, "The Law of Adultery and Ignominious Punishments—With Especial Reference to the Penalty of Wearing a Letter Affixed to the Clothing," *American Antiquarian Society Proceedings* 10 (1895):114.

10. *Mass. Assist. Ct. Recs.* 2:81 (1639), 124 (1642).

11. *Essex Ct. Recs.* 5:143 (1673), 291 (1674).

12. *Me. Ct. Recs.* 1:335.

13. *Ply. Col. Laws,* 251 (1671).

14. *Mass. Assist. Ct. Recs.* 2:34–35, 41 (1634), 62 (1636).

15. *Mass. Col. Recs.* 1:112, 118.

16. *Mass. Assist. Ct. Recs.* 2:86.

17. *Me. Ct. Recs.* 2:224 (1671).

18. *Essex Ct. Recs.* 6:265 (1677); 8:87–88 (1681).

19. "Suffolk Ct. Recs." 1:302.
20. *Mass. Col. Recs.* 1:12; 3:364. See chapter 2.
21. *Essex Ct. Recs.* 4:230–31.
22. *Mass. Assist. Ct. Recs.* 1:52–53 (1684); 2:108 (1641), 121 (1642).
23. "Conn. Part. Ct. Recs.," 268 (1663).
24. *Mass. Assist. Ct. Recs.* 1:29–30 (1674).
25. "Suffolk Ct. Recs." 1:82–83 (1672).
26. *Mass. Assist. Ct. Recs.* 2:19 (1631).
27. *Essex Ct. Recs.* 4:132 (1669); see chapter 9.
28. *Ply. Col. Recs.* 1:64 (1637), 131 (1639).
29. "Suffolk Ct. Recs." 1:26 (1671); 2:604 (1675), 674 (1676).
30. Alice M. Earle, *Curious Punishments of Bygone Days* (Chicago: Stone, 1896), 2–4.
31. *Mass. Assist. Ct. Recs.* 2:26, 32, 50, 65, 67, 74, 81.
32. *Mass. Col. Recs.* 1:75 (1630).
33. *Mass. Assist. Ct. Recs.* 2:21 (1632), 30 (1633), 53 (1635).
34. See *Ply. Col. Laws*, 41.
35. "Conn. Part. Ct. Recs.," 221; *Essex Ct. Recs.* 3:60 (1663), 343 (1666).
36. *Provid. Ct. Recs.* 1:78.
37. *Mass. Col. Laws* (1660), 127, 164–65, 171, 177, 194; *Ply. Col. Laws*, 59, 83–84; *New Haven Col. Recs.* 2:599, 606; *Conn. Laws* (1673), 35, 40, 58; *R.I. Col. Recs.* 1:186.
38. *Mass. Col. Recs.* 1:260 (1639); Powers, *Crime and Punishment in Early Massachusetts*, 196.
39. *Mass. Col. Laws* (1660), 164–65, 171, 194; *Ply. Col. Laws*, 65–66, 98, 247; *Conn. Col. Recs.* 1:547; *New Haven Col. Recs.* 2:599, 606; *R.I. Col. Recs.* 1:186.
40. Graeme Newman, *The Punishment Response* (Philadelphia: Lippincott, 1978), 115–16; Earle, *Curious Punishments of Bygone Days*, 46–47.
41. *R.I. Col. Recs.* 1:182 (1647).
42. *Mass. Assist. Ct. Recs.* 1:56–57, 145–46.
43. *Pyn. Ct. Rec.*, 278 (1673); *Essex Ct. Recs.* 6:386–87 (1677).
44. *Mass. Assist. Ct. Recs.* 2:63, 64 (1636), 74 (1638), 102 (1640).
45. *Essex Ct. Recs.* 1:99; John Winthrop, *History of New England* (or *Journal*), ed. James K. Hosmer, 2 vols. (New York: Scribner's, 1908), 285–86.
46. *Essex Ct. Recs.* 1:15 (1639).
47. Kathryn Preyer, "Penal Measures in the American Colonies: An Overview," *AJLH* 26 (1982): 348–49.
48. *Mass. Assist. Ct. Recs.* 1:56–57, 70, 73, 114.
49. *Essex Ct. Recs.* 3:17 (1662); *Ply. Col. Recs.* 4:106 (1665).
50. "Suffolk Ct. Recs." 1:82–83.
51. *Mass. Col. Laws* (1672), 208.
52. *Mass. Assist. Ct. Recs.* 1:138.
53. *Mass. Col. Laws* (1660), 119 (1661), 222 (1662).
54. Powers, *Crime and Punishment in Early Massachusetts*, 350.
55. *Mass. Assist. Ct. Recs.* 2:121.
56. *Mass. Col. Recs.* 4 (pt. 1): 212 (1654).

57. *Ply. Col. Recs.* 2:28 (1641).

58. *Provid. Ct. Recs.* 2:85–86.

59. *Conn. Col. Recs.* 1:115, 124, 129, 135.

60. *Provid. Ct. Recs.* 2:35, 66.

61. *Conn. Col. Recs.* 1:129, 143. See also chapter 8.

62. *Mass. Assist. Ct. Recs.* 2:3 (1630).

63. *Ply. Col. Laws*, 247 (1671).

64. *Mass. Col. Laws* (1660), 187 (1641, 1648); *New Haven Col. Recs.* 2:611 (1656); *Conn. Laws* (1673), 65.

65. *Mass. Col. Laws* (1660), 187; *Conn. Laws* (1673), 65.

66. Howard M. Chapin, ed., *Documentary History of Rhode Island*, 2 vols. (Providence: Preston & Rounds, 1916–19), 2:142.

67. *Provid. Ct. Recs.* 1:52–53; 2:56, 66, 71, 82, 85–86.

68. *Mass. Col. Laws* (1660), 43 (1641).

69. *Mass. Assist. Ct. Recs.* 2:19 (1631).

70. *New Haven Col. Recs.* 1:306–7.

71. Jules Zanger, "Crime and Punishment in Early Massachusetts," *WMQ*, 3d ser., 22 (1965): 473, 476.

72. *Mass. Col. Laws* (1660), 125, 137, 140, 149, 153, 158, 161–66, 171–72, 175, 177, 179, 182–83, 189–90, 200, 228–29, 241, 259.

73. *Ply. Col. Laws*, 30, 35, 44–45, 53, 65, 76, 81–82, 84, 87–88, 92, 98, 101, 103, 117, 125, 129, 131, 137, 140–41, 147, 156, 158, 160, 169, 171, 188–89, 198, 202, 247, 249–50, 252.

74. See Powers, *Crime and Punishment in Early Massachusetts*, 406.

75. *Mass. Col. Laws* (1660), 127 (1642); *Mass. Col. Laws* (1672), 204.

76. *Conn. Col. Recs.* 1:513–14 (1650); *New Haven Col. Recs.* 2:575 (1656).

77. *New Hamp. Laws* 1:16.

78. *R.I. Col. Recs.* 1:174 (1647).

79. *Ply. Col. Recs.* 1:74, 132, 143.

80. *Me. Ct. Recs.* 1:164.

81. *Ply. Col. Laws*, 246 (1671).

82. *Mass. Col. Recs.* 4 (pt. 1): 308–9 (1657); *Mass. Col. Laws* (1660), 220 (1661). See Powers, *Crime and Punishment in Early Massachusetts*, 328–29.

83. *New Haven Col. Recs.* 2:233–34n, 238–40 (1658), 363 (1660).

84. *Mass. Col. Recs.* 4 (pt. 1): 308–9 (1657).

85. *Mass. Col. Laws* (1660), 127 (1642).

86. "Suffolk Ct. Recs." 1:556–57.

87. *Conn. Col. Recs.* 1:513–14 (1650).

88. *Ply. Col. Laws*, 246 (1671); *New Hamp. Laws* 1:16 (1679); *New Haven Col. Recs.* 2:575 (1656).

89. *R.I. Col. Recs.* 1:166–67 (1647).

90. *Ply. Col. Recs.* 1:86–87 (1638); 3:207 (1661).

91. *Provid. Ct. Recs.* 2:56 (1667).

92. *New Haven Col. Recs.* 2:137–39 (1655).

93. *Mass. Assist. Ct. Recs.* 1–3; *Ply. Col. Recs.* 1:96–97; 2:44, 134; William Bradford, *Of Plymouth Plantation*, ed. Samuel E. Morison (New York: Knopf,

1952), 234, 320–21; *Conn. Col. Recs.* 2:184; "Conn. Part. Ct. Recs.," 251, 258; *New Haven Col. Recs.* 2:77–78, 81 n, 137–39, 440–43; *Provid. Ct. Recs.* 1:71–72; 2:97–98. See Appendices A and C.

94. See chapter 9; Winthrop, *Journal* 1:262–63.

95. Winthrop, *Journal* 2:161–63.

96. *Ply. Col. Laws*, 113.

97. William K. Holdsworth, "Adultery or Witchcraft? A New Note on an Old Case in Connecticut," *NEQ* 48 (1975): 394–406.

98. *New Haven Col. Recs.* 1:30–32.

99. Holdsworth, "Adultery or Witchcraft?", 407–8.

100. *Conn. Col. Recs.* 2:20–21; *Conn. Laws* (1673), 2–3.

101. Holdsworth, "Adultery or Witchcraft?", 408–9.

102. See chapter 7; Powers, *Crime and Punishment in Early Massachusetts*, 294, 302–3.

103. Powers, *Crime and Punishment in Early Massachusetts*, 294–95. See John Noble, *The Case of Maria in the Court of Assistants in 1681* (Cambridge, Mass.: Wilson, 1902), 3–16.

104. *Mass. Col. Laws* (1672), 129.

105. M. P. Baumgartner, "Law and Social Status in Colonial New Haven, 1639–1665," *RLS* 1 (1978): 168–69. See also Preyer, "Penal Measures in the American Colonies," 334–35.

106. Baumgartner, "Law and Social Status in Colonial New Haven," 169–70.

107. Adam J. Hirsch, "From Pillory to Penitentiary: The Rise of Criminal Incarceration in Early Massachusetts," *MLR* 80 (1982): 1179–80.

108. *Mass. Assist. Ct. Recs.* 2.

109. *Mass. Col. Recs.* 1:100, 158; 4 (pt. 1): 85, 214; (pt. 2): 21–22.

110. Powers, *Crime and Punishment in Early Massachusetts*, 219–21.

111. In 1785 Castle Island became the first institution in the United States to serve an entire state for long-term penal confinement. The name of the fort was changed in 1705 to "Castle William" in honor of the king, William III, and in 1799 to "Fort Independence" when ceded to the United States. See Powers, *Crime and Punishment in Early Massachusetts*, 241, 597 n.46.

112. *Ply. Col. Laws*, 67.

113. *Conn. Col. Recs.* 1:47, 430; 2:61.

114. *R.I. Col. Recs.* 1:65; Chapin, *Documentary History of Rhode Island* 2:143.

115. *R.I. Col. Recs.* 1:335.

116. *Mass. Col. Laws* (1672), 250 (1677); *Ply. Col. Laws*, 41 (1636), 126–27 (1660).

117. Powers, *Crime and Punishment in Early Massachusetts*, 222–23.

118. *Mass. Col. Laws* (1660), 186; *Mass. Col. Laws* (1672), 127, 152–53, 208, 234, 236.

119. *Ply. Col. Laws*, 120.

120. *Conn. Laws* (1673), 14.

121. *Mass. Col. Laws* (1672), 127.

122. *Ply. Col. Laws*, 120 (1658).

123. Ibid., 86.

124. *Mass. Col. Laws* (1672), 128.
125. *Essex Ct. Recs.* 2:39 (1657).
126. Ibid. 7:227.
127. Perry Miller and Thomas H. Johnson, eds., *The Puritans*, 2 vols. (New York: Harper & Row, 1963), 2:414.

Chapter 11: The New England Way

1. Babette May Levy, *Preaching in the First Half Century of New England History* (Hartford: The American Society of Church History, 1945), 171.
2. William E. Nelson, "Emerging Notions of Modern Criminal Law in the Revolutionary Era: An Historical Perspective," *New York University Law Review* 42 (1967): 451–52.
3. David H. Flaherty, "Law Enforcement and Morals in Early America," *PAH* 5 (1971): 216–17.
4. James F. Stephen, *A History of the Criminal Law of England*, 3 vols. (London: Macmillan, 1883), 1:476–77; Arthur P. Scott, *Criminal Law in Colonial Virginia* (Chicago: University of Chicago Press, 1930), 141–42.
5. Edgar J. McManus, *Black Bondage in the North* (Syracuse, N.Y.: Syracuse University Press, 1973), 129–30.
6. George W. Dalzell, *Benefit of Clergy in America* (Winston-Salem: John F. Blair, 1955), 27–29.
7. Edwin Powers, *Crime and Punishment in Early Massachusetts, 1620–1692* (Boston: Beacon Press, 1966), 523–25.
8. See Georg Rusche and Otto Kirchheimer, *Punishment and Social Structure* (New York: Columbia University Press, 1939), v–vi, 18–19.
9. Eli Faber, "Puritan Criminals: The Economic, Social, and Intellectual Background to Crime in Seventeenth-Century Massachusetts," *PAH* 11 (1978): 135–44.

Appendix A: Crimes Punishable by Death

1. Information for laws in New Plymouth can be found in *Ply. Col. Laws*, 42–43 (1636); 42–43, 113 (1658); 243–47 (1671); 178, 203–4, 243–47 (1684).
2. Information for Massachusetts laws of 1641 can be found in *Mass. Col. Laws* (1660), 55; for laws of 1648, in *Mass. Col. Laws* (1648), 4–6, 26; for laws of 1660, in *Mass. Col. Laws* (1660), 127–29, 152, 154, 156, 158; for laws of 1672, in *Mass. Col. Laws* (1672), 12–16, 52, 58–60, 62–63, 67; and for laws of 1686, in ibid., 12–16, 52, 58–60, 62–63, 67, 211, 315–16, and in *Mass. Col. Recs.* 5:194.
3. Information for laws in Connecticut can be found in *Conn. Col. Recs.* 1:77 (1642); 513–15 (1650); and in *Conn. Laws* (1673), 7–10 (1673).
4. Information for laws in New Haven can be found in *New Haven Col. Recs.* 2:575–78, 593, 605.
5. Information for laws in Rhode Island can be found in *R.I. Col. Recs.* 1:160–64, 166–68, 172–73, 182 (1647); and in *R.I. Col. Laws*, 1–4, 6–7, 33–34 (1684).

6. Information for laws in New Hampshire can be found in *New Hamp. Laws* 1:12–16.

Appendix B: Judicial Organization

1. Information for New Plymouth can be found in *Ply. Col. Laws*, 39 (1636); 149–50 (1666); 259–60 (1671); 208, 294–97 (1686).

2. The following are sources for information on the Massachusetts judiciary: for 1630, *Mass. Col. Recs.*1:74; for 1648, *Mass. Col. Laws* (1660), 122, 143; *Mass. Col. Laws* (1648), 2, 15; and *Mass. Col. Recs.* 1:169–70, 239, 264 (see also Thomas L. Philips, "Courts of Justice in the Province of Massachusetts Bay under the First Charter, 1630–1684," *ALR* 34 [1900]: 569); for 1660, *Mass. Col. Recs.* 4 (pt. 1): 61–63; *Mass. Col. Laws* (1660), 133, 137, 143, 164.

3. The following are sources for information on the Connecticut judiciary: for 1639, *Conn. Col. Recs.* 1:21, 24; "Conn. Part. Ct. Recs.," vii–viii; Herbert L. Osgood, *The American Colonies in the Seventeenth Century*, 3 vols. (New York: Columbia University Press, 1904–1907), 1:305–6; and Charles M. Andrews, *The Colonial Period of American History*, 4 vols. (New Haven: Yale University Press, 1934–38), 2:92; for 1650, *Conn. Col. Recs.* 1:522, 528, 537–38, 547, 558, 561; for 1673, ibid. 2:28–29, 34–35, 38, 53, 402, and *Conn. Laws* (1673), 3, 4, 17–18, 28, 31, 40, 58.

4. The following are sources for information on the New Haven judiciary: for pre-1643, Andrews, *The Colonial Period of American History* 2:156ff; for 1643, *New Haven Col. Recs.* 1:113–16; for 1656, *New Haven Col. Recs.* 2:570–71, 576, 585, 606.

5. The following are sources for information on the Rhode Island judiciary: for pre-1640, *R.I. Col. Recs.* 1:27, 52, 63, 70, 87; for 1640, ibid., 101–3 (for pre-1640 and 1640, see also Amasa M. Eaton, "The Development of the Judicial System in Rhode Island," *YLJ* 14 [1905]: 149); for 1647, *R.I. Col. Recs.* 1:191–92, 202; Andrews, *Colonial Period of American History* 2:28–29; Osgood, *American Colonies in the Seventeenth Century* 1:358; for 1664, *R.I. Col. Recs.* 2:26–27, 30–31; see also Stephen O. Edwards, "The Supreme Court of Rhode Island," *The Green Bag* 2 (1890): 526, and Andrews, *Colonial Period of American History* 2:48.

6. The source for information on the New Hampshire judiciary is *Provincial Papers: Documents and Records Relating to the Province of New Hampshire, from the Earliest Period of Its Settlement, 1623–1776*, ed. Nathaniel Bouton, 7 vols. (Concord and Nashua: Jenks, 1867–73), 1:373–82, 387, 395–96, 474.

Appendix C: Typical Crimes and Penalties

1. *Mass. Assist. Ct. Recs.* are the source for this and the following table.

2. Other penalties: confession of fault, humiliation, prison or house of correction, banishment, enslavement, branding, ear-cropping.

3. Miscellaneous offenses: adulterous behavior, disturbing church services, slan-

der, abusiveness, plotting piracy, assisting jail breaks, releasing servants before time, enticing servants to run away, morally suspect behavior, entertaining Indians, absence from military training, arson, conspiring against government, attempted infanticide, absence from jury duty, keeping bad company, bigamy, cheating, performing a marriage unlawfully, absence from guard duty, abusing parents, purchasing Indian lands unlawfully, violating the curfew, neglect of official duties, keeping a disorderly house, abuse of authority, playing unlawful games, illegal dancing, lying, quarreling, sale of firearms or liquor to Indians, disorderly conduct, idleness, breaking out of jail, fraud, bastardy, negligent homicide, wasting a master's goods, setting illegal traps, engaging in the fur trade without a license, sedition, unlawful entry, immodest speech, receiving stolen property.

4. Other penalties: confession of fault, property forfeiture, child support, compulsory service, prison or house of correction, ear-cropping, tongue-piercing, running the gauntlet.

5. Miscellaneous offenses: cursing, swearing, lascivious behavior, Anabaptism, disturbing church services, betraying the colony, sale of ammunition to Indians, enslaving Indians, assisting a jail break, card-playing, offensive speech, lying, smuggling, defying authority, slander, bastardy, settling in the colony without permission.

6. "Suffolk Ct. Recs." are the source for this and the following table.

7. Other penalties: confession of fault, property forfeiture, child support, compulsory service, humiliation, disfranchisement, disbarment, disqualification from testifying in any court, stocks, pillory, ear-cropping.

8. Miscellaneous offenses: absence from jury duty, receiving stolen goods, assisting fugitives from justice, slander, attempting suicide, antichurch activities, barratry, arson, advising offenders not to confess, keeping bad company, running away from service, keeping a disorderly house, offensive speech, disorderly living, unauthorized courtship, perjury, making a false confession, exporting goods illegally, negligent use of firearms, supplying prisoners with liquor, possession of leather without an official seal, neglect of family duties, spreading corrupt ideas, publishing marriage banns illegally, falsely asserting official authority, passing counterfeit money, retaining property unlawfully, embezzlement, robbery, bigamy, negligent homicide, deserting the militia, attempted bigamy, abusing a servant, seduction, malicious mischief, obstructing justice.

9. Other penalties: confession of fault, child support, stocks, pillory, compulsory service.

10. Miscellaneous offenses: absence from jury duty, unlawfully concealing goods, accosting females, contempt of authority, fraud, slander, illegal entry, suspected arson, suspected adultery, recklessness, working on a day of fast and humiliation, refusing to live with a spouse, wife-beating, deserting a wife, cohabiting after divorce, price-gouging, gambling, obscenity, illegal voting, running away from service, smoking in public, falsely denying criminal charges, making false claims, neglect of official duties, giving ambiguous testimony, dumping ballast in the harbor, attempted rape.

11. *Ply. Col. Recs.* 1.

12. Other penalties: bound to good conduct, public service, barred from owning land, disfranchisement, banishment.

13. Miscellaneous offenses: neglect of official duties, disturbing the peace, contempt of court, unlawfully contracting to marry, detaining a servant, running away from service, fraud, idleness, blasphemy, illegally killing animals.

14. *Ply. Col. Recs.* 3.

15. Other penalties: bound to good conduct, property forfeiture, banishment.

16. Miscellaneous offenses: cursing, swearing, slander, taking a false oath, offensive speech, disturbing church services, sale of liquor to Indians, derogating a minister, illegally proposing marriage, refusing to register a marriage, morally suspect behavior, deserting a wife, abetting adultery, threatening to kill someone, mistreating servants, assisting Quakers, refusal to assist public officers, absence from jury duty, defying orders of banishment, seizing Indian children for debts of parents, mixed dancing, usury, liquor violations, illegally entertaining servants, assaulting a spouse.

17. *Conn. Col. Recs.* 1, and "Conn. Part. Ct. Recs." are the sources for this and the following table.

18. Miscellaneous offenses: cursing, swearing, assisting escaped prisoners, striking law officers, absence from guard duty, misconduct by servants, unauthorized courtship, lying, price-gouging, illegally counseling prisoners, misconduct with a married woman.

19. Miscellaneous offenses: cursing, absence from jury duty, disorderly conduct, absence from guard duty, detaining animals illegally, sale of firearms to Indians, mistreating servants, breach of promise to marry, negligent homicide, false accusation of adultery.

20. *New Haven Col. Recs.* 1.

21. *Provid. Ct. Recs.*

Appendix D: Witchcraft Cases

Only accusations resulting in judicial proceedings are listed. For additional accusations involving only rumor and gossip, see John P. Demos, *Entertaining Satan* (New York: Oxford University Press, 1982), 401–9.

1. "Not convicted" includes both acquittals and dismissals.

2. No record of disposition, but conviction seems unlikely. A witchcraft conviction would have meant the death penalty, and Cole was not executed. See Demos, *Entertaining Satan*, 322. Cf. Richard Weisman, *Witchcraft, Magic, and Religion in 17th-Century Massachusetts* (Amherst: University of Massachusetts Press, 1984), 107.

3. Varlet's brother-in-law, Peter Stuyvesant, interceded with the Connecticut authorities on her behalf. See John M. Taylor, *The Witchcraft Delusion in Colonial Connecticut, 1647–1697* (1908; reprint New York: Franklin, 1971), 151–52.

4. Browne appeared before a local New Haven court but after the merger of the colony with Connecticut.

Bibliographical Note

Historians of early New England owe a heavy debt to the scholars and archivists who painstakingly transcribed and preserved the public records of the region in easily accessible printed collections. Since these records are the same whether cited in manuscript or in print, the latter have been used wherever possible for the convenience of readers wishing to check a particular citation. Court reports abridged or not included in the printed collections are available in catalogued manuscript form. Folio volumes of judicial proceedings in Massachusetts beginning in 1629 are in the Office of the Clerk of the Supreme Judicial Court of Suffolk County in Boston. The Greenough Collection, also in the Clerk's office, contains reports dating from 1647, most of which are available on microfilm. The Massachusetts Archives in the Office of the Secretary of the Commonwealth also contain valuable material. Volume 9 deals with domestic relations; volumes 38B to 44 cover crimes and prisons; and volume 135 has information on witchcraft proceedings. Similarly, the Connecticut Archives in the State Library at Hartford can be used to fill gaps in the printed records. Cases tried in the Particular Court can be found in volumes 1, 55, and 56, while those tried in the Assistants Court are in volumes 53, 56, and 58.

John D. Cushing's *A Bibliography of the Laws and Resolves of the Massachusetts Bay, 1642–1780* (Wilmington, Del.: Glazier, 1984) is a useful tool for locating early Massachusetts legislation. The complete text of the early Bay Colony statutes can be found in *The Colonial Laws of Massachusetts. Reprinted from the Edition of 1660, with the Supplements to 1672*, ed. William H. Whitmore (Boston: Rockwell & Churchill, 1889), which includes the *Body of Liberties* of 1641 and the code of 1660. For the first comprehensive compilation of Massachusetts law, see *The Laws and Liberties of Massachusetts, 1648* ed. Max Farrand (Cambridge, Mass.: Harvard University

Press, 1929), the most important and influential code of the seventeenth century. *The Colonial Laws of Massachusetts. Reprinted from the Edition of 1672, with the Supplements through 1686,* ed. William H. Whitmore (Boston: Rockwell & Churchill, 1887), contains the 1672 code and subsequent enactments through 1686. The laws passed during the provincial period are in *The Acts and Resolves, Public and Private, of the Province of the Massachusetts Bay,* 5 vols. (Boston: Wright & Potter, 1869–86).

The statutes of Plymouth Colony are in the *The Compact with the Charter and Laws of the Colony of New Plymouth,* ed. William Brigham (Boston: Dutton & Wentworth, 1836), which contains the codes of 1636, 1658, and 1671. Working with this collection requires caution, however, for it does not list all the code of 1658 under the code heading. All the laws passed between 1636 and 1658 are in the collection, but it lists under the code of 1658 only those laws which were new or different from the laws previously in force. Similarly, the code of 1685 lists only new or different legislation. It is necessary to refer back to previous enactments in order to ascertain the exact state of the law in 1658 and 1685. The complete 1658 code can be found in volume 11 of *Records of the Colony of New Plymouth in New England, 1620–1692,* ed. Nathaniel B. Shurtleff and David Pulsifer, 12 vols. (Boston: White, 1855–61).

Connecticut's early statutes can be found in *The Public Records of the Colony of Connecticut, 1636–1776,* ed. J. Hammond Trumbull and Charles J. Hoadly, 15 vols. (Hartford: Lockwood & Brainard, 1850–90), volume 1 of which contains the code of 1650. An indexed copy of the 1673 code for the combined jurisdiction of Connecticut and New Haven Colony is available in *The Laws of Connecticut: An Exact Reprint of the Edition of 1673,* ed. George Brinley (Hartford: Private printing, 1865). The laws of New Haven Colony as a separate jurisdiction can be found in *Records of the Colony or Jurisdiction of New Haven, 1653 to the Union,* ed. Charles J. Hoadly (Hartford: Case, Lockwood, 1858), which contains the code of 1656. The earliest laws of the jurisdiction are in *Records of the Colony and Plantation of New Haven, 1638–1649,* ed. Charles J. Hoadly (Hartford: Case, Tiffany, 1857). The colonial laws of Rhode Island are in *Records of the Colony of Rhode Island and Providence Plantations in New England, 1636–1792,* ed. John R. Bartlett, 10 vols. (Providence: Greene, 1856–65), volume 1 of which contains the code of 1647, and *Laws and Acts of Her Majesty's Colony of Rhode Island and Providence Plantations, Made from the First Settlement in 1636 to 1705* (Providence: Rider, 1896), which contains the 1665 code.

The records of the Massachusetts General Court and Court of Assistants are relatively complete for the period from 1630 to 1644, but the Assistants Court records thereafter become fragmentary. Most of the trial jurisdiction of both courts shifted after 1644 to the county courts. Judicial sessions of the General Court can be found in *Records of the Governor and Company of the Massachusetts Bay in New England, 1628–1674*, ed. Nathaniel B. Shurtleff, 5 vols. (Boston: White, 1853–54), and for the Assistants Court, see *Records of the Court of Assistants of the Massachusetts Bay, 1630–1692*, ed. John B. Noble, 3 vols. (Boston: Pub. by Suffolk County, 1901–28). The complete records of the Essex County Court have been preserved from its inception as an Inferior Court in 1636 to the end of the colony period. They are in *Records and Files of the Quarterly Courts of Essex County, Massachusetts*, ed. George F. Dow, 8 vols. (Salem, Mass.: Essex Institute, 1911–21). Court proceedings in Suffolk County during the 1670s can be found in "Records of the Suffolk County Court, 1671–1680," ed. Samuel E. Morison, 2 vols., in *Colonial Society of Massachusetts Publications* 29–30 (1933). Trials in the northern and western counties are covered in *Colonial Justice in Western Massachusetts (1639–1702): The Pynchon Court Record*, ed. Joseph H. Smith (Cambridge, Mass.: Harvard University Press, 1961); "New Hampshire Court Records, 1640–1692," in *New Hampshire State Papers Series* 40 (1943); and *Province and Court Records of Maine*, 5 vols. (Portland, Me.: Maine Historical Society, 1928–64).

Judicial sessions of the New Plymouth General Court and Court of Assistants can be found in *Records of the Colony of New Plymouth in New England, 1620–1692*, already cited. Criminal trials in Connecticut are in "Records of the Particular Court of Connecticut, 1639–1663," in *Connecticut Historical Society Collections* 22 (1928), and *The Public Records of the Colony of Connecticut, 1636–1776*, already cited. The latter covers trials in both the General Court and Court of Assistants. Court proceedings in New Haven Colony before the union with Connecticut can be found in *Records of the Colony and Plantation of New Haven, 1638–1649*, and *Records of the Colony or Jurisdiction of New Haven, 1653 to the Union*, both already cited. The judicial records of Rhode Island can be found in *Records of the Court of Trials of the Colony of Providence Plantations, 1647–1670*, 2 vols. (Providence: Rhode Island Historical Society, 1920–22); *Records of the Court of Trials of Warwick, 1659–1674* (Providence: Shepley Press, 1922); and *Records of the Colony of Rhode Island and Providence Plantations in New England, 1636–1792*, already cited. Trials in the Quarterly Courts of Newport and Portsmouth are in *Documentary History of Rhode Island*, ed. Howard M. Chapin, 2 vols. (Providence: Preston & Rounds, 1916–19).

Bibliographical Note

Numerous secondary works provide a useful introduction to the subject. Bradley Chapin's *Criminal Justice in Colonial America, 1606–1660* (Athens: University of Georgia Press, 1983) is a concise but comprehensive summary of American criminal law to 1660. While its attempt to quantify English, biblical, and indigenous law sources by exact percentages is questionable, this is a minor flaw and does not detract from the usefulness of the book. David G. Allen, *In English Ways* (Chapel Hill: University of North Carolina Press, 1981), and Joseph H. Smith and Thomas G. Barnes, *The English Legal System: Carryover to the Colonies* (Los Angeles: University of California Press, 1975), trace the translation of English law and customs to New England. Stephen Botein's *Early American Law and Society* (New York: Knopf, 1983) also contains much useful information. A comprehensive and highly readable survey of the rights of criminal defendants can be found in David J. Bodenhamer's *Fair Trial: Rights of the Accused in American History* (New York: Oxford University Press, 1992). The sixty years that have passed since its first publication have not diminished the value of Richard B. Morris's *Studies in the History of American Law,* 2d ed. (1930; reprint Philadelphia: Mitchell, 1959). It remains even today one of the best introductions to early American legal institutions.

Useful material on the English sources of New England law can be found in S. F. C. Milsom, *Historical Foundations of the Common Law* (London: Buttersworth, 1969); Frederick Pollack and Frederic Maitland, *The History of English Law before the Time of Edward I* (Cambridge, Eng.: Cambridge University Press, 1968); Julius Goebel, Jr., *Felony and Misdemeanor: A Study in the History of English Criminal Procedure* (New York: The Commonwealth Fund, 1937); A. L. Goodhart, *English Law and the Moral Law* (London: Stevens & Sons, 1953); Carl Stephenson and Frederick G. Marcham, eds., *Sources of English Constitutional History* (New York: Harper, 1937); and C. H. Firth and R. S. Rait, eds., *Acts and Ordinances of the Interregnum, 1642–1660,* 3 vols. (London: H.M.S.O., 1911). John H. Langbein's *Torture and the Law of Proof* (Chicago: University of Chicago Press, 1977) describes the connection between jury trial and the exclusion of judicial torture from Anglo-American law, and Thomas Green's *Verdict according to Conscience: Perspectives on the English Trial Jury, 1200–1800* (Chicago: University of Chicago Press, 1985) covers the origins of jury trial and the practice of jury modification of the law. Material on the English ecclesiastical courts can be found in Carson I. A. Ritchie, *The Ecclesiastical Courts of York* (Arbroath: The Herald Press, 1956), and Ronald A. Marchant, *The Puritans and the Church Courts in the Diocese of York, 1560–1642* (London: Longmans, Green, 1960).

While this is the only book currently available for all of New England, several excellent works on Massachusetts provide an introduction to the legal history of the region as a whole. By far the best is by George L. Haskins, *Law and Authority in Early Massachusetts* (New York: Macmillan, 1960), a brilliantly insightful study containing a wealth of information on both civil and criminal matters. Criminal issues have greater emphasis in Edwin Powers, *Crime and Punishment in Early Massachusetts, 1620–1692* (Boston: Beacon Press, 1966), which covers criminal law and justice in Massachusetts and New Plymouth. David T. Konig's *Law and Society in Puritan Massachusetts: Essex County, 1629–1692* (Chapel Hill: University of North Carolina Press, 1979) is an excellent study of how the justice system operated at the county level. Although written before the discovery of the important 1648 code, and therefore requiring cautious reading, Charles J. Hilkey's *Legal Development in Colonial Massachusetts, 1630–1686* (New York: Columbia University Press, 1910) still provides an excellent summary of early legal developments.

Specialized monographs contain a wealth of topical material on key subjects. Anton-Hermann Chroust's *The Rise of the Legal Profession in America*, 2 vols. (Norman: University of Oklahoma Press, 1965) describes the origins of the right to counsel, and Leonard W. Levy's *The Origins of the Fifth Amendment* (New York: Oxford University Press, 1968) is indispensable for understanding the privilege against self-incrimination in the seventeenth century. David H. Flaherty's *Privacy in Colonial New England* (Charlottesville: University of Virginia Press, 1972) is an excellent and highly readable account of Puritan attitudes toward privacy and social control, and George W. Dalzell's *Benefit of Clergy in America* (Winston-Salem: John F. Harper, 1955) traces the influence of an important legal fiction in colonial law. The role of the Puritan churches in punishing deviance is described by Emil Oberholzer, Jr., in *Delinquent Saints: Disciplinary Action in the Early Churches of Massachusetts* (New York: Columbia University Press, 1955). Useful material on colonial judicial procedure and the right of appeal can be found in Joseph H. Smith's *Appeals to the Privy Council from the American Colonies* (New York: Columbia University Press, 1950).

Kai T. Erikson's *Wayward Puritans: A Study in the Sociology of Deviance* (New York: Wiley, 1966) contains useful information on the social context of crime in colonial times. The scientific assumptions of law in the seventeenth century are examined in Sanford J. Fox's *Science and Justice: The Massachusetts Witch Trials* (Baltimore: Johns Hopkins University Press, 1968), especially with regard to the insanity defense in colonial courts. The use of criminal law to enforce religious conformity is covered by Emery Battis in *Saints and Sectaries: Anne Hutchinson and the Antinomian Controversy in the Massachusetts Bay Colony* (Chapel Hill: University of North Carolina Press, 1962). Williston Walker's *The Creeds and Platforms of Congregationalism* (New York: Scribner's, 1893) covers the roles assumed by church and state in the enforcement of Puritan social values. The execution sermons delivered at public hangings are covered in Ronald A. Bosco, ed., *The Puritan Sermon in America, 1630–1750* (Delmar, N.Y.: Scholars Facsimiles and Reprints, 1978), and Babette May Levy's *Preaching in the First Half Century of New England History* (Hartford: The American Society of Church History, 1945) describes the declining influence of religion as perceived by the Puritan clergy. Peter J. Coleman's *Debtors and Creditors in America* (Madison: The State Historical Society of Wisconsin, 1974) has material on imprisonment for debt and the sale of delinquent debtors into service for the benefit of creditors. The transportation of criminals to the colonies is dealt with by A. Roger Ekirch in *Bound for America: The Transportation of British Convicts to the Colonies, 1718–1775* (New York: Oxford University Press, 1987), and material on penal practices and social standing can be found in Georg Rusche and Otto Kirchheimer, *Punishment and Social Structure* (New York: Columbia University Press, 1939). While lacking documentation and flawed by flippant commentary, the study of Puritan morality by Gustavus Myers, *Ye Olden Blue Laws* (New York: Century Company, 1921), is still useful. The regulation of sex is dealt with by Roger Thompson in *Sex in Middlesex: Popular Mores in a Massachusetts County, 1649–1699* (Amherst: University of Massachusetts Press, 1986), an outstanding study of the subject.

Crimes by women are covered in N. E. H. Hull, *Female Felons: Women and Serious Crime in Colonial Massachusetts* (Urbana: University of Illinois Press, 1987), and Peter C. Hoffer and N. E. H. Hull, *Murdering Mothers: Infanticide in England and New England, 1558–1803* (New York: New York University Press, 1981). Both are excellent, though the latter, as already noted in the text, offers some questionable conclusions about infanticide convictions on the basis of circumstantial evidence. Roger Thompson's *Women in Stuart England and America: A Comparative Study* (London: Routledge & Paul, 1974) is very useful for the social and cultural subordination of women in the seventeenth century. How gender discrimination related to the prosecution of women for witchcraft is dealt with in Carol F. Karlsen's *The Devil in the Shape of a Woman: Witchcraft in Colonial New England* (New York: Norton, 1987), a book full of valuable leads and insights. Richard B. Morris's *Studies in the History of American Law,* already cited, has a useful chapter on the legal treatment of women in colonial times.

Several books deal with the legal treatment of blacks and Indians. The best for blacks is Lorenzo J. Greene's *The Negro in Colonial New England, 1620–1776* (New York: Columbia University Press, 1942), which covers both slaves and free blacks in the New England colonies. Useful information can also be found in Edgar J. McManus, *Black Bondage in the North* (Syracuse, N.Y.: Syracuse University Press, 1973), which covers the Middle Colonies as well as New England. Historians disagree, sometimes sharply, on the treatment of the Indians. Alden T. Vaughan, *The New England Frontier: Puritans and Indians, 1620–1675* (Boston: Little, Brown, 1965), takes the view that the Puritan justice system generally treated them fairly. Others reject this view. Yasuhide Kawashima, *Puritan Justice and the Indian: White Man's Law in Massachusetts* (Middletown, Conn.: Wesleyan University Press, 1986), Francis Jennings, *The Invasion of America: Indians, Colonialism, and the Cant of Conquest* (Chapel Hill: University of North Carolina Press, 1975), and Wilcomb E. Washburn, *Red Man's Land/ White Man's Law: A Study of the Past and Present Status of the American Indian* (New York: Scribner's, 1971), contend that Puritan law was an instrument of oppression and that white cultural chauvinism made equitable relations between the two races impossible.

The best starting point for the New England witch trials is John P. Demos's *Entertaining Satan* (New York: Oxford University Press, 1982), an exhaustive study of the phenomenon. Richard Weisman's *Witchcraft, Magic, and Religion in 17th-Century Massachusetts* (Amherst: University of Massachusetts Press, 1984) and Sanford J. Fox's *Science and Justice,* already cited, also contain valuable information. The misogynistic aspect of witchcraft is dealt with in Carol F. Karlsen's *The Devil in the Shape of a Woman,* already cited. Earlier works by Samuel G. Drake, *Annals of Witchcraft in New England, and Elsewhere in the United States, from Their First Settlement* (1869; reprint New York: Blom, 1972), and John M. Taylor, *The Witchcraft Delusion in Colonial Connecticut, 1647–1697* (1908; reprint New York: Franklin, 1971), are still useful. For comparisons with the later Salem witch trials, the studies by Paul Boyer and Stephen Nissenbaum, *Salem Possessed* (Cambridge, Mass.: Harvard University Press, 1974), Marion L. Starkey, *The Devil in Massachusetts* (New York: Knopf, 1949), and Chadwick Hansen, *Witchcraft at Salem* (New York: Braziller, 1969), are all valuable. Hansen's book is particularly interesting for its thesis that some of the accused were actually guilty of practicing witchcraft. An excellent summary of the numerous interpretations of the Salem tragedy can be found in Marc Mappen, ed., *Witches & Historians: Interpretations of Salem* (Huntington, N.Y.: Krieger Publishing Company, 1980). For the English background, Wallace Notestein's *A History of Witchcraft in England from 1558–1718* (New York: Russell & Russell, 1965) is the standard work on the subject. Much useful information can also be found in George L. Kittredge, *Witchcraft in Old and New England* (Cambridge, Mass.: Harvard University Press, 1929).

Journal articles contain valuable material on a wide range of topics. Three by George L. Haskins trace early legal developments: "The Beginnings of the Recording System in Massachusetts," *Boston University Law Review* 21 (1941): 281–304; "Codification of the Law in Colonial Massachusetts: A Study in Comparative Law," *Indiana Law Journal* 30 (1954): 1–17; and "Ecclesiastical Antecedents of Criminal Punishment in Early Massachusetts," *Massachusetts Historical Society Proceedings* 72 (1960): 21–35. Thorp L. Wolford's "The Laws and Liberties of 1648," *Boston University Law Review* 28 (1948): 426–63, deals with the most influential law code of the colonial era. Worthington C. Ford's "Cotton's 'Moses His Judicials,'" *Massachusetts Historical Society Proceedings* 16 (1902): 274–84; Isabel M. Calder's "John Cotton's 'Moses His Judicials,'" *Colonial Society of Massachusetts Publications* 28 (1931): 86–94; and Gail Sussman Marcus's "'Due Execution of the Generall Rules of Righteousnesse': Criminal Procedure in New Haven Town and Colony, 1638–1658," in *Saints and Revolutionaries: Essays on Early American History*, ed. David D. Hall, John M. Murrin, and Thad W. Tate (New York: Norton, 1984), 99–137, provide information of legal developments in New Haven Colony before its union with Connecticut. The influence of Massachusetts law on the rest of New England is traced by Stefan A. Riesenfeld in "Law-Making and Legislative Precedent in American Legal History," *Minnesota Law Review* 33 (1949): 104–44, and by George L. Haskins and Samuel E. Ewing, 3d, in "The Spread of Massachusetts Law in the Seventeenth Century," *University of Pennsylvania Law Review* 106 (1958): 413–18.

The influence of English law and Scripture on American legal development has been described in numerous articles and essays. Some of the most important are: H. D. Hazeltine, "The Influence of Magna Carta on American Constitutional Development," *Columbia Law Review* 17 (1917): 1–33; Paul S. Reinsch, "The English Common Law in the Early American Colonies," in *Select Essays in Anglo-American Legal History*, 3 vols. (Boston:

Little, Brown, 1907–1909), 1:367–415; Richard B. Morris, "Massachusetts and the Common Law: The Declaration of 1646," *American Historical
Review* 30 (1926): 443–53; George L. Haskins, "A Problem in the Recep-
tion of the Common Law in the Colonial Period," *University of Pennsylvania Law Review* 97 (1949): 842–53; and Zechariah Chafee, Jr., "Colonial
Courts and the Common Law," *Massachusetts Historical Society Proceedings*
68 (1945): 132–59. The influence of Scripture on Puritan homicide law is
covered by David H. Wrinn in "Manslaughter and Mosaicism in Early
Connecticut," *Valparaiso University Law Review* 21 (1986–87): 271–319.
Thomas A. Green, "A Retrospective on the Criminal Trial Jury, 1200–
1800," in J. S. Cockburn and Thomas A. Green, eds., *Twelve Good Men
and True: The Criminal Trial Jury in England, 1200–1800* (Princeton, N.J.:
Princeton University Press, 1988), 358–99, and Robert C. Palmer, "Conscience and the Law: The English Criminal Jury," *Michigan Law Review*
84 (Feb.–Apr. 1986): 787–800, contain useful information on jury modification of the law. John M. Murrin, "Magistrates, Sinners, and a Precarious Liberty: Trial by Jury in Seventeenth-Century New England," in
Hall, Murrin, and Tate, *Saints and Revolutionaries*, 152–206, already cited,
has material on jury trial in early New England. An especially valuable
article by Julius Goebel, Jr., "King's Law and Local Custom in Seventeenth Century New England," *Columbia Law Review* 31 (1931): 416–48,
emphasizes the contribution of English local law and custom to legal
developments in New England. The selected essays in George A. Billias,
ed., *Law and Authority in Colonial America* (Barre, Mass.: Barre Publishers,
1965), also contain a wealth of information.

Legal and judicial developments are traced in Zechariah Chafee's introduction to the "Records of the Suffolk County Court, 1671–1680," already
cited, and by Mark DeWolfe Howe and Louis F. Eaton, Jr., in "The
Supreme Judicial Power in the Colony of Massachusetts Bay," *New England Quarterly* 20 (1947): 291–316. Thomas L. Philips, "Courts of Justice
in the Province of Massachusetts Bay under the First Charter, 1630–1684,"
American Law Review 34 (1900): 566–72, is still useful. Trial practices and
legal due process are covered in E. M. Morgan, "The Privilege against Self-
Incrimination," *Minnesota Law Review* 34 (1949–50): 1–45; R. Carter
Pittman, "The Colonial and Constitutional History of the Privilege against
Self-Incrimination in America," *Virginia Law Review* 21 (1935): 763–89;
William Cuddihy and B. Carmon Hardy, "A Man's House Was Not His
Castle: Origins of the Fourth Amendment to the United States Constitu-
tion," *William and Mary Quarterly*, 3d ser., 37 (1980): 371–400; Edward J.

Bibliographical Note

White, "Benefit of Clergy," *American Law Review* 46 (1912): 78–94; and A. H. Carpenter, "Habeas Corpus in the Colonies," *American Historical Review* 8 (1902): 18–27. The right to counsel is covered in Nathan Matthews, "The Results of the Prejudice against Lawyers in Massachusetts in the 17th Century," *Massachusetts Law Quarterly* 13 (1928): 73–94; Max Radin, "The Ancient Grudge: A Study in the Public Relations of the Legal Profession," *Virginia Law Review* 32 (1928): 734–52; and Felix Rackow, "The Right to Counsel: English and American Precedents," *William and Mary Quarterly*, 3d ser., 11 (1954), 3–27. J. Hammond Trumbull's "A Sketch of the Life of Thomas Lechford," *American Antiquarian Society* 7 (1885): vii–xxviii, is a useful account of the first practicing attorney in New England.

The punishment meted out to offenders is dealt with in Kathryn Preyer, "Penal Measures in the American Colonies: An Overview," *American Journal of Legal History* 26 (1982): 326–53; Adam Hirsch, "From Pillory to Penitentiary: The Rise of Criminal Incarceration in Early Massachusetts," *Michigan Law Review* 80 (1982): 1179–1269; and Jules Zanger, "Crime and Punishment in Early Massachusetts," *William and Mary Quarterly*, 3d ser., 22 (1965): 471–77. Race as a factor in the sentencing of offenders can be found in William Wiecek, "The Statutory Law of Slavery and Race in the Thirteen Mainland Colonies," *William and Mary Quarterly*, 3d ser., 34 (1977): 258–80; Yasuhide Kawashima, "Jurisdiction of the Colonial Courts over the Indians in Massachusetts, 1689–1763," *New England Quarterly* 62 (1969): 532–50; and G. E. Thomas, "Puritans, Indians, and the Concept of Race," *New England Quarterly* 48 (1975): 3–27. Social status as a factor in the penalties imposed is covered in M. P. Baumgartner, "Law and Social Status in Colonial New Haven, 1639–1665," *Research in Law and Sociology* 1 (1978): 153–74.

The regulatory measures passed to safeguard social values are covered in David H. Flaherty, "Law and the Enforcement of Morals in Early America," *Perspectives in American History* 5 (1971): 203–53, and Douglas Greenberg, "Crime, Law Enforcement, and Social Control in Colonial America," *American Journal of Legal History* 26 (1982): 298–325. William E. Nelson, "Emerging Notions of Modern Criminal Law in the Revolutionary Era: An Historical Perspective," *New York University Law Review* 42 (1967): 450–82, a valuable study of the court records of Middlesex County, Massachusetts, traces the transformation of Puritan law into modern criminal law. Alcohol and sex, the two main regulatory problems, are covered in Edmund S. Morgan, "The Puritans and Sex," *New England Quarterly* 15

270

(1942): 591–607, and Dean Albertson, "Puritan Liquor in the Planting of New England," *New England Quarterly* 23 (1950): 477–90. William K. Holdsworth, "Adultery or Witchcraft? A New Note on an Old Case in Connecticut," *New England Quarterly* 48 (1975): 394–409, contains useful material on the punishment of adulterers. Caroline Bingham, "Seventeenth-Century Attitudes toward Deviant Sex," *Journal of Interdisciplinary History* 1 (1971): 447–72, and Robert F. Oaks, " 'Things Fearful to Name': Sodomy and Buggery in Seventeenth-Century New England," *Journal of Social History* 12 (1978): 268–81, deal with cases of aberrant sex. How class standing correlated with criminal misconduct is dealt with by Eli Faber in "Puritan Criminals: The Economic, Social, and Intellectual Background to Crime in 17th-Century Massachusetts," *Perspectives in American History* 11 (1978): 83–144. Finally, the role of the Puritan churches in law enforcement is described in Charles E. Park, "Excommunication in Colonial Churches," *Colonial Society of Massachusetts Publications* 12 (1909): 321–32, and Aaron B. Seidman, "Church and State in the Early Years of the Massachusetts Bay Colony," *New England Quarterly* 18 (1945): 211–33.

Index

273

Index